RUNNING SCARED

edward t. welch

RUNNING SCARED

fear, worry, and the God of rest

New Growth Press
Greensboro, NC

EDWARD T. WELCH is the author of such best-selling titles as: *Depression: A Stubborn Darkness, Addictions: A Banquet in the Grave, Blame It on the Brain,* and *When People Are Big and God Is Small.* He received a PhD in Counseling Psychology (Neuropsychology) from the University of Utah, and an MDiv from the Biblical Theological Seminary in Hatfield, PA. Welch is a licensed psychologist and works as a counselor, faculty member, and director of the School of Biblical Counseling at the Christian Counseling & Educational Foundation in Glenside, PA. His written work and speaking ministry, which are characterized by sound biblical exposition and paired with dynamic practical application, are in great demand by today's modern church. Ed is married to Sheri and has two amazing daughters. He is also the glad owner of a growing guitar collection and competes in the Master's swim event where he happily placed fourth in the country.

New Growth Press, Greensboro 27404
Copyright © 2007 by Edward T. Welch
All rights reserved. Published 2007

Cover Design: The DesignWorks Group, Nate Salciccioli and Jeff Miller, www.thedesignworksgroup.com
Typesetting: Robin Black, www.blackbirdcreative.biz

ISBN–10: 0-9785567-5-5
ISBN–13: 978-0-9785567-5-4

Library of Congress Control Number: 2007933627

Printed in Canada
20 19 18 17 16 15 14 13   9 10 11 12 13

To J. Alan Groves

A wise pastor
A loving father
My dear friend
(1952–2007)

TABLE OF CONTENTS

PREFACE

I HAVE LOOKED forward to writing about fear for years. I came close to it in *When People Are Big and God Is Small*, but all I could do was skirt the edges and savor the possibilities. I touched on it in *Depression: A Stubborn Darkness*, but since fear is not relevant to everyone who struggles with depression, all I did was raise a signpost and mention that there are beautiful words of comfort up ahead for fearful people.

Now I can graze on those beautiful words.

Like most writing projects, this book is aimed squarely at myself. Although I can be angry or melancholy, I am a fear specialist. In this I have found that I am not alone. Not everyone is a fear specialist, but there is no doubt that every single person who ever lived is personally familiar with fear. It is an inescapable feature of earthly life. To deny it is . . . well . . . to deny it.

I was initially intrigued by Luke's account of Jesus' command: "Do not worry." There was a time when the biblical commands "Do not worry" and "Do not be afraid" put a quick end to hopes that there was anything attractive to say to fearful people. It seemed as if the biblical counsel was "The law says don't fear, so don't. End of story." But there are at least two different ways to say "Don't worry." One is a judicial warning, which has a threatening overtone; the other is a parental encouragement, which aims to comfort. Scripture has both, but Luke placed the accent on parental encouragement. Those warm words from the loving Father were all I needed to notice God's passion for comforting fearful people.

Of course, Scripture took me to new places. I didn't anticipate being taught how to pray or how being an active peacemaker is a sure-fire way to know peace. I also didn't anticipate how the reading, writing, and arithmetic of the Christian life—Bible reading, prayer, and fellowship—would be the rudiments for our battle with fear and worry.

With that in mind, please don't think of the Scripture passages that you will find throughout these meditations to be mere filler. They are essential food. You probably already know most of them, but don't let your familiarity be an occasion for speed reading.

The Table of Contents will give you an outline, but this book is not exactly linear. It isn't a series of steps to follow. Instead, it is thirty meditations linked by a common theme. After you read the "Initial Observations," read a chapter a day. Don't read the next chapter until you have spoken to someone about what you just read.

ACKNOWLEDGMENTS

THE TIME IS COMING soon when the only words I will be able to write or speak are "thank you." I am becoming more indebted to other people every day:

To the Board of the Christian Counseling & Educational Foundation (CCEF), who approved and supported the sabbatical time needed to complete this book.

To my CCEF colleagues—David Powlison, Paul Tripp, Winston Smith, Bill Smith, Tim Lane, and Mike Emlet—whose ideas I shamelessly steal.

To Jayne Clark, who initially proposed CCEF's sabbatical plan.

To the CCEF staff, who make things run more smoothly in my absence.

To Westminster Theological Seminary, for the privilege of teaching so many wise and loving students.

To Sue Lutz, whose tireless efforts to shape my ideas and words continue to humble me.

To my daughters, Lindsay and Lisa, who have a part in everything I do but, as fellow fear specialists, even more so in this project.

To my wife, Sheri, who was always happy to speak with me about the ideas in this book and to read cumbersome sections. Somehow, she knows exactly when to laugh at my various anxieties and when to share my burdens. She should be listed as coauthor.

PART ONE

initial observations

PART ONE looks at our fears and worries with an unaided eye. Here is what stands out upon simple inspection.

- Fear and worry run deep in us all.

- Fear and worry have meaning. They say something.

- Fear and worry say that the world is dangerous.

- Fear and worry reveal us. They reveal the things that we love and value.

CHAPTER ONE

A WORLD OF FEAR

I like to scare people, and people like to be scared.
—STEPHEN KING

LOOK AT CHILDREN, see all humanity. Whereas adults cover up and hide, children are unadorned and open. They lack sophisticated facades and cultural trappings that quietly add layer upon layer to our adult experience. With children, you get the real thing.

Here is what you see.

> Children are profoundly needy but stubbornly independent: "No!" enters their vocabulary right after "Dada" or "Mama."
>
> They can be delightful and charming yet selfish and manipulative: "Mine!" comes right after "No!"
>
> When "Mine!" doesn't work, they throw temper tantrums, and they do this without ever having witnessed adults banging their fists on the floor and screaming bloody murder. Children don't have to learn anger.

Instead, anger can spring spontaneously from their already nascent minds.

They can tell lies, straight-faced, staring right at you, without blinking. Here again children need no teachers. They can lie without ever having been lied to.

And even if they live in an unassailable fortress, protected round the clock by loyalists who ward off all robbers, ghosts, and monsters, with loved ones always within calling distance, video cameras and alarms perpetually set, nightlights on before dusk, shielded from Stephen King, Walt Disney, Saturday morning cartoons, and all things creepy, they will—guaranteed—be afraid. Somehow, without anyone telling them, they know that they live in a world that isn't safe.

FEAR IN CHILDREN

One of the prized gifts of childhood is a grand imagination. Give a child any object and play happens. Dolls become treasured offspring; sticks transform into swords, guns, light sabers, and telescopes. The problem is that, coupled with a fearful heart, these wonderful imaginations can also envision the worst. Watch a child's imagination on the loose and you feel like you are watching an eight-year-old behind the wheel of an Indy race car. A dark room is all they need for their imagination to start careening out of control. Suddenly, clocks are watching them, as yet unclassified creatures scurry around inside the walls, and behind the closet door lurks a world of evil.

Consider Calvin of *Calvin and Hobbes*. He is certain that as soon as his parents are out of sight and the lights are off, there is something drooling under his bed. At a moment's notice—just a flick of the switch—young Calvin goes from world-class superhero to the local under-the-bed monster's supper. And, no doubt, he speaks on behalf of his peers.

If children's imaginations don't take them to these scary places, bedtime stories will. "Hansel and Gretel," "Beauty and the Beast," *Things That*

Go Bump in the Night. Why are there so many scary stories for children? Yes, in classic fairy tales the good people prosper and justice wins in the end. But who is to say if we are good enough to identify with Cinderella? What if we aren't? And even if we think we might be spared the witch's oven, we have still discovered that there are horrible things out there.

Consider these excerpts from popular children's stories from around the world. Notice how they hint of bad things to come and partner with the anxieties of even the most secure child.

> No one in the family ever went near the attic. They hoped the eerie sounds up there were made by branches scraping against the house. But they took no chances. And that was wise, for up in the attic an evil demonness awaited them.[1]

Nothing subtle about this opening to a popular German children's story. The strange sounds present in every house have just been identified, and no sane child will ever go up *any* stairs without an exorcist or parent. Forget about even closing his eyes for the next week! The attic apparition has nothing to do but wait until the family sleeps.

> Long ago in China there lived an old man with a heart of stone. He drove away every beggar who came to his door.[2]

This story starts off innocently enough. You might anticipate a morality tale about generosity. You aren't expecting the heebie-jeebies along the way. But this old man soon becomes a beggar himself. (Scary stories love symmetry.) And before he meets his end, which is assured, you will . . . not close your eyes for the next week.

> Once upon a time there was a widow who had a daughter of her own and a stepdaughter. Whenever her own daughter said or did anything, the

woman would pat her on her head and say, "Clever girl!" But no matter how hard the stepdaughter tried, she was always being called "foolish" or "lazy" by the woman, who often scolded her and sometimes beat her.[3]

In this case you certainly don't want to be the widow *or* her daughter. Their foolishness will be exposed, and then the axe will fall, perhaps literally. Meanwhile the stepdaughter, who (you *hope*) represents yourself, will marry someone rich and handsome.

Anya finally declared, "I am not afraid of anything!"[4]

This is a sure sign that in about three pages Anya will have the bejeebers scared out of her. Most likely she, too, will be dead in the end, and you will have the creeps. And notice the logic of the story. If you are *not* afraid, you are foolish and bad things happen. The only choice is, for our safety's sake, to be filled with dread.

What is going on? These are stories you can find in every known culture. Maybe Stephen King is right—we like to scare and be scared. After all, who hasn't enjoyed jumping out on an unsuspecting friend and saying, "Boo!"? And what American hasn't voluntarily entered a fun house or actually paid money to be scared on an amusement ride? As long as we know that there is really nothing to be scared about, we like to be scared. The adrenaline makes us feel more vital. A good scare can beat an extra-large coffee.

But we are talking about young children here. They don't yet take joy in scaring others or being scared (at least not until they are incited by mischievous siblings), and they don't need the extra energy. What else is going on? Why do their imaginations go so quickly to scary things, even if they have no acquaintance with them? And why do they seem to *like* scary stories?

One possibility is that children are scared *before* they ever encounter their first scary story, in which case the function of the story is to validate pre-existing primal fears. In other words, children already feel as if there are dangers lurking in every dark room. These fears came with the package of being human. The scary stories don't create fear; they simply offer explanations for it: "Yes, there are reasons why you are afraid. You feel *as if* there are monsters under the bed, and you are right. There really *are* monsters under the bed." Children might not be pleased to discover that the noise in the wall is a boogeyman, but at least they have an explanation for their fear, and now they understand why they need a nightlight. (Monsters, of course, are strictly nocturnal.)

Fear is natural to us. We don't have to learn it. We experience fear and anxiety even before there is any logical reason for them. Children's fears predate their acquaintance with scary stories.[5]

FEAR IN TEENS

When children become teens, they take their scary stories with them, but these fortified stories are no longer cute. Gone are the good fairies and kind strangers with unusual powers. Now it is just in-your-face horror: *Goosebumps*, Freddy Krueger, Chuckie, and chainsaws.

A few teens—maybe two or three—refuse to watch these movies. They already have plenty of fears. Why add to them? The rest seem to *need* these nightmarish tales. For some, fear makes them feel alive. It functions in the same way as extreme amusement rides. The guys laugh and the girls scream, which is one reason the guys laugh. But the horror genre serves more purposes than an adrenaline rush or getting a date to hold onto you during an especially chilling scene. These stories say, "It isn't safe out there! Something is watching!" And they are more accurate than they know. Being good, which was your protection in the children's stories, doesn't seem to matter now. Whatever is lurking out there seems incapable of judging between who has been naughty and who has been nice. It has no prejudices or preferences. Teens are not so naïve as to think that their own good deeds will somehow protect them.

Maybe teenagers will be protected if they act out their fears. At least that seems to be the logic behind Halloween. How many emotions have their own national holidays? All around the world there are variations of Halloween. People dress up and do something either to scare off or to make peace with the spirits that allegedly walk among us. In the United States, as secular and scientific as we think we are, the spiritual overtones of Halloween are right on the surface. The costumes are increasingly macabre. A quick walk down the street and you see zombies, mutilated bodies, devils, and your walking nightmares. The costumes are not exclusively ghoulish; there are adorable angels galore. But the angels have a purpose. Angels are spiritual beings, sent from God to protect us. They are part of the supernatural ethos of the evening. Fear is, indeed, a spiritual matter.

FEAR IN ADULTS

As adulthood nudges its way into our lives, one would assume we would put away childish fears and anxieties. But have we? Though adults might not go door-to-door to ask for candy, more dress up for Halloween and Mardi Gras events than ever before. Prime-time television programs feature vampires, mediums, ghosts, and other visitors from the afterlife. The murder mystery is requisite beach reading. Adult horror stories take our senses to the limit. The evening news continues to be a horror reality show. Although there are occasional attempts at positive news, no one tunes in if the news gets too warm and fuzzy. As a culture, young and old, we are groping for a venue to portray the unreasonable, mysterious, risky, and downright scary essence of daily life.

Our cities have random shootings and the threat of *jihad* adds to our anxieties. It would seem that increased freedom would help, but it doesn't. Both oppression and freedom can incite fear. Freedom resolves the fear and anxiety associated with persecution and oppression, but it increases the fear of personal failure, which is one reason Soren Kierkegaard said that anxiety is the dizziness of freedom. With freedom come more choices, which mean more opportunities to get it wrong. Freedom or oppression—pick your poison. They both contribute to our fears and anxieties.

In short, nothing happens to assuage our fears when we turn twenty, and much in our society assumes that fact. Politicians, for example, count on them. It is axiomatic that the candidate who taps into our fears is the one who wins. Once it was the Communist menace. Now politicians predict fiscal catastrophe or increased terrorism or WMDs—unless, of course, they are elected.

All this happens in countries where there is relative peace and prosperity. How much more intense fear must be in less stable regions! Consider those living in the Sudan, where Omar al-Bashir's campaign of ethnic and religious persecution killed over 180,000 in two years. Over two million were driven from their homes; the burning of villages lessened only because there were so few villages left to burn. Such oppression breeds paralytic fear.

As we might guess, far from gradually becoming extinct in adulthood, our fears increase throughout our lives. What was once a small family of worries quietly conducts an aggressive breeding program to become a teeming community of palpable fears and private anxieties. The code by which fear and anxiety live is primal: multiply. As we possess more things, care about more people, accumulate more bad experiences, and watch *Fear Factor* and the evening news, it is as if we absorb fear. If they are not obvious in your own life, perhaps it's because you have been living in a war zone your entire life. At first you noticed every gunshot. After a while the mayhem blends in with the rustle of the trees, the TV, and the children playing in the other room. Fear gradually becomes the background noise of everyday life.

Yet it doesn't take much for that background noise to jump to the forefront of our attention. When the town fathers in Sarasota, Florida, announced a proposal to place a few lifelike clowns around town, subterranean fears erupted.

When coulrophobes [those who fear clowns] there learned that city officials were about to approve a plan to put 70 life-size fiberglass clowns in the downtown area, they inundated agencies with calls, e-mails, and in-person protests.[6]

The proposal went down in flames because one in seven of us is a certifiable coulrophobe.

Ask a friend if he or she has a particular phobia and your own fears won't seem quite as silly. There are names for literally thousands of fears.

Have you ever read a book or seen a movie about submarines? Stories such as Alistair MacLean's *Ice Station Zebra* are scary stories for adults because they arouse our claustrophobia, fears of suffocation, and fears of being buried alive. The submarine doubles as a coffin. The children's writer, Hans Christian Anderson, was always afraid he would be buried alive. His practice was to leave a note on his bedside table explaining that he may "seem dead" but that he was merely sleeping.

There was a time when adults were neatly categorized into one of two groups: you were either neurotic or psychotic. Psychotic meant that you were out of touch with reality and afraid; neurotic meant that you were *in* touch with reality and afraid. Today we are much more enlightened and offer many more diagnostic possibilities. There are scores of psychiatric disorders from which we can select. Yet by far the largest category remains fear. Notice how fear and anxiety are central to this list of modern psychopathologies.

Generalized anxiety disorder

Agoraphobia

Social phobia

Obsessive-compulsive disorder

Sexual aversion disorder

Sleep terror disorder

Avoidant personality

Persecutory delusions

Panic disorder

Paranoid schizophrenia

Other specific phobias

Post-traumatic stress disorder

Nightmare disorder

Paranoid personality

Separation anxiety disorder

About one in ten experiences more extreme versions of these problems. But if we look closely at ourselves, we will notice something in every description that feels familiar.

Obsessive-compulsive Disorder (OCD), in its pronounced form, affects about one in fifty people. It is worry run amok. The obsession is an intrusive idea that feels impossible to dislodge. The compulsion is the action intended to neutralize the obsession. In its less disruptive form it is fairly common: Most people think about germs and contamination, and it's not unusual to triple-check the alarm and double-check the stove. But it can become life-dominating. The obsession of germs can lead to the compulsion of endless hand-washing that leaves the skin bleeding and sore. The imaginary fear that you might have witnessed or caused an accident keeps you circling back to the side of the road where you think it all happened. You check the scene until the compulsion is dislodged by another. Religious doubts and fears are handled by repetitive counting. Hours of each day are filled with rituals that hopefully will nullify those fears.

One in fifty is the statistic for the more severe form of OCD, but traces of it can be found everywhere. Worries come to us covered in sticky paper; they aren't shaken off easily.

Panic is another common form of fear and anxiety. It is fear that utterly explodes in physical symptoms: heart palpitations, shortness of breath, dizziness, shaking, fear of dying, fear of going crazy. After the initial episode, we add the fear that it could happen again, which makes it all the more likely that it will.

There are, of course, treatments for fears and anxieties. Medication dulls the physical symptoms; psychological treatments address the thoughts. If you are afraid to fly because you keep thinking the plane will crash, you can replace that thought with another. *I've flown many times before and nothing has happened. It's the safest way to travel.* This might help, but it rests on the premise that fear submits to logic, which is a dubious assumption. In reality, fears are rarely logical. Or, as fearful people might protest, they are *very* logical. If the statistics on plane crashes indicate that they are extremely rare, the statistics also say that planes *do* crash and people actually die in plane crashes. *Someone* is going to be that 1 in 100,000; and you aren't feeling very lucky. You have a foreboding sense that the odds are against you.

Other treatments, such as *systematic desensitization,* focus on the body's response to fear. The goal is to teach your body how to relax as a way to distract a mind locked into a potential catastrophe. After you learn to physically relax, you then either imagine or actually face a series of lesser fears while you maintain physical calm. Once you master those, you graduate to the greater fears. You might be encouraged to add a pleasant mental image to your bodily relaxation. Tropical islands are popular. The basic idea is that you can't multi-task. If you are thinking about balmy breezes on a perfect beach, your mind won't have room for your fears.

These versions of fool-your-body-into-thinking-everything-is-okay can help some people cross bridges or even fly; but, when examined closely, they seem superficial and thus rather hopeless. They reduce fear to a series of physiological responses. Meanwhile we suspect that there is a deeper reality to our fears and worries. Listen to your fears and you hear them speak about things that have personal meaning to you. They appear to be attached to things we value.

One of the things we value is life, so it isn't surprising that death hovers right below the surface of many fears. Neither thought control nor physical relaxation can ward off this monster. If we want fear to loosen its grip, we have to deal with death head on. Bridges, planes, and many other fears are the fear of death in disguise. Given such a potent adversary, we can't simply gloss over it with mental trips to Tahiti unless we have already decided that there are no answers and denial is our only hope.

These deeper meanings in our fears suggest that we will have to look in two directions. As we look outward, we will see real dangers: disease, death, war, economic collapse, and a host of other ills. That, however, is only part of the story. Why do we all have different *responses* to possible dangers?

And why are some people petrified of some things, such as mice, that aren't dangerous?

To deeply understand fear we must also look at ourselves and the way we interpret our situations. Those scary objects can reveal what we cherish. They point out our insatiable quest for control, our sense of aloneness. Even the vocabulary of fear indicates that the problem can be deeper than a real, objective danger. While "fear" refers to the experience when a car races toward us and we just barely escape, "anxiety" or worry is the lingering sense, after the car has passed, that life is fragile and we are always vulnerable.

The terrain is fear and anxiety. You are familiar with it, and you are not alone.

CHAPTER TWO

YOUR FEAR

I have a new philosophy. I only dread one day at a time.
—CHARLIE BROWN

"NO, I DON'T really have any fears." He was casual and confident.

Maybe he would reveal his secrets of fearlessness to the rest of us. But you have your doubts. You wonder what would happen if he teetered on the ledge of a tall building or was strapped in the passenger seat while a newly-minted, sixteen-year-old driver, with four boisterous friends in the back, gazed into the rearview mirror to join in the backseat fun and blindly made her way onto the fast lane of the expressway, assuming that other drivers…well, not thinking about other drivers.

Then he explained.

"When I have to fly, I get sweaty palms and usually think about how the plane is too heavy to lift off. When my children are out, I notice all the police and ambulance sirens. I can't stand thinking about the possibility of my wife dying before me. I worry about money all the time, and how I might die. But, no, I'm not a fearful person."

His standard must have been hourly panic attacks and full-blown paranoia. He had all the normal fears, maybe more than most. He was just saying that he wasn't quite certifiable. Yet.

Please don't follow his lead. Rather than minimize your fears, find more of them. Expose them to the light of day because the more you find, the more blessed you will be when you hear words of peace and comfort.

BACKGROUND FEAR AND ANXIETY

Start by rounding up the usual suspects.

Fears for your safety and the safety of those you love.

Fears about how you will die: a progressively debilitating disease, cancer, Alzheimer's disease, being alone, being penniless.

Fears about what happens after death: being forgotten, being maligned, being judged, being extinct.

Fears about living a meaningless life. Extensive resumés seem more and more hollow when we consider the end of life.

Fears about being unloved or alone.

Fears about being in love and the high probability of being hurt.

Fears about what you might lose: your figure, boyfriend, girlfriend, hair, youth, mind, money, job, spouse, health, hobbies, purpose, faith.

Any time you love or want something deeply, you will notice fear and anxieties because you might not get them.

Any time you can't control the fate of those things you want or love, you will notice fears and anxieties because you might lose them.

Good insurance policies might help, but they only lessen the risk on things that aren't our real worries. They can't insure that our loved ones will outlive us or keep us from the ravages of age.

Control and certainty are myths.

PHOBIAS

Now take a look at your phobias. Our frailties and eccentricities are plentiful, easy to locate and (when they aren't too extreme) easy to poke fun at. You should be able to come up with twenty or so within a couple of minutes. If you have trouble getting started, ask some friends to prime your pump by naming some of their own specific fears. Once you can name the first ten, you shouldn't have any problem identifying dozens more. For those on the cutting edge of anxiety, *arachibutyrophobia* is a recent one: the fear of peanut butter sticking to the roof of your mouth. Think about it long enough and you could probably wind up claiming it as your own.

Here are some of the more common fears.

Heights	Needles
Paper cuts	Cancer
Suffocation	Terrorism
Mice and other rodents	Insects
Snakes	Baldness
Fat	Germs
Flying	Vomiting
Driving in bad weather	Drowning
The dark	Dentists
Bridges	Crowds

For bonus points, take your top three fears and ask what they say about you. What do you really want? What is important to you? What do you value? What do you love? But that is jumping ahead.

DREAMS

Next, consider your actual dreams and nightmares. Do you have any fear and anxiety dreams?

I was in a house and saw a person being murdered. The murderer was trying to drown someone in the bathtub. When I ran in to try to help, I saw that the person in the bathtub was me.

Just another night's sleep for a healthy college student!

Most of us have anxiety dreams, such as dreams of being pursued, unprepared, overwhelmed, or out of control. The most frequent of my anxiety dreams is one in which I find myself at a podium in front of thousands of people. I am slated to give a speech and my topic is being introduced. As I listen to the title, I hear a string of multi-syllabic words. I assume they are English but I can't be sure. I can't even identify the general category: physics, medicine, astronomy, world peace, fat-free cooking? And if I had the presence of mind to look down, I would probably find that I was naked or dressed in some way that insulted everyone in the audience. I have ten seconds to organize my thoughts.

I can smile about these when I wake up, but they always reveal that I am, indeed, anxious.

What are your dreams saying? The content can be silly and inscrutable, but listen for the emotional tone of your dreams. What do they feel like? Being pursued? Missing deadlines? Spinning endless plates? Being exposed and embarrassed? Keep track of them and in the course of a week you will hear them speak: "I am afraid," "I am anxious," "I'm feeling pressure."

PHYSICAL CLUES

Now notice your body. We can distract ourselves mentally from our anxieties, but our bodies can stay focused on them even when our minds aren't. Our bodies are always scanning our inner emotional terrain. At the first hint of a threat, our bodies are mobilized: palpitations, sweaty palms, perspiration, tension headaches, clenched jaws, impotence, rapid breathing, loss of appetite, increased appetite, problems sleeping, high blood pressure. Our bodies can tell us we are anxious even before we are aware of it.

Take a quick inventory of your physical tension. Start at the top of your head and go to your toes. Unless you are actually on the tropical beach you once imagined or in a backyard Jacuzzi, you will probably notice that your forehead and neck are tightened. If you relax, your shoulders will drop a good inch or two. Your arms are much more constricted than they need to be in order to hold a book. Try to make yourself a little heavier by letting your muscles relax. A brief physical scan makes you wonder who told your body that the sky is falling.

STRESS

When we are aware that anxiety has registered at a physical level we call it stress. Stress usually means that there is too much to do in too little time, or the things we have to do are beyond our competencies. There is no way we are going to get children off for school on time, meet that deadline at work, or call the plumber about the leak that is starting to come through the ceiling—and that is just the to-do list before lunch. The frenetic pace of life was intended for those with twenty-four-hour secretaries and chauffeurs who double as grocery go-fers. If you listen a little more closely, you will probably detect the theme of control. Stress is saying that life is teetering on the brink, right at the farthest reaches of your ability to maintain some control. What would happen if you really lost control? You don't know, and you don't *want* to know.

Stress can also signify that there is something on your to-do list that will be inspected by others. You feel stress before an important test or before anything done in public, such as athletics, speaking, or performing. Any occasion for evaluation can be stressful. If you listen to this type of stress, it whispers, "Life is risky. Your most treasured dreams rise or fall on your performance." Is failure really that bad? If someone doesn't think you are great, will life rip apart at the seams? Again, you aren't sure, but you don't have time to consider it. Anxiety and fear prefer to stay on the surface rather than linger to consider something more deeply. And you are too busy anyway. If you think about these things, you will just get farther behind.

BUSY AND DRIVEN

When you have to manage the world, please everyone, earn more than you did last year, and work off five pounds, you will be driven. If not, you run the risk of being un-American or even un-Christian because our economy and churches rely on such people. Even when paralyzed by circumstances, a stressed person is a driven person.

Always busy, never enough time, pushing toward deadlines, fitful sleep, working late, intolerant of interruptions, puts projects over people: You could be talking about the CEO, the middle manager, or the stay-at-home mom who is homeschooling three children. For some, it feels like life is driving them; there is simply so much to do. For others, there is a curious love-hate relationship with their lifestyle. So much of their busyness is self-imposed. Their "yes" to every request suggests that they prefer a driven lifestyle. Or perhaps they value personal achievement and a robust resumé because these might shield them from financial disaster or, worse, the disdain of others.

Maybe the anxiously driven person is running from something. Blaise Pascal was one of the first to suggest that personal character can be assessed by how people handled rest and solitude. Do you avoid quiet? When you are alone, is either the iPod or TV always on? It should make you wonder: *What am I avoiding? What is it about quiet places that is so scary?*

DEPRESSION

Drivenness and depression, on the surface, have little in common. One is active, the other passive. But both can be ways of responding to fear. Listen carefully to depression and you often hear fear and anxiety: *I am not strong enough to handle the despair any longer. I am afraid all the time. I am losing my ability to hide my true self. I am afraid I'll be exposed. Underneath the emotional pain is terror.*

Depression is rarely sought. It finds you and covers you in darkness. But in the history of literature it is, along with alcohol abuse, romanticized as a kind of poetic muse. Sylvia Plath, Anne Sexton, Virginia Woolf, Edgar Allen Poe, and Robert Lowell are all people who could express tragedy with elegance. But especially in Plath's case, fear was the deeper problem, and there was nothing romantic about it. After her father's death she was terrified of abandonment and responded by running. She threw herself into study, tennis, and writing. "I want to kill myself, to escape from responsibility, to draw back into the womb."

Notice the depressed person who can't get out of bed. Is it possible that he or she doesn't want to face the dangerous world? Outside the covers is a world that is out of control with the potential for failure, rejection, and endless surprises we can't even imagine, so depression opts for paralysis.

Freedom and its pitfalls show up again here. In an authoritarian context you make very few decisions, but with freedom you decide how you will spend your time and money. If you choose to do one thing with your time, you are saying no to something else. You can invest your money in the stock market, open a savings account, put it in a certificate of deposit, or stuff it under the mattress. Each has its risks; none carries a guarantee.

What is more, each choice sets you on a different life trajectory. Choose one IRA over another and you just made a decision that will eventually keep you from a decent house or a high-end retirement home. Decide to work at one company because the benefits are better and embezzlers hijack your retirement account. Will you find a relationship if you keep saying no to coworkers who invite you to a popular bar? Did you allow your son to take the car at the same time a drunk driver was on the road? Should you marry this guy even though you have heard plenty of Jekyll and Hyde stories? It's enough to make all of us want to stay in bed and yearn for simpler times when we didn't have to make decisions.

ANGER

Many people are familiar with depression. We are all familiar with anger. Anger says, "You are wrong, I am right." But if you listen closely, it can say more.

How do you explain an overly aggressive animal? If it is domesticated or accustomed to sharing its space with humans, you suspect that fear is the problem. Though some run in fear, others attack, defending something important that is at risk. Listen to anger and you will frequently find fear. A woman rages at her husband for coming home late with alcohol on his breath. Sure, there is the "You are wrong" component. But there is also "I am afraid you are losing interest in me. I am afraid you could be tempted by another woman. And when you add alcohol, I get even more afraid."

The problem is compounded with men because men aren't supposed to be afraid. With no permission to discuss fears, men opt for anger. Sometimes their anger says, "This is the only way I know to get some control in an out-of-control world." But it's a stopgap measure. Control that emerges out of anger is strictly temporary.

Scripture says this about anger: "What causes fights and quarrels among you? You want something but don't get it" (James 4:1–2). You want power, love, the TV remote, perfect children, but you don't get them.

Fear and anxiety say this: "You want something, and you might not get it." You want power, love, the TV remote, perfect children, but you might not get them. You want financial security, health for yourself and those you love, safe passage to work, and you know you can't presume any of it.

Fear and anger can be the same words spoken with a different attitude.

OVERPROTECTION

You wouldn't think that protective and involved parents would be driven by fear, but look more closely. Today's parents were an under-protected lot. They grew up during a time when the divorce rate had spiked; they came home to empty houses. Not only were many of them self-parented, they also parented their parents, which means that they had no parents. So naturally, they are protective now as parents, involved and exhausted. They are looking into preschools before their child is born because they sense that the wrong one could forever handicap his or her future. Fear has given birth to extreme parenting. It looks like love, but it is love mingled with fear.

SUPERSTITIONS

Do you have any superstitions? (Assume yes.) When my wife and I visit a particular relative, we can't leave without salt flying, a cryptic comment about cats and ladders, and an incantation or two. And never, ever say *pig*. The neutralizing ritual for such a cosmic *faux pas* would extend your visit an extra day.

Superstitions are personal routines you hope will bring good fortune or avoid bad. "Don't step on the crack or you'll break your mother's back" only morphs with age. It doesn't disappear. World Cup soccer coaches, even of championship teams, won't allow a Scorpio in the locker room for fear that the astrological balance of the team would be forever disrupted. Baseball players wear that one unwashed sock in hopes that it will grant them a big hit. Every major newspaper has its astrology section. Every telephone directory has pages devoted to fortune-tellers and palm readers.

We make light of the idol worshiper, but at least an idol worshiper is appealing to someone personal for good luck. Somehow that makes more sense than trusting in a dirty sock or the gravitational pull of a nearby planet. Superstitions and eccentric habits are a Western substitute for actual idols.

LIFE WITHOUT FEAR?

Could you imagine life without fear? Maybe, but only if you have retained some of that turbo-charged imagination from childhood. What can you imagine? You walk on an airplane and it feels no different from walking into someone's office. Your kids are out late and you still sleep like a baby. Economic indicators predict the worst but you are focused on more important things.

It's not that you want to be without all fear. It's just that some fears are more of a nuisance than others. There are some fears you'd prefer to keep in a less extreme form. For example, you want to be concerned about reckless drivers so that you will wear a seat belt and drive defensively. You prefer to maintain a healthy respect for all animals very large and very small. You just want courage that is not overcome by fear. You don't mind having fear in dangerous situations. It is the nagging background anxieties that you would gladly jettison.

We are in this together, so there is no reason to be shy in acknowledging our multitude of fears and worries. W. H. Auden wrote a poem about our era entitled, "The Age of Anxiety." Albert Camus spoke about the "century of fear." But every age is an age of anxiety, every century a century of fear.

CHAPTER THREE

FEAR SPEAKS

THERE IS NO DAWDLING in the face of fear. When we perceive it creeping up on us we want to keep moving. To slow down and listen to what it might be saying is counterintuitive.

But fear is speaking, and we should listen.

One useful life skill is to know when to listen to our feelings and when to ignore them. As a general rule, the first step is to listen. There is a logic—a language—to fear and anxiety, just as there is to most emotions. Anger says, "You are wrong." Embarrassment or shame says, "I am wrong." Fear says, "I am in danger," but it also says much more.

Don't forget, listening for fear is like listening to background noise. At first you think there is nothing to hear, but then you notice the wind in the trees, birds calling for a mate, cars passing by, a plane overhead, creaks in the floors, the water heater kicking in. At first we might deny any palpable fears and their logic, but then we listen more carefully and notice that they are everywhere, speaking loudly.

Eventually we can start to detect some general themes.

"I AM IN DANGER"

Here is the obvious starting point. You don't have to listen long to know that fear says, "Life is dangerous." We might not have Genghis Khan sweeping across the plains, prepared to destroy everything that moves, but life is dangerous no matter when and where we live. There are real reasons to be afraid.

Our world is uncertain and accidents happen. Cuts, bruises, broken bones, and life-threatening injuries are daily occurrences, even without sworn enemies to worry about. You could argue that accidents are even more dangerous than enemies because, with enemies, at least you have some warning. You know when to be vigilant and when to be at rest, but accidents by their very nature are haphazard and unpredictable. They come without warning. Although we recognize that there are steps we can take to lower the risks of life, such as wearing a seat belt, not riding a motorcycle, and avoiding certain places late at night, we also know that we are ultimately powerless. Something bad might happen today. If we live long enough, something bad will *certainly* happen, and there is nothing we can do to keep it at bay.

"Danger" has been a cry of the heart throughout human history. Page through Psalms, the most recited book in Scripture, and you will find timeless expressions of human experience. Its prominent themes are danger, fear, and anxiety.

> O LORD, how many are my foes!
>   How many rise up against me!
>   —Ps. 3:1

> Answer me when I call to you,
>   O my righteous God.
> Give me relief from my distress;

be merciful to me and hear my prayer.
How long, O men, will you turn my glory into shame?

—Ps. 4:1–2A

Why, O Lord, do you stand far off?
Why do you hide yourself in times of trouble?
In his arrogance the wicked man hunts down the weak.

—Ps. 10:1–2A

The psalmists invite you into perilous situations with them. They have real questions about whether or not they will be alive tomorrow. Their situations are probably more extreme than our own, but the psalmists rarely mention the specifics because they don't want the details of their personal stories to bar us from entering in with our own. Instead, they invite us to participate whenever possible. They are choirmasters who want us to join them in their chorus to the Lord.

The psalmists recount times when they had enemies who hunted and maligned them. To join in, we could insert our own experiences of being wounded by critical or hateful comments. We might incorporate stories about past abuse and victimization. Have you ever thought your life was hanging in the balance? You could bring that into the psalm.

"I AM VULNERABLE"

Implicit in "Life is dangerous" is "I am vulnerable." We wouldn't be scared of an enemy if we knew we were much stronger. If you live in a trailer park in hurricane alley, during the humid days of summer you will be on the edge of your seat with each forecast. But if you live in the same area in a house made to withstand the worst of high winds and rain, and if that house has already proven its mettle, you won't be afraid. Something can be dangerous, but you can still be safe.

This is where fear gets interesting. Danger points at the threatening world around us. Vulnerability points to ourselves. If fear were only about dangerous people and difficult circumstances, we would just take precautions and live the best we can. But fear is about us.

Listen and you hear: "I am not in control." You don't have to be on the verge of a world apocalypse to feel this one. All you have to do is get out of bed on a fine spring day when everything seems to be going fine.

Take someone who is accustomed to driving and put him in the front passenger seat. Get someone else behind the wheel, and see what happens. Watch his left foot nearly do a Fred Flintstone as he puts all his weight on an imaginary brake. Listen to his ongoing advice to (and commentary on) the driver, even when the driver is the more careful of the two. That person is saying that he is vulnerable and out of control—but enough about me.

Behind this desire for control is the gnawing awareness that we are merely human. Although we might dream about superhuman powers, by design we are limited and we know it. No matter how much we rail against our dependency on other people, we really *are* dependent people with limited control. We *have* to rely on other people. Like it or not, that's the system.

Listen more carefully and you might hear a faint whisper that we are creatures, and we have a complicated relationship with God. Superman, the Incredibles and the Fantastic Four are fiction, but they suggest that, given a choice, we would prefer to *be* God. Without that option we dabble in trusting him. Even agnostics will turn to God in difficult situations. When the captain of a jumbo jet announced that he would be forced to make a "hard" landing because all hydraulics had failed, a stewardess who survived reported that the announcement was followed by a strange quiet. Everyone, it seemed, decided it was time to trust God rather than pursue their own means of controlling the world. Everyone was praying.

Here is where fear is a door to spiritual reality. It suggests that authentic humanness was never intended to be autonomous and self-reliant. Humans are needy by design.

Will we abandon the myth of independence and seek God? Fear, control, God—they are all linked together. Since independence only works during the really good times, the obvious answer would be to seek God. The problem is that God, the One in control, does not *seem* to exert much control. Trust him or not, bad things will happen. (More on this later.) At this point, just realize that fear is saying something about you.

"I NEED (AND I MIGHT NOT GET)"

Another way of expressing our personal vulnerability is through our experience of need. There is a close connection between what we fear and what we think we need.

> If we need comfort, we will fear physical pain.
> If we need approval from others, we will fear being criticized.
> If we need love, we will fear rejection.
> If we need admiration for our attractiveness, we will fear getting fat.

Whatever you need is a mere stone's throw from what you fear.

Two prominent categories of fear are those fears related to money and people. Their power to provoke fear is directly related to how much we need them. If we need what people can give us, *they* are in control and we will fear them. If we need what money can give us, we will notice rising insecurities whenever we do the bills.

Let's follow the path of money for a moment. Money is believed to have unusual power to satisfy our many needs and wants, so it is a target for endless fears.

With money we can get adequate medical treatment, love, respect, and care in our old age. Nothing else in creation can offer so much control and power. Without it we are vulnerable and powerless. No wonder our fears attach themselves to our net worth.

A hundred-dollar bill may look like only a hundred-dollar bill, but in it you place your hopes and dreams, your desire for influence, your independence, your legacy, your security, and that of your family members. It looks like a hundred-dollar bill, but it is a symbol that represents what you feel you need.

Watch your confident friend when her bank account is headed down rather than up. (It is not so much the amount of money a person has as it is the increase or decrease of one's net worth that calms or excites anxiety.) If she has lost money, your friend will no longer have the brave façade. Instead, every bill she receives will be met by a churning stomach and a fitful night's sleep. She needs the security of knowing there is enough money for today, tomorrow, and next year.

Not everyone imposes so much meaning on a buck. My father saw money very simply. For him, it was a God-given means to avoid being a burden on other people, and it was a way to bless others. From my teen years on, his bank account headed in a downward direction. His response was that he felt privileged to give away as much as he did. A few years later, when I encouraged him to take nice vacations or at least be less generous with those he didn't even know, he would say, "I will be faithful with what God gives me, and he will be faithful to me." And he was right. Old age found him penniless, but he was cared for in a style that was more than he could have imagined, and he was never a burden on anyone. He was, simply, a blessing.

Did he need money? Yes. But needs are prioritized. The greater ones make the lesser ones less significant. My father needed money, but he had a greater need to be generous. As a result, never once did I see him fret about money. He fretted about other things, such as physical health, but never about finances.

My wife Sheri is another member of that elite group that views money as a gift to be stewarded, and since it is a gift it should be freely given to others. Whenever our personal finances are threatened or seem to be in a downward spiral, she never frets or grasps. Instead, she maintains a simple confidence in her Creator and Father, and doesn't miss a step in her generosity.

I, on the other hand, am patiently waiting for such fearlessness to rub off on me. I have both nature and nurture covered—I have generous genes and I live with a generous wife—but so far that has not been enough. I still find many perceived needs that are symbolized by that hundred-dollar bill. It will, indeed, take a more powerful hand than theirs to loose me from money's grip.

Fear, control, God, anger, and need—they are all part of the same cluster.

"I AM NEEDY, BODY AND SOUL"

Our neediness or vulnerability comes in two forms: physical need and soul or psychological need.

A seventh-grade boy accidentally bumps into the junior-high bully who immediately reacts. "You just got yourself a fight. See me on the playground after school. If you don't show, I'll find you and hurt you even worse."

The boy turns pale; his stomach goes into spasms, and anxiety reigns. The need he feels is for physical well-being. He couldn't care less about the potential psychological humiliation of being pummeled. All he can think of is pain.

A seventh-grade girl is the only girl in school to dress for color day. Her friends said they would be wearing red and white but, in a flurry of late-night phone calls, decided that color day was lame. The girl feels vulnerable and exposed. She comes home from school and insists that she can never go back. Her anxiety level is off the charts.

In both cases there is danger. Both are vulnerable; both feel needy. The boy fears physical danger; the girl feels social disgrace. Given a choice between the two, most of us would choose the pummeling because the wounds heal faster.

Included in the list of physical dangers are snakes, any large beast, dogs that bite, heights that make you dizzy, aging, and physical disease. The psychological or spiritual danger is of a different ilk. This danger includes loss of reputation, influence, love, respect, admiration, security, and other desires that are intangible but often the center of our lives. Guilt can be folded in here as well.

Where do people and money fit? They span both categories, hence their power. We feel physically needy and vulnerable; money can buy food, people can defend or attack us. We feel psychologically needy; money buys reputation, people can give or withhold love and respect.

"THAT IS VALUABLE TO ME: I LOVE IT AND HAVE PUT MY TRUST IN IT"

Fear links with *danger. Danger* links with *God*, being *vulnerable,* being *out-of-control,* and *need. Need*, then, links to other experiences. When we need money, we are saying that money is especially *valuable* to us, and anything especially valuable is something we *love*.

I crave or love respect, so I am undone when I don't receive it. I fear not getting it.

I love comfort, so physical discomfort is terrifying. Our fears point to what we really care about.

For decades my wife and I never locked our house. We couldn't even find a key. When we went away we never thought twice about burglaries because there was nothing we needed in the house. There was nothing we really loved. Everything was worth fifty dollars or less, and if anyone stole some of it, we might have been grateful.

Then we began to amass a few things that were important to us. To be forthcoming, I should say they were important to *me*. Now before we leave for a trip, I package those items and hide them. I have even considered purchasing a safe—all of which my wife finds pitiful and humorous. I never really loved anything in our house until now. I never had fears of robbers until we accumulated a few items that I love.

Love, an intimate relationship, is linked to *trust*, a personal allegiance. Trust reveals the center of our worlds. When we have fears about our financial position, we might be revealing that we trust in our money. The phrase evokes images of authority, even kingly authority. When we are afraid we don't have enough money, money is probably enthroned in our lives.

The cluster of things attached to fear is growing. What began as a study of fear and danger has enlarged to include God, control, need, love, trust, and being ruled or owned by something else.

"I COULD DIE"

Our need for (love for, trust in) prestige and reputation seems so essential. Our vulnerability in the face of uncertain investments keeps us watching the stock reports every day. Then a day comes when we learn that death is close. It may be our own death or the death of someone we love. Either way, other fears now seem trivial. Death is a stalker that pursues us as a vague presence. Once we see him, our fears are concentrated on death alone.

Horror movies are frightening not because a person was rejected or someone met financial disaster. They are horrifying because they bring death close. No one cares about their reputation or their bank account when they find themselves in the shadow of death. If you could erase all other fears except death, persistent anxiety would still be our common lot.

Much of our anxiety over death stems from the *way* we might die. How many times have you heard people say that they want to die suddenly, in their sleep, from a heart attack, while they are still otherwise healthy? How many of us envy those who die peacefully, without pain and surrounded by family and friends? We tremble at the thought of a long-term, debilitating disease. We watch the courage of Lou Gehrig and Morrie Schwartz from *Tuesdays With Morrie*[1] and stand amazed that humans can be so vital in the face of ALS. But we still dread the thought of ALS. We read the book because it gives us hope that maybe we too can go through the valley of the shadow of death with a certain dignity.

A friend calls with fear in his voice. He says that he feels less competent at his job. He can't learn new tasks. At other times we might have joked about getting old, but not this time. His father died of early-onset Alzheimer's disease, and he is scared to death that he might follow the same path.

Now add the other side of death. How much of our fears and worries are connected to concerns about what might happen *after* we die? Some believe that there will be nothing after death which, given our fundamental conviction that life is good, is not very encouraging because we are losing something good. Most of us believe that there is some kind of life after death and, if you believe the statistics, most of us believe that we will go someplace pleasant. This can assuage our fears, but we also realize that, apart from divine revelation, we are making it up as we go. If we believe that there is a heaven, we believe there are entrance criteria as well. What are those criteria? Those who are "good" make it and those who aren't don't? Or maybe it's by percentages—the top 80 percent make it. None of us feel like moral superstars, but we hope that we are one of the crowd and can slip in unnoticed. But are we really that confident in our afterlife theories? Is it possible that the bar is higher than we think?

If uncertainty and powerlessness are basic to fear and worry, then the far side of death is enough to make anyone afraid. Why don't we all acknowledge it? If we don't, death will announce itself in other ways.

An atheist professor delighted in tearing down the Christian faith of zealous freshmen. By his own admission, he was arrogant, selfish, and intolerant of anything that didn't measure up to his standards of reason. His wife agreed, adding that he was chronically grumpy and often angry. Everything changed, however, after a near-death experience. During routine surgery, something went wrong and the surgical team thought they lost him. Meanwhile, the professor was witnessing bright lights and warmth, which he subsequently attributed to an afterlife vision. After his recovery, he was a changed man. He tolerated the Christian beliefs of his freshman students, and his wife confirmed that he was less cranky with her and others.

Do you remember how anger, especially in men, can be a cover for fear? Perhaps the professor's near-death experience did only one thing for him: It took away his fear of death. He interpreted his near-death experience as an accurate vision of the afterlife. Since it turned out to be warm and fuzzy, there was nothing to fear.

Among those who follow Christ, we would expect death to hold no fear. This is true for some, but for many the fear of death still has its talons in us. We know that there is no condemnation as we put our trust in Jesus Christ, but theory is easier than practice. Heaven holds many mysteries and some of us don't like surprises. There are times when we wonder if it is all too good to be true. We wonder what God will really say to us when we first see him face to face.

All this listening to fear brings both clarity and confusion. It brings clarity because we hear important messages that call for a response, but the process can become confusing because we hear so much. If it feels a little overwhelming, take encouragement in this: The reason we are investigating some of the hidden features of fear is because God has beautiful words of comfort for fearful people. After you listen to your own heart, listen to God.

A PERSONAL RESPONSE

There are times when fear says that something is just plain dangerous and I should be afraid. But my goal in listening to my fears is to learn how to decipher what else they are saying. When I pause and listen, I might find that fear says a lot and it speaks clearly. What it says can provide me with immensely helpful direction.

I have been doing that. I have paused and listened. I have located fears—lots of them. So far the exercise has been more helpful than I expected. For example, I wasn't anticipating the connection with my fear and my desires, wants, needs, and loves. When I see this stew of activity within me, I am much more hopeful. If fear were just about a dangerous world, there would be little I could do. But if it is about me, maybe there is a way through it.

Of the different words and ideas that cluster around fear, work with *trust*. Review some of your fears and ask: *What do these fears say I trust in? What do my fears say I love?*

CHAPTER FOUR

ANXIETY AND WORRY CHIME IN

HAVE YOU NOTICED that when you are actually overtaken by your fear, it is rarely as bad as anticipated?

A skier in search of a thrill pushes off and drops forty feet to the steep, powdered slope below. He loses his balance on impact and begins careening out of control into either a stand of trees or a field of boulders. Whatever he hits, he knows the impact will kill him. But he is surprisingly objective about it. He wonders if the impending crash will hurt. He wonders about life after death. He wonders about the bill on his desk that remains unpaid. And he muses about all this without any alarm. Somehow he avoids both trees and rocks and walks away unscathed.

A twelve-year-old girl, who was always scared of the water and never learned to swim, is beckoned by friends to cool off in a relatively shallow area of a bay. Reluctantly, clutching a boogie board, she ventures out. All is well until she loses her grip on the board and slips into a small hollow on the water's bottom. As she sinks beneath the surface she experiences a surprising calm. Here she is facing her worst fear and it seems peaceful. When she looks up, she notices two white pillars above her. They are the legs of a friend who doesn't even know she is drowning. The drowning girl gets her hand on one leg and pulls herself up to the surface.

The stories are nearly archetypal. When you are actually in the battle you aren't thinking about fear. The hard part is the night before. Your anxiety level rises when you hear the drumbeat of the opposing army getting closer and closer and all you can do is wait. Anxiety about the future event is usually worse than the event itself.

WORRIERS LIVE IN THE FUTURE

There is a story line to human life that includes a past, present, and future. Fear spans them all. Fear can be triggered by the past, react to crises in the present, or anticipate them in the future. Its preferred time zone, however, is the future. Dread, panic, nervousness, worry, and anxiety all speak of our potential future vulnerability. Our word *fear* doesn't discriminate between threats that are present or future, real or perceived, but it usually says, "I *am* in danger." *Anxiety* and *worry* are less oriented to the present. They say, "I *think* there *will* be a danger"; "Something or someone I love might be threatened in the future."

Here is where adult imaginations show their mettle. Imaginations are our ability to consider things that don't presently exist. Sometimes we call it vision. A visionary is one who looks ahead and envisions the trajectory of a church, business, or individual life. A talented visionary is one who can see future possibilities and persuade others of that future. Visionaries are rarely right (at least in the details), tend to be optimistic, and are always confident.

WORRIERS SEE THE FUTURE IN MINUTE, GORY DETAIL

Worriers are visionaries minus the optimism. An experienced worrier can go for days leapfrogging from past to future and back again, never landing in the present. When they travel into the future they see it in Technicolor and vivid detail. Before they go for a routine physical they can hear the doctor pronouncing the dire diagnosis. They see the twisted metal of the imagined car accident. They watch the course of their life change after they fail a biology test, and they haven't even taken it yet. They hear the pastor saying "dust to dust" at a spouse's graveside service. They see the house being sold and watch the grieving children console themselves in drug abuse.

It isn't only children who should have warning labels put on their imagination!

WORRIERS ARE FALSE PROPHETS

Of course, such scenarios are possible. No one can prove worriers wrong, so there is a veneer of reasonableness to every worry. Aliens *could* invade. An errant meteor could destroy civilization as we know it, though the meteor would spare incorrigible worriers because they have made adequate preparations. We can't prove otherwise. Where worriers show their irrationality, however, is in their success rate: They are always wrong, at least in the specifics. They think the worst about tomorrow, and it doesn't happen. Then, when their prophecy doesn't come to pass, they don't say *mea culpa* or place less credence in their next worry. There isn't time for such things because there is too much to worry about for tomorrow.

Advanced worriers worry about everything, and if you worry about everything you will occasionally stumble upon an approximation to a real event. Worry that someone you love will be in a car accident, and worry about that every day—every hour—for a decade, and someday you might get a call from a friend who needs a ride because her car battery went dead. This event will then justify every worry you ever had.

Or let's say that there actually was a car accident, and your worries began there. Now you are scared to drive, and you worry when anyone you love goes faster than twenty-five miles per hour. Worry has become your talisman to ward off future catastrophe.

Can you see how worries multiply? Suddenly you are a gifted prophet and it is your God-given duty to worry. You see the future; others are blind to it. You must sound the alarm for the people you love. Compassion *demands* that you worry.

So goes the natural history of a professional worrier.

If you are looking for a way out, consider starting with a name change. In the Old Testament, prophets were the ones who talked about the future, and, much like worriers, what they foretold was often bad. The only way you could remain in good standing as a prophet was if your predictions were infallible. Err once and you were forever banned from making future prophecies (Deut. 18:22). Using this standard, worriers are certifiable *false prophets.* Their peer group is not so much those with psychiatric diagnoses as they are astrologers, tarot card readers, and Ouija board devotees. How much better off we would be if all our future predictions were declared illegal and we were forever banned from making any others.

WORRIERS ARE IMMUNE TO REASON

As worry veers out of control, cool heads try to help. First, they state the obvious: Worry doesn't help. Second, they add that worry has more in common with astrology than it does careful weather forecasts. Then, if nothing else works, helpers try to assuage the worrier by making the environment more secure, if possible.

An empty-nest wife was petrified to be alone. She had visions of murderers, robbers, and rapists invading her home. Her husband asked the local police for records of crimes committed within a three-mile radius. Other than the disappearance of a Game Boy and a case of beer, the area had been remarkably free of crime over the last five years, but this did not ease her fears. Then her husband installed alarms in the house and positioned motion detectors outside, but her fears only grew while their bank account shrank. Don't forget, there is a strange confidence that lies behind all worry. To put it bluntly, worriers don't listen very well. It takes something more powerful than logic and statistical probabilities to assuage our fear and anxieties. This husband was giving his wife security through what the world offers. In that, he was not helping her, he was hurting her.

GENETICS OR DEEPER PURPOSES?

Our habitual worry or anxiety could suggest a genetic cause. It seems to fit the criteria: it resists change, it happens even when we don't want it to, reasonable counsel doesn't help, and inveterate worriers can usually be found somewhere in the family tree. Some medications even take the edge off.

But whether there is a genetic contribution or not, don't let the first hint of a genetic link abort all other promising leads. Don't let the rationale, "Mom worried a lot," be the end of your examination of worry. When you listen to worry and witness its stubborn grasp, you find something that is most assuredly *you*. You have your *reasons* for worrying. You have purposes in your anxieties.

One message is obvious: *If I imagine the worst, I will be more prepared for it.* Worry is looking for control. It is still irrational because worry will not prepare us for anything, but at least it has its reasons.

Going one step further to track this message back to its origins, there is an entire worldview implicit in some worry. It cries out about an ultimate aloneness. There is no one who can really help. No one can rescue. No one is really looking out for you. You are an orphan in a chaotic universe that operates according to chance. Who wouldn't be worried given such a view of reality?

When a person constantly practices and reinforces his or her own worry, the motives may be darker. Human beings are naturally self-oriented. Some people are unusually altruistic, but we can easily find a selfish bent to our lives. If that is true, it is likely that even our worry reflects some self-centeredness: Worry puts the focus on me.

Worry lets me indulge in self-pity. When I worry, people listen.

These elements aren't present in all worry. But there is no reason for us to shy away from these harsher possibilities because we want our feelings to be spared. It is true that humans are selfish. So when we look for opportunities to unmask it, we will most likely see it. But then we can battle against it.

All this is just skirting the edges of fear, worry, and anxiety, but it is enough to show why some of the famed psychic explorers, most recently people like Rollo May and Freud, saw anxiety as "the Holy Grail of the soul." As Freud put it:

> There is no question that the problem of anxiety is a nodal point at which the most various and important questions converge, a riddle whose solution would be bound to throw a flood of light on our whole mental existence.[1]

Let's look for some light.

A PERSONAL RESPONSE

Guilty. I am, indeed, a false prophet. Sadly, that new name will not stop me from making a few more prophecies in the next hour or two, but it will slow me down and make me think about what I am doing.

The plan? Here it is so far. Take a hard look at yourself instead of your circumstances when worry is blaring. Ask yourself what you are trusting in. Consider your poor track record for predictions, yet recognize that all these steps, while they may give some hope, still don't push back the boundaries of fear and worry. Reason alone can't do it. Face the reality that we have to go outside ourselves for an answer and seek the God who is in control.

PART TWO

God speaks

PART TWO adds the glasses of Scripture to the study of fear and anxiety. Without them we might have insights but no firm answers.

Chapters 5 through 8 review most of the essentials to meaningfully address our fears and anxieties. They appear in one particular story: God's gift of manna to a worried people. Other Scripture will then build on and enrich the details of this story.

CHAPTER FIVE

DO NOT BE AFRAID

There is a limit to pain, but no limit to fear.
—SIR FRANCIS BACON[1]

QUICK. WHAT IS, by far, God's most frequent command?

The usual suspects include "Do not commit adultery," "Have no other gods before me," and "Love one another." The next group includes whatever commands you know you have violated, in which case they only *feel* as if they appear on every page of Scripture.

The actual answer is "Do not be afraid."

Here is a sampling (italics added) of its over three hundred occurrences.

> After this, the word of the LORD came to Abram in a vision: "*Do not be afraid*, Abram. I am your shield, your very great reward" (Gen. 15:1).

> God heard the boy crying, and the angel of God called to Hagar from heaven and said to her, "What is the matter, Hagar? *Do not be afraid*; God has heard the boy crying as he lies there" (Gen. 21:17).

That night the LORD appeared to him and said, "I am the God of your father Abraham. *Do not be afraid*, for I am with you" (Gen. 26:24).

"I am God, the God of your father," he said. "*Do not be afraid* to go down to Egypt, for I will make you into a great nation there" (Gen. 46:3).

The LORD said to Moses, "*Do not be afraid* of him, for I have handed him over to you, with his whole army and his land" (Num. 21:34).

The angel of the LORD said to Elijah, "Go down with him; *do not be afraid* of him" (2 Kings 1:15).

He said: "Listen, King Jehoshaphat and all who live in Judah and Jerusalem! This is what the LORD says to you: '*Do not be afraid* or discouraged because of this vast army. For the battle is not yours, but God's'" (2 Chron. 20:15).

Be careful, keep calm and *don't be afraid*. Do not lose heart because of these two smoldering stubs of firewood—because of the fierce anger of Rezin and Aram and of the son of Remaliah (Isa. 7:4).

"*Do not be afraid*, O worm Jacob, O little Israel, for I myself will help you," declares the LORD, your Redeemer, the Holy One of Israel (Isa. 41:14).

Do not tremble, *do not be afraid*. Did I not proclaim this and foretell it long ago? You are my witnesses. Is there any God besides me? No, there is no other Rock; I know not one (Isa. 44:8).

Do not be afraid; you will not suffer shame. Do not fear disgrace; you will not be humiliated. You will forget the shame of your youth and remember no more the reproach of your widowhood (Isa. 54:4).

"*Do not be afraid* of them, for I am with you and will rescue you," declares the LORD (Jer. 1:8).

Then he continued, "*Do not be afraid*, Daniel. Since the first day that you set your mind to gain understanding and to humble yourself before your God, your words were heard, and I have come in response to them" (Dan. 10:12).

Do not be afraid of those who kill the body but cannot kill the soul (Matt. 10:28).

But Jesus immediately said to them: "Take courage! It is I. *Don't be afraid*" (Matt. 14:27).

Then Jesus said to them, "*Do not be afraid.* Go and tell my brothers to go to Galilee; there they will see me" (Matt. 28:10).

Peace I leave with you; my peace I give you. I do not give to you as the world gives. Do not let your hearts be troubled and *do not be afraid* (John 14:27).

Now envision pages more of such references. Do you get the sense that God is alert to your fears?

THE GOD WHO HEARS AND CARES

"Don't be afraid." "Don't worry." They can be said so casually. I have said them to my wife when we have been on airplanes together and her palms were sweating before takeoff. My words, of course, were meaningless. They veered off into self-serving platitudes because I didn't really want to hear about her fears. Already engrossed in the flight magazine's crossword puzzle, I didn't want to be bothered. But God's words are nothing like my own.

Think about them. God never says anything just to get you off his back. The sheer number of times he speaks to your fears says that he cares much more than you know. He is not so busy that he attends only to macro-level concerns. Instead, he is close and speaks to the details of your troubles.

Do your troubles seem trivial, at least when compared to the dangers other people face? He knows you and has compassion. He does not compare your worries to those of others, decide which ones get priority, and then give everyone a number based on need. The way he repeats himself suggests that he understands how intractable fears and anxieties can be. He knows that a simple word will not banish our fears. He knows that our worries aren't patiently waiting for permission to leave.

Search Scripture and find that our fears are not trivial to God. "Do not be afraid" are *not* the words of a flesh-and-blood friend, a mere human like yourself. They are not the hollow words of a fellow passenger on a sinking ship, who has no experience in shipwrecks, can't swim, and has no plan. These words are more like those of the captain who says, "Don't be afraid. I know what to do." When the right person speaks these words you might be comforted. Remember, "Do not be afraid" are the words of the One who can match speech with action. He is the sovereign King who really *is* in control. The efficacy of the words is directly related to the authority, power, and love of the One speaking them.

So far so good. But the exhortation still doesn't grab you. Perhaps you remember times in your life when God did not hold a fearful situation at bay. Perhaps the thing you dread has already hit you full force. Long ago you observed that those who worship God are not spared the horrors of life. With that in mind, "Do not be afraid" sounds well-intentioned— maybe—but it doesn't help much in real life.

FEAR'S IMPATIENCE

There are two things you should know about fear or worry.

First, like any strong emotion, it wants to be the boss. It wants authority. It claims to tell us how life *really* is, and it won't be easily persuaded otherwise. If my experience of fear says that there is danger and you say there isn't, my fear wins. If my experience of fear says that there is danger and God himself says he is with me, my fear wins. Fear doesn't trust easily. It tenaciously holds onto its self-protecting agenda. Think about it. When was the last time God's comforting words made a difference to you?

Second, when fear escalates, it wants relief and it wants it now. Fear is impatient. Of course, we are all impatient, and whenever we experience something uncomfortable we want to get rid of it as quickly as we can. Fear is no different. It will alight on a promising treatment, give it a few seconds, then flit to something else without ever returning. Fear has tried God and God didn't work. To reconsider God goes against fear's manic style.

Why highlight this? Because one of the first steps in combating fear and worry is to slow down. "Be still" (Ps. 46:10) is another of God's exhortations to fearful people. *Quiet!* is the way some have translated it, and you can understand why.

A PROPOSAL

You can't blame fear for wanting a place of peace and rest, and wanting it fast. The odd thing is that fear and anxiety are running away from something, but they don't know what to run *to.* They know danger, but they don't know where to find peace and rest. If fear slows down for a minute, it realizes that peace and rest can only reside in some*one* rather than some*thing*, in people rather than pills. A fearful child wants to sleep with her parents. On a walk through dark woods, our fears ebb in the presence of a companion—in a pinch, we will even settle for a small dog. Over the short run, anything alive will do, but we prefer an actual person who is big and strong. If the threat is to our bank account, we prefer someone rich. If our sense of well-being is at risk, we want someone who loves and affirms. Fear calls out for a person bigger than ourselves.

Then, just as fear and anxiety are about to embrace another human being who almost fits the bill, they remember that people are unreliable. Fear quickly hits the default switch and opts for independence, control, and self-protection.

The problem is that our worries and fears remind us of our own smallness, so to rely on ourselves takes us back to where we started. But what else can we do?

At this apparent cul-de-sac we find God. If you are jaded because you feel as though God has been unreliable, look at it this way: There are no other choices. Other people can't quite be trusted, and we are not in control. That limits the field to God himself. Not gods, only God. A pantheon of gods will not do, because none of them may have jurisdiction over your particular dilemma. The greatest possibility for rest and comfort lies in the knowledge of the true God. And who can resist the One whose self-given name is Mighty God, Everlasting Father, Deliverer, Lord of Hosts, Rock of Ages, Faithful One, and Good Shepherd?

Don't forget, fear's interpretations are not always to be trusted. You might *feel* abandoned so you believe you *are* abandoned. But you don't know the entire story.

So here is the proposal: let fear point us to the knowledge of God, and let the Spirit of God, by way of Scripture, teach us the knowledge of God. When fear is the problem, our typical approach is to follow action steps. If we are on our spiritual game, we can pray with thanksgiving (Phil. 4:6), we can cast our cares on him (1 Peter 5:7), or we can heed his command to not be afraid. These are good things, but they are *responses* to our growing knowledge of God. The knowledge of God comes first. Apart from this personal knowledge, Scriptural advice is no different from the thought stoppage or imaginary vacations that secular treatments offer.

If fear is a personal matter, we must set off to know a person.

"DO NOT BE AFRAID," AND WHAT THAT SAYS ABOUT GOD

Think of the entire Bible as the unfolding story of God's revelation about himself. As such, "Do not be afraid" says something about him even before it speaks to us.

At first, it could sound like God is the exalted King firing off edicts from his heavenly throne. He is the Lord; his word is final. When he speaks, he speaks with authority. We don't necessarily like being bossed around, but we begrudgingly acknowledge that if anyone has the right to issue commands, the God who created us has that right.

But there are two different ways of saying, "Don't be afraid." One is as an edict to be obeyed, in which case it is a peculiar edict. It sounds like the King actually cares about us. He isn't ordering us to make bricks without straw. Instead, it sounds as if he wants his people to know peace. So, even when seen as an authoritative command, this reveals something lovely about God. Unlike other kings, at least those who have despotic authority, God knows the concerns of those in his realm and commands things that are in their best interest. That is the most severe way to understand "Do not be afraid."

Here is the other way: "[Jesus said] 'Do not be afraid, *little flock*, for your Father has been pleased to give you the kingdom'" (Luke 12:32).

It echoes the way God spoke to Israel hundreds of years before: "'Do not be afraid, O worm Jacob, *O little Israel*, for I myself will help you,' declares the LORD, your Redeemer, the Holy One of Israel" (Isa. 41:14).

No one inserts "little flock" into an inviolable command. No king talks about being "pleased" to give anything, let alone the kingdom itself, to his subjects. Jesus is invoking kingly imagery, indeed. But the One who sits on the throne is the Father, and that changes everything.

He is your Father. I would do anything for my daughters and sons-in-law within the bounds of wisdom and love. I would sacrifice (and have) time, money, and anything else necessary for their welfare. And I am just an ordinary, somewhat selfish father. If there is anything good in my fathering, it is because I mirror something of my good Father.

When Jesus spoke about God as our Father, we can refer back to the entire Old Testament record of his fatherly care. Jesus summarizes the Old Testament story in his remarkable parable of the prodigal son.

Jesus continued: "There was a man who had two sons. The younger one said to his father, 'Father, give me my share of the estate.' So he divided his property between them.

"Not long after that, the younger son got together all he had, set off for a distant country and there squandered his wealth in wild living. After he had spent everything, there was a severe famine in that whole country, and he began to be in need. So he went and hired himself out to a citizen of that country, who sent him to his fields to feed pigs. He longed to fill his stomach with the pods that the pigs were eating, but no one gave him anything.

"When he came to his senses, he said, 'How many of my father's hired men have food to spare, and here I am starving to death! I will set out and go back to my father and say to him: Father, I have sinned against heaven and against you. I am no longer worthy to be called your son; make me like one of your hired men.' *So he got up and went to his father.*

"*But while he was still a long way off, his father saw him and was filled with compassion for him; he ran to his son, threw his arms around him and kissed him.*"

—LUKE 15:11–20, *author's emphasis*

In the ancient Near East, the children's job description was to enhance the reputation—the glory—of the father. The father cared for the children and blessed them so they could continue the family line. The children honored the father by loving and obeying him. Clearly, this child was not a dutiful son. To make matters worse, the father was a prominent person who lived in a culture where everyone was watching. The actions of the son would and did bring great shame.

Who could have predicted that the father, on hearing the news that his son might be returning, would run to meet him? Important people don't run anywhere. That's the job of servants. If an important person ran toward anyone, it would be undignified and, in this case, compound his shame.

This father, however, threw reputation to the wind. He wasn't interested in meeting his son halfway, even though that would have been embarrassment enough to a normal father. In his delight, he ran until he embraced his bedraggled son and kissed him.

This is a story that the Father gave us to help us understand him better.

He is the King. Now consider that the Father is also the King. "Your Father has been delighted to give you the *kingdom*." As Father, God comes close to you. He knows your needs and you take comfort in his love. As King, he sovereignly reigns over his kingdom, and his bidding will come to pass. You take comfort in his power. If he is going to speak effectively to your fears, he must be both loving and strong, and indeed he is.

Yet there are questions about jurisdiction. A king's power is relevant only within his domain. Outside the boundaries of his kingdom, you are on your own. So how big is the kingdom?

Throughout Scripture, God insists that he is one God, and "apart from me there is no God" (Isa. 44:6). In other words, there is no other kingdom. Satan, to be sure, has presented himself as a rival, but there is ultimately one King and one kingdom. Everything belongs to him. "This is what God the LORD says—he who created the heavens and stretched them out, who spread out the earth and all that comes out of it, who gives breath to its people, and life to those who walk on it" (Isa. 42:5).

I was walking through the nearby woods with our friend's six-year-old son. All was well until he noticed that dusk was setting in. With that, his fears announced that danger was close at hand. Whatever it is that happens in the dark was about to happen. Seeing an opportunity to teach him about God's care, I picked him up, put him on my shoulders and countered his increasing fears: "Don't be afraid because I am with you. I'll defend you."

My intent was to create an analogy that pointed him to God's care. I could already picture the eternal crown waiting for me, which, as I understand it, might be even weightier after I've blessed young children. His response, however, was to cry louder. No doubt he hoped his ear-piercing screams would summon someone more powerful than I.

He knew I loved him, even in a fatherly way, but he also knew that the woods were not my domain. If he had been sitting in my house and lightning had taken out the electricity, I would have had a better chance of comforting him, but he knew that I was not the lord of the woods.

God reveals his fatherly love *and* kingly authority to fearful people. And there is more.

He is generous. "Your Father has been *pleased* to give you the kingdom." Fathers can give begrudgingly and kings can give simply because they made an oath, but God gives out of his pleasure and delight.

When we see the similarities between ourselves and the prodigal son, it is natural to doubt God's munificence. After all, we certainly wouldn't open the treasury to indifferent or treasonous people, even if they were our children. But God not only opens the doors to the entire kingdom, he is delighted to do so.

Sound too good to be true? Please understand that when God speaks in ways that are completely contrary to our expectations, then we have encountered something genuine. No one could invent a god who, in response to rebellion, is so generous that he gives his entire kingdom. Since this is too good to be true, it *must* be true. This, indeed, must be the Holy One.

All this inverts our normal way of thinking. We tend to judge God's words by our own feelings and sensory observations. If we *feel* orphaned, we believe we *are* orphaned. If we *feel* a sense of impending doom, the worst will in fact happen. If we are told that God reigns, but everything seems to be in chaos, we twist God's revelation about himself to fit our understanding of the data. Scripture, however, reveals the things we can't see with the naked eye, and God's self-revelation is a higher authority than our feelings. When our feelings conflict with God's communication, we must side with God's interpretation. Any other decision puts us above God, which we already know isn't true because fear reminds us of our own puniness. We certainly are not gods!

IS IT WRONG TO WORRY OR BE AFRAID?

It is wrong to be afraid? Is it sinful? Maybe, but put these questions on hold. The emphasis in Scripture is, "When I am afraid, I will trust in you" (Ps. 56:3). The issue isn't so much whether or not we are afraid and worry. Scripture assumes that we will be afraid and anxious at times. What is important is *where* we turn, or *to whom* we turn when we are afraid.

The God who calls you to trust in him when you are afraid will spend a great deal of time showing you that you *can* trust him. He doesn't ask you to live with your eyes shut. Faith is not blind. The Hebrews—who first received Scripture—were very big on eyewitnesses, accurate testimony and evidence. Faith was about knowing God in an intimate, personal way and trusting him because he is trustworthy. Faith sees more, not less.

Think of the child who wakes up toward the end of a long trip and begins to cry because she doesn't want to be in the car any longer.

Her mother tries to comfort her, "We are almost at Grandma's house."

But the child's tears betray disbelief.

The mother tries again. "Sweetheart, you know I don't lie to you. I am telling you the truth. Stop crying for a moment and look outside. Do you see that store? We walked there from Grandma's house one time. Do you remember? And look, does that street look familiar? Maybe *you* could give us directions to Grandma's. Look and see. We are almost there."

Yes, we are being taken to places we can't yet see. We are asked to live by faith. But God's communication allows us to see. It might all look like a bloomin,' buzzin' confusion, but when our eyes are opened, we will see much more.

A PERSONAL RESPONSE

The more you read Scripture, the more you actually talk to God rather than think about fear.

God, open my ears. I don't clearly hear your care and compassion when you tell me not to worry or be afraid, but I know they are there.

Father, open my eyes. I act like I see all reality. I act like I can see even more than you do. But I am seeing now that there is an entire world that is blurry to me, and that world is you. It is you I don't see well.

I want to trust in what you say and see the things you have revealed. That leaves me no choice but to start with humility. This is the way all journeys with you begin. Please teach me humility so that what you say overrules what I feel.

CHAPTER SIX

THE MANNA PRINCIPLE

"DO YOU REMEMBER when I had to rescue you after you were toppled by that wave?"

"Yeah, that was really scary. It was a good thing you were there, Dad."

In good relationships there are scores of stories available to illustrate trustworthiness and love. But then there are the classic stories, which are recounted at every opportunity. Our family remembers water rescue(s), getting lost and found at swap meets, getting lost and found at malls, getting lost and found at…these are some of our stories of danger and rescue. We tell these stories at birthdays and other family events as a way to rehearse our children's history of being loved and protected—or at least loved and searched for.

Scripture too is crammed with stories about God's faithfulness, stories that are meant to be retold because, in our fear, we are so quick to forget. Open your Bible anywhere and you will land on a story of faithfulness. Some stories, however, are more seminal than others. Some are so important, so defining, that they deserve to be remembered at every family function. One such story recounts the way God brought his people out of Egypt. Before leading them to the land in which they would settle, he first led them into the wilderness and cared for their daily needs. This story reveals details of God and his parenting methods, and he invites us to listen and learn.

GOD HEARS

A twenty-one-year-old woman, fresh out of college, is planning to move to a new place. She has no idea how she is going to do it. She has never rented a truck. She doesn't know who will help her move all her furniture, and she doesn't know where to stay when she moves to the new city.

A friend learns of her worries and says, "Why don't you just call your parents? You know they would be glad to help." This friend has met the parents and knows they enjoy serving their children. So she did call, and her parents were glad to help.

Most human beings respond to cries for help. When they do, it is because they are in some small way chips off the old block. They are looking like their Father.

The deliverance of the Israelites from Egypt began when God heard their cries: "The Israelites groaned in their slavery and cried out, and their cry for help because of their slavery went up to God. God heard their groaning and he remembered his covenant with Abraham, with Isaac and with Jacob" (Ex. 2:23–24).

Notice two things about this. First, there is no reason to believe that the Israelites' cry for help was directed to God. More likely, they were just groaning to no one in particular. In other words, God rescued his people even before they called out to him. If you think about it, you have witnessed that many times yourself.

Second, whenever Scripture says anything about God hearing, watch out, because you know something is about to happen. When God hears, he acts. In the Israelites' case the deliverance began immediately, and the people left Egypt without lifting a finger in their own defense. But their groaning wasn't over yet. Once safe from Pharaoh and his armies, they next faced dehydration and starvation. As their food reserves waned they began crying out with complaints directed against Moses and Aaron, their leaders: "In the desert the whole community grumbled against Moses and Aaron. The Israelites said to them, 'If only we had died by the LORD's hand in Egypt! There we sat around pots of meat and ate all the food we wanted, but you have brought us out into this desert to starve this entire assembly to death'" (Ex. 16:2–3).

This is not exactly a model prayer. There is complaining, grumbling, self-pity—all the things that can drive us crazy about other people. And don't forget that "grumbling" is a euphemism for "holding God in contempt" (Num. 14:11). Given such self-centered insolence, you would at least expect God to say, "I'm not listening until you ask nicely." But this is not an invented story where the god is like us. This is *the* God.

> Then Moses told Aaron, "Say to the entire Israelite community, 'Come before the LORD, for he has heard your grumbling.'" While Aaron was speaking to the whole Israelite community, they looked toward the desert, and there was the glory of the LORD appearing in the cloud. The LORD said to Moses, "I have heard the grumbling of the Israelites. Tell them, 'At twilight you will eat meat, and in the morning you will be filled with bread. Then you will know that I am the LORD your God.'"
>
> —Ex. 16:9–12

This response goes against all our expectations. God truly is not like us.

It is as if God says to us, "Let me remind you of how I listen and see if you think I could listen even to you." Then he recounts stories of adulterers like King David, murderers like the apostle Paul, and grumblers like newly delivered Israel. If he hears and loves them, he will hear and love us. The lesson is clear: He doesn't hear because of *us* and the quality of our prayers. He hears because he is the God Who Hears.

Need more? "Does he who implanted the ear not hear?" (Ps. 94:9). God has created our capacity to hear because *he* hears and we are his offspring.

Ask any Christian where he would like to grow and he or she will say, "I would like to pray more." As a remedy, some seek accountability or discipline themselves to pray and pray longer. A better strategy is to know God as the One Who Hears and remember the many stories of how he listens. Let it sink in that God is not like us. While we can "merely listen" (James 1:22) in the sense that we can hear the words but not respond, when God hears, he acts. Every instance of God hearing is followed by his mighty acts.

GOD DELIVERS

In the exodus, one mighty act followed another. The story goes like this: Combine the most powerful king in the known world, slaves who stood no chance of successful insurrection because all they knew was slavery, and oppression that was getting worse. You now have the perfect ingredients for God's decisive act of deliverance. It was the event on which God staked his reputation until it was superseded by his even more cosmic deliverance through Jesus Christ.

Here is what we learn: God prefers the impossible. Although he often cares for our needs before we know we have them, his mighty acts are showcased best against the backdrop of insurmountable odds. Anything less would detract from his greatness. In this case, all Moses did was stretch out his hand—his empty hand—and watch a mighty deliverance.

Having seen God's authority over all living things, we might expect the Israelites to turn quickly to their Deliverer when they were hungry. But the lessons of yesterday don't always carry into today, to which we can all attest. Worriers go right back to their worry, and God repeats his mighty acts. In this case, he rained manna on the hungry people.

To reinforce that this second deliverance was also from him alone, God provided food that, though delicious, was new to their diet. Manna was a heavenly recipe as noted by its name, which means "What is it?" (Ex. 16:15). It was a tasteful reminder that said, "God alone is the Deliverer."

GOD IS NEAR

When God's mighty acts are on display, it means he is near. Kings can do their bidding from a distance through intermediaries, but God chooses to come close. He sits on the throne of the universe, but he also dwells with commoners. This is music to the ears of worriers. "Then Moses told Aaron, 'Say to the entire Israelite community, "Come before the LORD, for he has heard your grumbling."' While Aaron was speaking to the whole Israelite community, they looked toward the desert, and *there was the glory of the LORD appearing in the cloud*" (Ex. 16:9–10, author's emphasis).

The glory of the Lord means the presence of the Lord.

Nearness and presence will be recurring themes in God's words of comfort to fearful people. Of course, the earth belongs to the Lord and, as Spirit, God is not bound by the limitations of space. He is everywhere at all times. When he underscores his presence, as he does here, it means that he is working on behalf of his people. It means that he is for them. He is an active, protecting, comforting presence. When he says he is near, watch for his mighty acts. When he is near, he is *really* near.

GOD TESTS

Now comes a key feature of this story. Expect to find it in your story as well: God is the One Who Tests, and he will test you. Don't think of final exams and test anxiety. Think of this test as a way to expose traitors during wartime. We are the potential traitors and don't even know it. God tests us because we are so oblivious to the mixed allegiances in our hearts. The purpose of the test is to help us see our hearts and if they are found traitorous, we can turn back to God. God is not playing mind games with us; he is forging a relationship.

Then the LORD said to Moses, "I will rain down bread from heaven for you. The people are to go out each day and gather enough for that day. *In this way I will test them and see whether they will follow my instructions.*"

—EX. 16:4, *author's emphasis*

Remember how the LORD your God led you all the way in the desert these forty years, to humble you and *to test you in order to know what was in your heart,* whether or not you would keep his commands.

—DEUT. 8:2, *author's emphasis*

Control freaks and worriers are being told that the challenges of life are ordained by the Father and King. They are neither random nor accidental. The outcome of these daily tests doesn't give God any new information about us. He is the Searcher and Knower of hearts. At least one of their purposes is to reveal us to ourselves. In that, they have the potential to reorient us and send us back to the true God.

Only enough for today. The tests follow a particular pattern: God will give us what we need for today and today alone. No mystery here, it is all spelled out.

This is what the LORD has commanded: "Each one is to gather as much as he needs. Take an omer for each person you have in your tent." The Israelites did as they were told; some gathered much, some little. And when they measured it by the omer, he who gathered much did not have too much, and he who gathered little did not have too little. Each one gathered as much as he needed. Then Moses said to them, "No one is to keep any of it until morning."

—EX. 16:16–19

"Take as much as you want, but don't keep even a crumb for tomorrow." In various forms, this will become God's plan for human life. You will encounter it again when Jesus trains his disciples and sends them out on a missionary journey with no extra supplies (Mark 6:7–9). The plan, of course, is genius. Dump a year's supply of manna into cold storage and, guaranteed, you will forget God until the supply disappears (Deut. 8:10–14). Such prosperity would be a curse. God's strategy is to give us enough for today and then, when tomorrow comes, to give us enough for that day too.

Do you see how this is exactly what we need? Fears and worries live in the future, trying to assure a good outcome in a potentially hard situation. The last thing they want to do is trust anyone, God included. To thwart this tendency toward independence, God only gives us what we need when we need it. The emerging idea is that he wants us to trust *him* in the future rather than our self-protective plans.

The Sabbath test. One curious feature of Scripture is the prominence of the Sabbath. It figures prominently in the Ten Commandments, and has been arguably *the* distinguishing feature of Judaism throughout the centuries. The need for a Sabbath day of rest makes its first appearance in the manna story, even before the people heard about it through the Ten Commandments.

> He said to them, "This is what the LORD commanded: 'Tomorrow is to be a day of rest, a holy Sabbath to the LORD. So bake what you want to bake and boil what you want to boil. Save whatever is left and keep it until morning.'" So they saved it until morning, as Moses commanded, and it did not stink or get maggots in it. "Eat it today," Moses said, "because today is a Sabbath to the LORD. You will not find any of it on the ground today. Six days you are to gather it, but on the seventh day, the Sabbath, there will not be any." Nevertheless, some of the people went out on the seventh day to gather it, but they found none.
>
> —Ex. 16:23–27

Imagine that you are self-employed with very tight financial margins. Miss a day's work and your competitors get the upper hand. Miss a day's pay and you wonder if you will be able to buy groceries. Time is money.

Now consider an agrarian economy. Here time might mean survival. Delay planting and you might miss the rain. Take a day off in the midst of harvest and your produce might overripen or even rot. With these risks in mind, the Sabbath was a big deal. It was a test, a weekly tutorial for anxious people. God was saying through it, "I am the Creator God who will care for your needs. Embedded in the rhythm of your week will be an opportunity to rest. You will do this because I rested on the Sabbath, and you will do it because I continue to be at work on your behalf on the Sabbath."

Just when you think you are getting the knack of the manna and are not worrying about tomorrow, you are told to trust your heavenly Father for today *and* tomorrow. Once again, we can't help but be astonished at God's strategy. Worry and fear are about danger, perceived needs, and being out of control. By incorporating the Sabbath into the normal rhythms of life he gives us weekly opportunities to say, "You, God, are in control, and I will practice trusting you by honoring your Sabbath and resting today."

GOD'S GENEROSITY KNOWS NO BOUNDS

On the surface, the story is all about manna and our daily needs. The plot line is simple: hungry people get fed. But when you follow the larger story line of Scripture, you find that the good life is not simply about free food and durable clothes. As every person with a stocked refrigerator and full closet knows, there must be something more.

> Remember how the LORD your God led you all the way in the desert these forty years, to humble you and to test you in order to know what was in your heart, whether or not you would keep his commands.

He humbled you, causing you to hunger and then feeding you with manna, which neither you nor your fathers had known, to teach you that *man does not live on bread alone but on every word that comes from the mouth of the LORD.*

—DEUT. 8:2–3, *author's emphasis*

God made us physical beings, and he cares for us physically. But we are also spirit, which means that we are made of God's stuff. We are his offspring. And spiritual people need spiritual food.

When Jesus cited this passage (Matt. 4:4) it was in the context of a much larger reality. Jesus was being accosted by the Tempter—Satan himself. Fittingly, Jesus hadn't eaten for forty days. No doubt, food was his primary need. But in the midst of near starvation, he said that there was something more important than food: to be strengthened by the Spirit of God as he rested on the very words of the Father.

Spiritual food can seem unsatisfying at first, but have you ever had someone say to you, "I love you"? Wouldn't you gladly pass on a buffet in order to hear such words? In Jesus' case, this spiritual food was more important than physical life itself.

Now we begin to understand how God remains faithful to his promises even when his people go hungry. The physical food points to something better. The apostle Paul often went hungry but he saw absolutely no contradiction between that and God's generous care for his truest needs. Paul knew that, no matter how well-fed, the physical body was inevitably going to die. But a fed spirit is satisfied for this life and the life to come. To make it more personal, if Paul had God, what else did he really need?

A sentimental line from the movies is: Whenever I am with you, I am home. The person is trying to say that whatever the hardships, the presence of a loved one makes all the difference. It means there is peace.

God's deliverance is better than food, a clean medical scan, or having our candidate win the election. His deliverance means he will be with us;

we will be able to withstand temptation without giving in to sin; and we will be able to stand firm even when attacked by our fiercest adversary, Satan the Accuser.

Yes, you can trust God today. Trust him for your physical needs. But now there is a rich new agenda for fearful people. We are fearful when something we value is in jeopardy. How can we spiritually grow to the point where we see there are things more valuable than food, shelter, reputation, even life itself? That is where we will uncover the mysteries of dealing with fear and anxiety. Through that process we have the potential to say with the apostle Paul, "I have learned the secret of being content in any and every situation, whether well fed or hungry, whether living in plenty or in want" (Phil. 4:12).

A PERSONAL RESPONSE

The manna story is *the* story for all worriers. I love how God broadcasts his ways with us. That certainly doesn't mean that he is predictable, but it does mean that I can be better prepared during those back-against-the-wall times.

Consider a few possible responses.

1. In the manna story, God gives specifics about how he will work. Though the future—maybe even ten minutes from now—might look bleak, he will give us what we need right now. There are times when I should expect to feel surrounded with no way out. But this is *not* a time when God is distant or silent. *Things are not always the way they appear.* Instead, it is a time when God is especially close. He is teaching me to call out to him and trust him.

2. The Deliverer and the One Who Hears is the same now as he was then. In a very real way, I am continuing the story that stopped with the book of Revelation. I will still trudge through the wilderness,

wondering if God will care for me. I, however, have the benefit of learning from history. While the Israelites had an excuse, since theirs was the first real mega-deliverance, I have already witnessed the mighty acts of God. My goal is to contribute to a story where I imitate *Jesus* in the wilderness, not the Israelites.

3. I want to keep better track of the many mini-deliverances in my life. I can look back on days when there was too much work, too much pain, too many expenses, too little wisdom; and I can see how God delivered me.

4. "Trust me" is starting to make more sense. That exhortation is the mother lode of comfort for fearful people. I want to remember that trust can be fed with the evidence that God, indeed, is trustworthy. This is God's method with us. He asks for no leap of faith, no blind trust, only our acknowledgment of his history of faithfulness.

5. I want to learn how to pray.

CHAPTER SEVEN

THE GOD OF SUSPENSE

DELIVERANCE IS GRAND except for one thing: It isn't deliverance unless it's the eleventh hour. There first has to be some kind of danger for there to be deliverance. Such drama is fun to watch in movies and great to hear in other people's stories, but we would prefer not to experience it in our own lives.

Doesn't this get to one of the essential features of fear and anxiety? You don't feel danger until the threat is a palpable presence. That is when you panic, feel alone, and want to run. But imagine what it would be like if that same moment—that eleventh hour—evoked an awareness of the God who was present and active. If called upon, you could fall fast asleep because you knew your God was awake.

In the wilderness story, God tells us up front that he is the God of suspense. In the course of that story, he assures us that there will be times when we feel surrounded, facing insurmountable odds with no apparent way out. That, in fact, is part of his good plan for us. He also tells us that he will bring us to the end of our own cleverness because that is when we are most apt to acknowledge his strong hand alone.

When Sheri and I were buying our first house, we worked with a real estate agent who knew my parents. We told him how much money we had and how much I earned, which he used to gauge what homes we could afford. We also told him that some of our money had been loaned to friends, but we expected it back in time for settlement. The first day out we saw a house we liked, signed a letter of intent, and put down a deposit.

Two days before settlement the money was not in hand, and we wouldn't have it for at least another week, maybe longer. When we informed the agent, he was quite casual about it and assured us that everything would be fine. Not being savvy in real estate, we assumed that everyone in the business was this wonderful embodiment of "no worries." It was as if he was saying, "You don't have the money today? No problem. Just mail it to me when you get it." If only all businesses could be so friendly and laid back!

The morning of settlement we telephoned to shore up last-minute details and let the agent know that the money still hadn't come. Once again he assured us that all was well.

Fifteen minutes before we left to close on the house, a cashier's check was delivered.

After a smooth settlement we asked the agent, "What would have happened if we hadn't had the money?"

"Oh, I wasn't worried about that. I know your parents, and they know God. I knew they would be praying about this, so I knew the money would come."

Here was a man who had minimal religious inclinations of his own, but he knew better than we did that God hears the prayers of his people, and he often chooses to deliver with a certain amount of drama.

GOD'S QUIET CARE: DELIVERANCE BEFORE WE KNOW WE NEED IT

Last-minute deliverance is not God's only means of care. More often his care is less obvious.

He waters the earth and causes it to be fruitful for everyone, whether he is acknowledged or not.

Every meal we eat is an expression of his sovereign care. Sometimes we pray and give thanks; more often we just eat and assume that the grocery store will have what we need for tomorrow.

He heals us day after day. Some researchers believe that cancer is always present in our bodies, but God sustains our bodies in a way that wards off its advances.

How many times have you had colds, infections, food poisoning, and a host of other physical maladies that you no longer have?

He protects us, without us knowing or asking, while traveling on an interstate when everyone around us is engrossed in their cell phone conversations.

How many times has the Good Shepherd fought wild beasts to keep us safe while we peacefully grazed, unaware of his heroic care?

Even before we get to the fullest expression of God's love and care through Jesus Christ, we have reason to live in thankful dependence. As God has already demonstrated to us in the exodus, he doesn't wait for crises to happen before he acts. He doesn't wait for us to call out to him. Instead, he is always on the move, always sustaining, giving every breath to every living being every day.

GOD'S ELEVENTH-HOUR DELIVERANCE

It is against this backdrop that God chooses to show his mighty acts of deliverance. His quiet daily care is the rule. Not many people are called to a life where mighty acts of deliverance are daily necessities, but the evidence is that, at some point, we all will have that opportunity.

Notice how God orchestrated this opportunity during the exodus. What looked like a clean getaway from Egypt was foiled when God told Moses to double back. Predictably, the route trapped them. With the Red Sea behind, Pharaoh's army in front, and no fighting men to speak of, they seemed doomed within days of their miraculous escape.

Then and only then did the sea open up and become dry land. A tradition has begun; then one piles upon another. God waits until Sarah is well past childbearing age to give Abraham and Sarah the promised son.

Abraham lies to save himself and says that he is Sarah's brother. Pharaoh, believing that Sarah is unmarried, brings her into his household. Only a last-minute disease that God brought on Pharaoh's household kept Sarah from being defiled. (Sometimes deliverance is from a mess of our own making.)

Gideon's army is reduced to 300 unarmed men before God gave him victory over Midian (Judg. 7).

Naomi is widowed in a foreign country, without any land. She sneaks back to her people shamed and destitute. Her daughter-in-law Ruth chooses to stay with her, thus also resigning herself to a life of poverty and widowhood. Just before their ruin, God raises up a kinsman who marries Ruth. Ruth bears a child who is the grandfather of King David, and Naomi is now assimilated into the royal line, and the line of the Messiah.

Elisha is being pursued by the enraged king of Aram. The enemy armies are in sight. There is no escape, and Elisha's servant is absolutely freaking out. But Elisha knows God and his penchant for impossible deliverances. He prays that the servant's eyes would be opened and, not a moment too soon, his servant sees the immense army of the Lord of Hosts. Elisha then prays that the enemy army's eyes would be shut, which they are, and the solitary prophet escorts the entire army to the king of Israel (2 Kings 6).

Jesus' ministry was replete with miracles, the New Testament equivalent of mighty acts of deliverance. Some were accomplished as part of his strategy of quiet care, although there is nothing quiet about being given sight when you have been born blind. Some miracles are last-second deliverances, such as when Jesus calmed the storm with a simple rebuke to the wind and seas.

GOD'S DELIVERANCE *AFTER* HOPE DIES

Eleventh-hour deliverances, spectacular as they are, were actually just a prelude to something even more dramatic. As you read through Scripture, there is a gradual progression. Initially the deliverances are at the last minute. By the time of the New Testament, they are delayed to the point where even those who are tenacious in clinging to God have lost hope.

A New Testament woman loses her husband in a day when husbands were the primary form of social security for women. Most likely some townspeople also assumed that her husband's death was God's judgment against her for some past sin. She is left with only one son. You hear that the son is sick, but you have no worries. Surely God will show up just in the nick of time. So you watch and wait. Any second now, fortunes will be reversed, and the sick son will get rich, have famous children, or something like that. But the son gets sick and dies. End of story.

So you grieve and wail with the widow and her friends. Your faith is shaken, especially because you were so certain that God would heal her son.

Meanwhile, Jesus "happens" to be walking through the town at the same time as the funeral procession. He could have been there at the eleventh hour and healed the son, but now it's too late. Then, recalibrating eleventh-hour deliverance, Jesus walks over to the lifeless body, touches it, and brings the son back to life (Luke 7). This is a deliverance you never anticipated.

With Lazarus he follows the same pattern. This time Jesus deliberately waits until Lazarus is dead and the grieving has begun. His rationale: "For your sake I am glad I was not there, so that you may believe" (John 11:15).

"For your sake"? I don't think so! If it were up to me, Lazarus would be resting comfortably in his home after a brush with death. Everyone would be sitting around giving thanks to God for his eleventh-hour deliverance.

We must be missing something.

Apparently, these after-the-fact deliverances are heralds of what was to be *the* deliverance that would forever change our definition of "the last minute." No doubt, many people who witnessed Jesus' ministry were persuaded that the Roman occupation was about to end. Here was the Messiah, the One who would overthrow Roman oppression and bring Israel back to its former glory. Many held onto that hope to the very end, recognizing that God specializes in last-minute surprises. Their hopes crashed, however, when Jesus died a shameful death.

Little did anyone realize that all the stories of deliverance had just reached their climax. In the death and resurrection of Jesus, the hinge of history turned. Captives were freed. The poor were made rich. Invalids were made whole. And there was no longer any condemnation for those who followed King Jesus and put their trust in him rather than themselves.

The *real* deliverance was not the manna in the wilderness, but the Bread of Life given for us. The ultimate deliverance was not our rescue from the jaws of death, because any temporal deliverance from death meant only that death was postponed. The real deliverance was the death of death secured by the death of Jesus Christ.

Abraham somehow grasped this, even though he did not have the evidence we do. When told to sacrifice his only son, he never hesitated. He set out early in the morning in obedience to the divine word and his arm was raised. He was *not* expecting an angel to stop him or provide a ram in

Isaac's place. Instead, "Abraham reasoned that God could raise the dead" (Heb. 11:19). He anticipated deliverance *after* the crisis.

The people of faith who have gone before us had a different sense of time than we do. For me, the eleventh hour is when the check comes in the mail with only fifteen minutes to spare. If Abraham were in my position, the check could have never come, he could have been jailed for reneging on his commitment to buy the house, he could have faced abuse from other prisoners, and he *still* would be anticipating eleventh-hour deliverance—and he would have received it.

What would Abraham have received? As Hebrews observes, he would have received a resurrected son, since God had promised to establish a nation through Isaac. But there were other promises God made that Abraham did not see fulfilled in this life. Most notably, Abraham lived as an "alien and stranger" on this earth (Heb. 11:13) despite God's promise that the land of Canaan was his. By faith he saw beyond the uncertainties of real estate transactions and was willing to live in a tent, "for he was looking forward to the city with foundations, whose architect and builder is God" (Heb. 11:10).

These words *sound* good—a son resurrected, a much better home— and they were more than enough for Abraham. But they might not seem like enough for you. They may fall short of actual comfort, at least for now. They might inspire hope, as you encounter a normal, fallible human being who could look past the tragedy of the moment to see things the way God sees them. But whatever grace Abraham had is elusive for most of us. Abraham had a spiritual vision that allowed him to see beyond the eleventh hour, but the rest of us live with reading glasses that exaggerate what is in front of us and blur everything beyond three feet.

What do we tend to see?

Bills

An uncertain economy

Sick family members

Children wandering down a dangerous path

Aloneness

Emotional or physical pain that will be more than we can bear

Against all that, a nebulous future, even one with promise, doesn't have enough weight to tip the scales in its favor.

Then what do we do?

First, consider how you might have already experienced post-eleventh-hour deliverances.

A woman went through a deep depression. She hoped and prayed for deliverance but she didn't receive it, at least not in the way she desired. Instead, depression raged for months that felt like lifetimes before it finally lifted. Now she is headed down that same downhill course again. Yet what should terrorize her is actually being welcomed. As she looks back on her previous depression, she can see deliverance in a way she didn't expect: God gave her the gift of faith to cling tenaciously to the One who holds her. Yes, it takes a certain amount of spiritual maturity to appreciate such things, but even those who know her recognize that she has been transformed into an increasingly glorious woman through her trials. She has seen a redemptive deliverance. The thing she feared did happen, but God did something in her in the midst of it that she recognized was for her good and his glory. It was worth it to her.

A man recently lost his dream. He believed that God had given him a vision for a business. When he acted on that vision, God brought unimaginable success. Why then did a groundless lawsuit cause him to lose everything? The businessman assumed that God would vindicate him in court. Instead, he lost the case and the entire business.

This meant he had to learn about a new eleventh hour. The eleventh hour, whatever it was, was still to come. He asked God to search his heart, and he began to consider his fears and worries. He came to the conclusion that God had given him a great gift. He saw that he had wanted to do great things *for* God more than he wanted God himself.

Now, he says, he couldn't be happier or more content. *That* turned out to be his eleventh-hour deliverance. At first he thought God would vindicate him in court, restore his fortune, and allow him to serve as he had previously. But God's deliverance was on a different plane. It led him to know God in an entirely different way. Yes, genuine pain and loss coexisted with the deliverance, but it did not have the last word. Its power to hurt him was weakened because he could see the bigger things God was doing in, for, and through him.

You can probably find similar events in your life. Hard things persisted, there was no apparent deliverance, but, with closer inspection, you notice a deliverance that went much deeper.

And these are eleventh-hour deliverances on *this* side of death and eternity. Imagine if you gradually developed the spiritual skill to see beyond the immediate moment and catch a glimpse of the glories to come. The basic outline is clear: if you have thrown your lot in with Jesus, everything he has is yours, even the kingdom itself. It would be impossible to ask for more.

Those who imitate Abraham's faith are always pushing the last minute farther out until it comes even after physical death. Such a person is fearless.

A PERSONAL RESPONSE

The God of suspense is delivering left and right.

For his daily, less noticeable deliverances I want the Spirit to open my eyes so I can be thankful.

For his mighty acts that appear at the eleventh hour, I want grace to trust him. I want to learn how to express faith in simple obedience amid uncertain situations.

But these after-the-fact deliverances? I hardly know what to ask. What if you actually went through your worst nightmare—sexual violation, death of a loved one, divorce? What then? Where was the deliverance? What difference does the after-the-fact deliverance make then?

It means that there will be lots of sorrow as we walk through life, but we aspire to know sorrow that is mingled with hope. For subjects of King Jesus, death and tragedy are *never* the last word. The goodness of our God is certain. He has given up his very Son for our redemption. There is no reason to doubt him. The resurrection punctuates how the last word is one of blessing and joy.

> The resurrection of Jesus issues the surprising command: don't be afraid. Because the God who made the world is the God who raised Jesus from the dead and calls you now to follow him. . . . Believing in this God means believing that it is going to be all right, and this belief is ultimately incompatible with fear.[1]

So we don't reset our watches. We throw them away, and then we wait.

> Out of the depths I cry to you, O LORD;
>> O Lord, hear my voice.
> Let your ears be attentive
>> to my cry for mercy.
> If you, O LORD, kept a record of sins,
>> O Lord, who could stand?
> But with you there is forgiveness;
>> therefore you are feared.
> *I wait for the LORD, my soul waits,*
>> *and in his word I put my hope.*
> *My soul waits for the Lord*
>> *more than watchmen wait for the morning,*
>> *more than watchmen wait for the morning.*
> O Israel, put your hope in the LORD,
>> for with the LORD is unfailing love
>> and with him is full redemption.
> He himself will redeem Israel from all their sins.
>
> —PSALM 130, *author's emphasis*

The psalmist introduces a new kind of waiting. He holds loosely onto his personal dreams and tightly onto his God who, if he forgives sins, must be good.

How do we wait? In our grief we rest in the promise of renewal that is packaged with the resurrection. Along the way we ask for prayer and search out companions from Scripture, such as the psalmists, who have learned the secrets of waiting on the Lord.

Are you a pessimist or an optimist? Silly question—worriers by definition expect the worst. Bad things certainly can and will happen, but there is a resurrection ending. So your task is not to transform into a superficial, sunny optimist. It is to grow to be an optimist by faith. The kingdom is advancing; God's reign is spreading; there will be justice; and when we belong to Christ, it will end with joy.

As for me, I want to watch and endure, not worry. I want to be like the night watchmen who are waiting to see first light. God is the God of suspense, but it is a suspense that teaches us peace. He is the God of surprises, but the surprises are always better than we could have dreamed. I can't put him in a box and assume that he should act according to my time schedule and according to my less sophisticated version of what is good. I need the mind of Christ. I can do with nothing less.

> Let us fix our eyes on Jesus, the author and perfecter of our faith, who
> for the joy set before him endured the cross, scorning its shame.
>
> —HEB. 12:2

Say it: "Lord, I trust you."

CHAPTER EIGHT

WORRY ABOUT WORRY

ONE MORE THING before getting into some of God's specific words to fearful and anxious people: Worry is dangerous. It is not to be trifled with. When you find worries, anxieties, and fears, pay attention.

God repeats "Do not be afraid" for more reasons than one. Certainly, he is the God of comfort who assures his children that they can trust him. But there is another reason why he repeats himself. When someone—a teacher, a spouse, a child—keeps saying the same thing over and over, you have to wonder why. At first you think that the person is being a nag. Then you get upset because you feel like you are being treated like a little kid: "I heard you the first time!" But if you have a smidgeon of humility you begin to understand that what is being repeated must be very important, and the person speaking must see that you are not responding appropriately.

Listen to God's words and you will hear a hint of urgency. Yes, one of the background images for "Do not worry" is a pasture. The Shepherd is caring for us and we don't have to be afraid. But the Shepherd seems awfully determined to calm our fears. It makes you wonder if there is something dangerous about fear and worry in and of themselves.

To give Franklin D. Roosevelt a nod, the only thing to worry about is worry itself.

> The farmer sows the word. Some people are like seed along the path, where the word is sown. As soon as they hear it, Satan comes and takes away the word that was sown in them. Others, like seed sown on rocky places, hear the word and at once receive it with joy. But since they have no root, they last only a short time. When trouble or persecution comes because of the word, they quickly fall away. Still others, like seed sown among thorns, hear the word; *but the worries of this life, the deceitfulness of wealth and the desires for other things come in and choke the word, making it unfruitful.* Others, like seed sown on good soil, hear the word, accept it, and produce a crop—thirty, sixty or even a hundred times what was sown.
>
> —MARK 4:14–20, *author's emphasis*

This is a parable of the kingdom. It is Jesus' explanation of a story he told the disciples. Worry's appearance is shocking.

What are killers of spiritual life and growth?

> "Satan." We knew that.
>
> *"The deceitfulness of wealth."* There are plenty of warnings about this in Scripture. Most notable is the case of the rich young man who, although a fine, moral person, walked away from the kingdom of God. "I tell you the truth, it is hard for a rich man to enter the kingdom of heaven. Again I tell you, it is easier for a camel to go through the eye of a needle than for a rich man to enter the kingdom of God" (Matt. 19:23–24). No surprise here.
>
> *"The desires for other things."* This is another phrase for lust. We are all familiar with it and there are many warnings about it. Covetous desires are caused by sin (Rom. 7:8). Left unchecked, they will master us.

"Worries." What? No way. Worries feel so bland and harmless. This is the last thing we would expect to make the list. Everyone has worries, and they seem so . . . ordinary. Worries are our "legitimate concerns." But Jesus is saying that when you see worry—and you will see it—be careful.

It makes sense when you think about it.

Worry is focused inward.

It prefers self-protection over trust.

It can hear many encouraging words—even God's words—and stay unmoved.

It can be life-dominating.

It is connected to your money and desires in that it reveals the things that are valuable to you.

It can reveal that you love something more than Jesus. It crowds Jesus out of your life.

This adds some oomph to our strategy with fear and worry. It would be easy to sit back and let Jesus take his best shot at them, all the while being fairly sure that he won't have much success. He speaks, we passively listen. But now we find that we are actually in danger. This is no time to be casual. We must be doers of the word of Christ to us.

> Do not merely listen to the word, and so deceive yourselves. Do what it says. Anyone who listens to the word but does not do what it says is like a man who looks at his face in a mirror and, after looking at himself, goes away and immediately forgets what he looks like. But the man who looks intently into the perfect law that gives freedom, and continues to do this, not forgetting what he has heard, but doing it—he will be blessed in what he does.
>
> —JAMES 1:22–25

A PERSONAL RESPONSE

This parable is alarming. At first, my interest in fear and worry was limited to quieting them for the sake of my own personal well-being. Now the stakes are much higher. My worry is a sign that I am in danger.

When in doubt, pray. I am not sure of all the ways I am called by God to act, but I am certainly feeling more desperate, so I can pray.

> Lord, help me. I worry and I am worried about it. I didn't realize that my worry and fears were so much about you and your kingdom. Now is the time for me to be a true hearer of the Word. Forgive my passivity and indifference.

GOD SPEAKS

on money and possessions

WORRIES attach themselves to the things we value, so it's not surprising that Scripture often addresses our fears and worries about money. Some things never change. Be prepared to have your eyes opened as you hear God speak to this universal struggle. You will be expecting him to reduce the issue to right and wrong: It is right to be generous with your money; it is wrong to worry about it. But God will talk about entire kingdoms and ask us to consider in which kingdom we want to live. Money points to our kingdom allegiances.

CHAPTER NINE

"DO NOT WORRY"

FEAR IS NURTURED by ignorance. If you know very little about snakes, you will panic when you see a garter snake slithering through the garden. But a herpetologist will be delighted by the cute little creature. When you see that the 747 is full and every overhead bin stuffed, you can't imagine such a heavy machine getting off the ground and staying aloft. But if you know the rudiments of aerodynamics, you catch a nap before takeoff.

When we don't know the true God, we assume that he is like ourselves, which is a terrifying thought. What if he is impatient, incapable of multitasking, and prone to taking time off for naps—or worse? But as you listen and come to know him, as you learn about his ways, you can rest. In the story about manna we are no longer ignorant about the ways of God.

He is near.

He hears.

He tests us.

He gives us grace for today.

He delivers.

His earthly deliverance has an even better deliverance in view.

The manna story provides the basic melody for the Bible's song about God's ways with fearful, anxious people. Other stories will add embellishments and variations, but you will usually be able to hear the old melody.

The New Testament variation on this theme is found in Jesus' collection of teaching referred to as the Sermon on the Mount.

> Therefore I tell you, do not worry about your life, what you will eat or drink; or about your body, what you will wear. Is not life more important than food, and the body more important than clothes? Look at the birds of the air; they do not sow or reap or store away in barns, and yet your heavenly Father feeds them. Are you not much more valuable than they? Who of you by worrying can add a single hour to his life?
>
> And why do you worry about clothes? See how the lilies of the field grow. They do not labor or spin. Yet I tell you that not even Solomon in all his splendor was dressed like one of these. If that is how God clothes the grass of the field, which is here today and tomorrow is thrown into the fire, will he not much more clothe you, O you of little faith? So do not worry, saying, "What shall we eat?" or "What shall we drink?" or "What shall we wear?" For the pagans run after all these things, and your heavenly Father knows that you need them. But seek first his kingdom and his righteousness, and all these things will be given to you as well. Therefore do not worry about tomorrow, for tomorrow will worry about itself. Each day has enough trouble of its own.
>
> —MATT. 6:25–34

Notice how Jesus' sermon stands on the shoulders of the manna story. We learn more about the God who hears and cares, who gives enough for today, and who has something even better in mind. But since Scripture provides us with a gradual unfolding of God's character, this New Testament story reveals even more than the Old Testament prequel.

JESUS SPEAKS TO YOU

Throughout Israel's wilderness journey, God was close to his people by way of a pillar of fire at night and a cloud by day. He communicated through Moses. He even invited a select group from Israel to climb the mountain and witness his presence, though only Moses was allowed to come near (Ex. 24:1–2). To get too close would have been deadly.

Now picture yourself on a hillside—a more gentle and hospitable version of Sinai. There are no shadows or crags in the rock where robbers can hide. The lake below adds to the peacefulness of it all. You are listening to the greater Moses. As we know now, he is the Lord, but his identity is not yet fully known. Certainly his true identity wouldn't be revealed by this pastoral scene because no one would catch the connection to Sinai. This time there is a crowd, and they are sitting close. Everyone is invited to draw near. As it was at Sinai, there is law giving: He elaborates on murder, sexual sin, truthfulness, and justice, and he seems to set the bar even higher than Moses did. But it is all unmistakably personal, especially when he teaches us how to pray. He insists that the One we pray to is our Father.

With Jesus' words about worry, you feel as if he is talking to you alone. Have you ever heard a preacher speak on a topic that made you think he was listening to your thoughts? That's what is happening here. Jesus essentially says, "I know something about you." He knows that you struggle with financial fears, threat of job loss—anything related to money and the insecurities we experience when we are on the financial edge.

Picture yourself on a hillside. The living God is speaking about real daily struggles, and he is speaking to you. The One who is risen from the dead, who is the same today as he was when he was sitting on the hillside, is speaking to you.

JESUS SPEAKS PERSUASIVELY

When Jesus speaks, he decides to use lots of words. He could say "Don't worry" and let the Old Testament background carry the rest, but you can hear him working hard to persuade you. He knows you have reason to worry. He even knows that fear and worry aren't conquered easily, so he perseveres in trying to reach your heart. As a way to keep you engaged, he is going to ask you a number of questions along the way.

"What is important?" Every question and sentence you hear from Jesus will be good for hours of meditation, especially this first one: "Isn't life more important than food, and the body more important than clothes?"

Trick question. Life *certainly* is about food and shelter. So, no, there is nothing more important. When I am really hungry I am a burger-seeking missile that can't be disarmed. When more money goes out than comes in, my finances are a "legitimate concern," though my concerns might look like an obsession to my wife.

But I am missing the point. Jesus' question implies, "Yes, there is something more important." Even if I forget the Old Testament commentary about the manna story, which says that manna is really about being sustained by the very words of God, Jesus has already talked about what is more important: "Blessed are the poor in spirit, for theirs is the *kingdom of heaven*" (Matt. 5:3). "Your kingdom come" (Matt. 6:10). "Store up for yourselves treasures in heaven" (Matt. 6:20).

Why am I so concerned about a meal, which will fill me for about an hour, when the kingdom is coming? One of the strategies for dealing with worry is to be overtaken by something more important than the object of your worries. Jesus is showing us what is more important. A new kingdom was being inaugurated, and it was present even as Jesus spoke those words because he is its King. This new kingdom is so beautiful and important that it can override our worries about everyday concerns like food and clothing.

Does this sound familiar? Moses already spoke about a better and more satisfying food, and Jesus is pointing the way. He actually *is* that food.

I am listening, King Jesus, keep going. Just wake me from my stupor when I think that there is nothing more important than basic physical needs, and keep talking.

*"Your **Father** cares for the needs of birds."* The rebuke, however, doesn't come. I had it doubly wrong. Not only did I think that basic physical needs were primary, I also assumed that Jesus was just a human being who would respond in annoyance to my failings. Instead, Jesus actually hears my myopic concerns and sets out to prove that our daily needs—our physical needs—*are* important to God. More specifically, in keeping with the highly personal nature of Jesus' teaching, he says that our daily needs are important to our heavenly *Father.*

There is something familiar in what Jesus says, but it should sound new. "Father" is not a new way to address God. God himself said, "How gladly would I treat you like sons and give you a desirable land, the most beautiful inheritance of any nation. I thought you would call me 'Father' and not turn away from following me" (Jer. 3:19). But there are only a handful of direct Old Testament references to God as Father. Jesus exceeds that number in the Sermon on the Mount alone. "Heavenly Father" is Jesus' preferred way to talk about God, and it is how he teaches us to address God in prayer. His emphasis on our Father encourages us to listen even more attentively.

How perfect for those who worry! The term *Father* immediately connotes care, compassion, and strength. In those days, the father was committed to protecting his children so that the family line could continue and the father's name would receive praise. The son or daughter was always welcome, always loved. Do you remember seeing pictures of John F. Kennedy's son John-John playing in the Oval Office? A father is to be respected and obeyed, even feared, but he is accessible and welcoming to his children. He delights in blessing them.

"You are more important than birds." Jesus continues his appeal by saying that our Father cares for the birds that were flying overhead. They don't ask for help but they receive it. Jesus is assuming that we remember that, in contrast with the rest of creation, we are made in the image of God. We have a unique relationship with the Creator.

If he cares for the birds, and he is not their Father in the way he is *our* Father, how much more will he care for us, his own children? The Father loves his creatures but not all creatures are made in his image or called his offspring. Only *we* are created in the image of God. Only we call him Father. The Creator and Sustainer of all things has a unique interest in caring for us.

"He clothes non-human creation in beauty. He will certainly do the same and more for you." Shifting his attention to clothing and, by extension, any form of shelter, Jesus again uses creation to illustrate his next point. Notice the beauty of the wildflowers, he says. These living things do absolutely nothing to attain their beauty. It is a gift to them from God. And notice their ephemeral nature. They are here today and gone tomorrow. They do not consist of eternal substance like we do. The argument is that if God cares for these transient aspects of creation, won't he care much more for children who share in his eternal kingdom?

So we will be cared for. But how? Don't think our clothes will be the standard issue, drab uniforms of old communist China. Some people might be satisfied with purely functional clothing, but most men are discriminating about what they wear, and most women would like something that enhances their beauty. Trivial, you think. Who cares about beauty when our hearts are destined for things that are not of this earth? Not so. Jesus is making a point about beauty. His kingdom is not merely drab and functional; somehow the kingdom he is announcing is a kingdom of beauty. The Beautiful One is King, and his children are and will be reflections of his beauty.

It is hard to imagine these things, but one thing is clear: The King is extravagant. That is the good news for fearful people. Most fears link to our doubts about God's generosity and attention to detail. In response, God decks his halls with beauty, which means that he freely gives what is costly. And, as the true expert craftsman, he attends to every last detail.

"O you of little faith." Given such generosity, will we trust him? That's the obvious question after God reveals himself to fearful people. Whose kingdom are you seeking? Do you trust the King who is also your Father? Dangers abound, and life is comprised of hourly risks, but the real issue behind worry is that of spiritual allegiances.

Our answer? "Sort of . . . a little . . . usually." We *sort of* want the kingdom, and we sort of want to trust the King—until life gets precarious. When everything is going well and the storehouses are full, we trust him. But when there is nothing for tomorrow, we panic and track down the address of another god who can give us enough for tomorrow and the next day too. It might not be Baal or Vishnu; but, in the context of Jesus' words, the god will have something to do with money and possessions.

Our natural tendency is to be fair-weather fans. When the team is doing well, that is, when they are giving us what we want, we follow them religiously. We never miss a game. When the team wins, we win. But when their losses outweigh their wins, we shift allegiances to another team with a better chance at a championship.

Whom do I trust? Where is my faith? Those are the questions that all worriers must ask, yet all of us already know the answer. Our trust is divided. We don't put all our eggs in one basket—even God's—because that's too risky. Our trust might not pay off the way we hope. We are reluctant to simply say to our Father, "I am yours," and stop worrying. Jesus knows this. Fear and worry reveal that our faith is indeed small.

If you are looking to plumb the depths of worry, you can find it in your mixed allegiances. You trust God for some things but not others. You trust him for heaven but not for earth.

"Seek first his kingdom." Can you see the universe taking shape? It is not just your own heart that wavers between two kingdoms. All creation is structured according to rulers and kingdoms. Worry points us to these realities.

With our ambivalent allegiances exposed, everything should now be simple. All that's left to do is trust God. But that just happens to be the hardest thing for a human being to do. If it were natural to us, everyone would happily follow Jesus, and divided allegiances would be an aberration. But trust isn't natural, and divided allegiances are the norm. We are all guilty of little faith and, to make things worse, it isn't enough to simply understand this. Acknowledging the diagnosis does not automatically lead to a cure. You can confess it, and worry will creep in even during your confession!

The cure is not to simply know what the problem is. The cure is to know the One we are called to trust. Keep looking at the triune God and how he has revealed himself throughout history. Don't spend your time focusing on your wavering allegiances.

How do you seek the kingdom? When you seek the King, you are seeking his kingdom. This kingdom includes everything that comes from him. It includes his law, his grace and mercy, his blessings of life, adoption, and holiness, and all his promises throughout Scripture. Those who seek him feed on his Word and seek to imitate him.

Are you worried? Jesus says there is nothing to worry about. It isn't our kingdom, it is God's. We take our cue from the King, and the King is not fretting over anything. He is in complete control.

"Therefore, don't worry about tomorrow." Here Jesus makes a reference to the original story of the manna, when Israel was only supposed to gather food for one day, and not store it up for the future. Worry is focused on tomorrow and God has already promised us that he will care for us tomorrow. A fair interpretation of Jesus' words could be, "Don't worry about tomorrow because your Father will care about tomorrow." He is taking care of both the big picture and the details. This frees us to focus on the work of the kingdom today. Even in human relationships, if someone competent and reliable is going to take care of future details, you are freed from worry and able to focus on the matters that are right in front of you.

When our two daughters married, my wife managed the details of their weddings. For one of the weddings, a good friend offered to take care of every last flower. On the day before the ceremony, we went to the church and saw hundreds of flowers being maintained, or refreshed, in dozens of twenty-gallon buckets of cold water. For anyone taking a quick inventory, the conclusion was simple: There simply was not enough time to organize these flowers into bouquets, table arrangements, and church beautification. Worry was the only logical response. Except that this was a good friend and a person of her word. She said, "Don't worry, they will be beautiful." So we didn't, and they were. Of course, it meant round-the-clock work for her while we enjoyed a good night's sleep, but all we needed to know was that someone trustworthy and capable was worried about the flowers. For us to worry would have been to doubt her word, and we never worried.

A PERSONAL RESPONSE

If I can trust the word of a friend, why do I question the word of the God of the universe? Go figure. Sin is truly bizarre.

It's time to distinguish between memorizing and meditating. Most people who have read the Bible know this passage on worry. Chronic worriers like myself have probably memorized much of it. Memorizing certainly can be useful, but the purpose of memorizing Scripture is to keep the passage handy so that we can meditate on it even when a Bible is not available.

One way to meditate is to say, "Yes, Lord, I believe," after each section of Scripture. Another is to teach and talk about this passage. I find that it is one thing to think about something, but another thing altogether to write it or explain it to others.

As a way to meditate, talk about this passage with a friend. Pray through it with someone else. Your entry point is money and the ways you can trust in it, but Jesus is also talking about the entire world of worries.

CHAPTER TEN

THE MESSAGE OF THE KINGDOM

THE PLAN IS simple: Don't worry, seek the kingdom. But what exactly *is* this kingdom and his righteousness? If the kingdom is our alternative to worry, we should learn more about it. And since the emerging data indicates that God communicates clearly and richly to us, we should expect to be able to understand the kingdom.

In the Sermon on the Mount, Jesus' teaching about the kingdom is at the center. For example, with regard to money, he begins and ends by talking about the kingdom.

In which kingdom do you invest? "Do not store up for yourselves treasures on earth" (Matt. 6:19). If you do, these treasures will not last and you will have no choice but to worry because your treasures are always at risk. But if we store up treasures in the kingdom of heaven, they are absolutely secure and there will be no reason to fret.

Which king do you serve? "No one can serve two masters. . . . You cannot serve both God [the King] and Money [the usurper king]" (Matt. 6:24). You cannot have simultaneous allegiances to two kingdoms. "Therefore

I tell you, do not worry [about money]" (Matt. 6:25). "Seek first his [my Father's] kingdom" (Matt. 6:33).

In other words, worry is usually about seeking something other than God's kingdom. Worry is a sign that we are trying to have it both ways, with one foot in the kingdom of the world and the other in the kingdom of heaven.

What is the way out of worry? We must become students of the King and his true kingdom so that we see its beauty and glory and become enthralled by it. It is hard to worry about money when you know about the riches within the kingdom of heaven.

WHAT IS THE KINGDOM?

When we think about the kingdom of heaven, everything gets a little fuzzy. We imagine clouds with enough density to hold disembodied spirits, though we suspect that spirits are very light and the clouds we see from airplane windows will be enough. We also envision this kingdom as very far away in time and space. Between now and then there are all kinds of bad things that can happen.

Fear and worry are not eager to wait for this kingdom. You are vulnerable right now; an intangible future hope isn't comforting. A future inheritance in a spiritual kingdom doesn't pay the rent today.

But the kingdom is *more* real than our day-to-day world, not less. Jesus announced that it was near (Matt. 3:2). He said that many of those listening to him would witness the kingdom in its glory.

Do you remember the children's game "hot-and-cold," where you try to find a hidden object? When you get closer, the leader says, "Warmer." When you move further away, the leader says, "Cooler." If you could have asked Jesus "Where is the kingdom?" he would have said, "You're getting warmer" every time you took a step toward him. If you touched him he would say, "You're burning up!" Jesus was and is the embodiment of the kingdom because he is the King. How much more real could the kingdom be?

He [Jesus] went to Nazareth, where he had been brought up, and on the Sabbath day he went into the synagogue, as was his custom. And he stood up to read. The scroll of the prophet Isaiah was handed to him. Unrolling it, he found the place where it is written: "The Spirit of the Lord is on me, because he has anointed me to preach good news to the poor. He has sent me to proclaim freedom for the prisoners and recovery of sight for the blind, to release the oppressed, to proclaim the year of the Lord's favor." Then he rolled up the scroll, gave it back to the attendant and sat down. The eyes of everyone in the synagogue were fastened on him, and he began by saying to them, "Today this scripture is fulfilled in your hearing."

—LUKE 4:16–21

Jesus is saying, "The kingdom has come." "Do you want evidence?" he asks. Watch and see if the poor are cared for, the blind receive sight, and the oppressed are liberated. His kingdom is the kingdom of heaven, not because it is far away and ethereal. Instead, it is where the King dwells, and the King now dwells on earth in a new way. He is firmly establishing his reign where his will is done.

The kingdom is the place where the King has all authority and power and, with the advent of Jesus' public ministry, he is proclaiming his kingdom authority against a usurper and a false kingdom. The world is no longer under enemy control.

Don't lose the connection to worry and money. Worry and fear say that the world is threatening and you are alone. But when the kingdom of heaven pierces the earth, God is establishing his control in a new way. Now that the King has come, you will never be alone.

THE STORY BEHIND THE KINGDOM

There is a history to the kingdom that you should understand. It begins with God creating all things. By definition, therefore, all things are his. He is the King; we are his subjects and owe him our allegiance. But there was insurrection in the kingdom as Satan—a creature—wanted a kingdom for himself. By successfully tempting Adam and Eve, Satan secured a following and laid claim to the earth. Once he had followers, he was the ruler of the kingdom of the air (Eph. 2:2), and fear became the norm for human experience.

The kingdom of God, however, was neither defeated nor dormant. Immediately after humanity's insurrection, God set about to restore his kingdom with an even greater grandeur. God determined to work through an insignificant group of people to usher in the eternal reign of his Son, the Messiah.

> Then Moses went up to God, and the LORD called to him from the mountain and said, "This is what you are to say to the house of Jacob and what you are to tell the people of Israel: 'You yourselves have seen what I did to Egypt, and how I carried you on eagles' wings and brought you to myself. Now if you obey me fully and keep my covenant, then out of all nations you will be my treasured possession. Although the whole earth is mine, you will be for me a kingdom of priests and a holy nation.'"
>
> —Ex. 19:3–6

All he asked was that this chosen people act as if they were his subjects, which they did not. Instead, they imitated the kingdoms around them by following their gods, pursued an earthly king (1 Sam. 8:7), and basically did everything possible to trash their status as a kingdom of priests and a holy nation belonging to God.

But while the Hebrew kingdom was shrinking with the compounded evil of Israel's kings, the real kingdom, with all its splendor, was going to come no matter what. Sin, the evidence of Satan's kingdom, was not powerful enough to hold back the work of God. God would establish his kingdom, and the fact that he would do it in the face of betrayal would make the kingdom that much more magnificent. It would clearly be God's work, without human strength or ingenuity.

God would do what he had promised.

> [To David] "Your house and your kingdom will endure forever before me; your throne will be established forever."
>
> —2 SAM. 7:16

> Your throne, O God, will last for ever and ever; a scepter of justice will be the scepter of your kingdom.
>
> —Ps. 45:6

> In the time of those kings, the God of heaven will set up a kingdom that will never be destroyed, nor will it be left to another people. It will crush all those kingdoms and bring them to an end, but it will itself endure forever.
>
> —DAN. 2:44

All this points to Jesus, the cross, his resurrection, and his present reign.

THE KINGDOM HAS ENEMIES

Make no mistake, the two kingdoms are spiritual. But that doesn't mean they are ethereal and unearthly. Spiritual means *more* real. "Spiritual" gets stuck with the same connotations we attach to heaven: It's ghostly, otherworldly, and boring. The reality is that "spiritual" is more like when someone lifts the fiberglass shell off a NASCAR contender. The fiberglass shell helps with aerodynamics, and it's the part of the car we see, but the real action is just below the shell. That's where you see the huge engine, the reinforced side panels and roll bar, and a cockpit designed for pure speed. Underneath the fragile shell is the real world of NASCAR.

The spiritual world is our world—under the hood. You might not actually see it, but every single movement in life is inspired by it. We are human beings—spiritual/physical beings—who are all connected in some way to the true God, who is the Spirit. In everything we do, we make *spiritual* decisions: we live in dependence on the Spirit and imitate our God, or we set off against the Spirit, in which case we are separating ourselves from the Life-giver to go on end-stage life support. When we live apart from the Spirit, we are still connected to a spiritual being, but the spiritual being is Satan, the Evil One. One kingdom is ruled by fear, the other by mercy and grace.

If we have any doubts about how the world is organized into king-doms and how these kingdoms are ruled by spiritual heads, take a look at what happens immediately after Jesus is proclaimed as the rightful heir to the true throne: spiritual battle breaks out (Matt. 3:16). Satan tempts Jesus with promises of food, authority, and power, but Jesus defeats him by spiritual means. That is, he trusts his Father and obeys him. When Jesus casts demons out of man, he is announcing that "the kingdom of God has come upon you" (Matt. 12:22–28). And notice what happens even today whenever the reality of the kingdom of Christ is proclaimed: The Evil One quickly tries to snatch away what was sown in the heart (Matt. 13:19).

All we can see with the naked eye is our own particular frets and fears, but there is something much bigger taking place. Worries are a way that we doubt the King's presence and power. Our doubts could come from our own stubborn commitment to the myth of personal autonomy, or they may come from satanic accusations that question God's generosity and our unworthiness. Either way, anxiety and worry are spiritual wake-up calls that must be handled by spiritual means.

When you wake up to kingdom realities, you find that you are tracing the steps of both the Israelites and Jesus himself into the wilderness. Can you sense it? Wild animals, robbers, unreliable food supplies. But there is more. The wilderness is the place where God meets his people, Satan attacks, and kingdom allegiances are revealed. If the only footprints in the desert were those of the ancient Hebrews, we would have no choice but to imitate their worry. All good intentions to trust wholeheartedly would disappear at the first sign of hardship. But the King has gone where others failed, and he shows us another way. He has even given us the Spirit to give us the power to be Jesus' followers.

This explains one of the paradoxes of all kingdom life. On one hand, there is rest and peace: The King has come, and we enjoy the benefits of the kingdom. But at the same time, we live knowing that we are in the enemy's crosshairs. Satan is ready to engage us in battle. The two kingdoms are in conflict. With all this going on behind the scenes, don't think you can simply say no to fear and worry, and that will be the end of them.

IT IS HARD FOR THE RICH TO INHERIT THE KINGDOM

Money complicates things even further. It doesn't matter whether you have a lot or a little. The poor can covet as much as the rich, but, as a general rule, the more you have, and the longer you have had it, the more you have fallen into the habit of valuing money above the King.

Children in the kingdom of God hold onto possessions loosely. They know that the King is powerful and generous, and they know that what they have is on loan anyway. They are quick to help those in need. The rich, on the other hand, are sorely tempted to trust in their riches.

> Jesus answered, "If you want to be perfect, go, sell your possessions and give to the poor, and you will have treasure in heaven. Then come, follow me." When the young man heard this, he went away sad, because he had great wealth. Then Jesus said to his disciples, "I tell you the truth, it is hard for a rich man to enter the kingdom of heaven. Again I tell you, it is easier for a camel to go through the eye of a needle than for a rich man to enter the kingdom of God."
>
> —MATT. 19:21–24

Now we understand even more why Jesus makes such a passionate appeal to not worry. He knows that worry, especially about money, draws us to the kingdom of earth, a.k.a. the kingdom of this world, our own kingdom, and the kingdom of the Evil One. This anti-kingdom perpetrates a lie that says God is not generous and, when it comes to our wants, we are on our own.

Can the rich enter the kingdom? Yes, but only because all things are possible with God (Matt. 19:25–26) who transforms us by his Spirit (John 3:5).

Once again, fears that are connected to money will not just drift away. Unless they are attacked through spiritual means they, like all fears, will multiply.

It makes you feel a little desperate for help, doesn't it?

THE KINGDOM IS ABOUT ALLEGIANCE TO AND IMITATION OF THE KING

Think of the kingdom as a family on a very large scale. Like the father of the ancient Near East, the king's task was to love, protect, and bless his subjects so that the kingdom—his kingdom—prospered. Subjects of the realm, for their part, acknowledged their allegiance to the king and demonstrated that allegiance by living according to his laws.

In the kingdom of God, the King has made extravagant promises to us—promises of protection, liberation, and peace. We respond with our allegiance, which we typically call faith or trust. The essence of faith is *not* that we trust without evidence but that we choose sides: In whom do we trust? Our allegiance to the kingdom of God is nurtured by the very words of God, especially as they are spoken by King Jesus, and it is demonstrated in our obedience. And since God's laws are a systematic expression of his character, we become more like the King when we keep his laws.

God's kingdom has been moving forward since the beginning of creation, but its inaugural moment was the resurrection of Jesus. The resurrection was the Father's confirmation that this was indeed his Son, the only

One worthy to sit on the throne. It announced the inauguration with fanfare. But since then, as is characteristic of God's ways, the actual building of the kingdom is gradual. It moves forward by small, individual acts of our obedience.

Does that seem somehow disappointing? This gradual growth of the kingdom is the way of God. Miracles happen—and they can happen in a moment—but God's favored method is to bring change with less fanfare. Don't expect all of your fear and worry to be extinguished by the time you get to the end of this book. The kingdom is a field that grows (Matt. 13:24–29), the tiniest mustard seed that becomes the largest of all the garden plants (Matt. 13:31–32), the yeast that gradually but thoroughly permeates the loaf and transforms it (Matt. 13:33). The kingdom unfolds this way in our own personal lives and in history. So, when in doubt about how to seek first the kingdom, choose the path of persistence and endurance. Don't wait for the occasional spectacular mighty acts of today.

Life in the kingdom consists of humility, peacemaking, mercy, and a heart for the poor and oppressed (Matt. 5:1–10). It delights in studying the words of God in order to obey them. We keep our word, even when it is inconvenient (Matt. 5:33–37), forgive as we have been forgiven (Matt. 6:9–15), love our enemies (Matt. 5:43–46), and pursue justice (Ps. 45:6). We invite others to live under the King, knowing that we have been given a gift of inestimable worth and we want others to receive it (Matt. 22:1). We shun any hint of exclusivity (Matt. 23:13). Our models are little children, with their love and dependence toward their parents (Luke 18:17). In general, we look for opportunities to show grace and mercy so we will be a light to others. This means that, unlike the rest of the world, we are not going to assume that fear and worry are staples of human life. Instead, we are going to set out on a path to trust more and worry less.

Let's get more specific. One way to test our kingdom allegiances is to look at our budget. For example, do you tithe? Do you freely give ten percent of your income to God's work in its many forms? That was the Old Testament guideline. And when we get to the New Testament, when the riches of the kingdom are unveiled, Jesus invited people to give God everything: "Sell your possessions and give to the poor. Provide purses for yourselves that will not wear out, a treasure in heaven that will not be exhausted, where no thief comes near and no moth destroys" (Luke 12:33).

If you don't tithe, your faith is more than likely small. You hoard because you don't believe the Father is generous. You don't share in the king's heart of self-sacrifice. As a result, worry and fear will be an uneasy undercurrent in your life.

Tithing, of course, is not the central issue in the kingdom. The kingdom is first about what God gives, not what we give. Giving is merely our response to his ongoing generosity. We already know that his generosity to us is boundless—it is the kingdom itself (Luke 12:32). But what *is* this kingdom that he is giving us?

The answer, like his promises to us, is a list that is endless. He gives forgiveness, reconciliation, love, power, meaning, purpose, sanctification, glorification, peace, and more. But all the gifts of the kingdom are gathered together in Jesus the King.

WHEN YOU RECEIVE THE KINGDOM, YOU RECEIVE A PERSON

When people see death approaching, no one yet has said that they wished they had worked longer hours or amassed more goods. A colleague of mine was trying to motivate another colleague to write more books. He was saying, "At the end of your life, what do you really want? Lots of people at your funeral or a shelf full of books?" The one speaking, as you can imagine, was a bit full of himself. He had never really considered the end of life. But when he heard the words come out of his mouth, he realized that people were more important than productivity. Talk to someone with wisdom and you will hear that friends and family are what's important. How much more important is a relationship with the King himself! With that in mind, only an immature child would be disappointed to hear that his parent, who had been away for some time, would be the big Christmas gift.

A PERSONAL RESPONSE

There are times when the kingdom seems elusive and I attribute it to the kingdom being…elusive. Since it is hard to see, I don't expect myself to fully understand its reality. I have picked up books on quantum physics that I don't expect to fully grasp because, although the authors talk about real matter, I can't see it. But my kingdom denseness is neither a result of the kingdom being invisible nor my own intellectual deficits. The kingdom is elusive to me because I am in a spiritual battle and I don't even realize it, which makes me even more vulnerable to the enemy's attacks.

If the kingdom doesn't sound good to you yet, if you are still hoping for health, wealth, and prosperity, then you can be sure that the spiritual battle is raging. The Accuser wants nothing less than your spiritual death. Don't stand for it! Satan is a liar who perpetrates injustices. You want nothing to do with him.

Let's talk about the kingdom with each other. Let's pray for each other that we would see clearly.

> Lord, give me eyes for the kingdom. Show me where my own sin is keeping me from seeing. Please give me your Spirit so I can witness the beauty of the kingdom of heaven.

CHAPTER ELEVEN

WHEN THE KINGDOM ISN'T ENOUGH

LET'S THINK a bit longer about kingdom conflict. Worry about money is located right at the crossroads of the two kingdoms. It is strategic ground, so we expect the battle to be fierce. From the Accuser's perspective, we couldn't be any more susceptible to defeat. When trouble is on the horizon, we already feel alone. We feel like we have to rely on ourselves. We might know what God says but it doesn't seem relevant to the emerging crisis. We have a sense that the kingdom is for the future but our needs and worries are in the present. In other words, the Evil One doesn't have to do much more than say, "Yes, you are right to think that you have to hoard to protect your own kingdom."

The kingdom of heaven, however, has clearly foreseen that this is where the battle would rage, and it is prepared. It is as though every page of Scripture has been looking to this moment—all three hundred-plus exhortations to fear not, the tradition that began with manna, and Jesus' very personal words about worry.

With this battle in mind, let's listen in on what our hearts are saying when the temptations come. If the kingdom doesn't sound that good to us, the problem most likely can be found in our own hearts.

THE KINGDOM DOES NOT GIVE US ALL WE NEED

Will the King really care for our needs? He says he will, but we aren't so sure and we have our reasons. Didn't the apostles go hungry on more than a few occasions? Jesus and his disciples were often without shelter. When famine strikes a country, God doesn't partition those who trust him from those who don't and then care only for his children. Fires aren't limited to pagan homes.

Thus we find ourselves turning toward the kingdom of the earth and its ethos of self-protection. We know that self-protection hasn't helped in the past, but we aren't so sure that faith in the King has either. In this spiritual no-man's land, the lure of money is strong. Although wealth can't protect my material possessions from being stolen or set ablaze, it can at least replace most of them.

Some kings would say good riddance to us in the face of such treasonous reasoning. After all, God receives no real benefit from our allegiance. He doesn't need us. But our King responds to us with more persuasive words, though they might not be persuasive at first. He brings us back to Deuteronomy 8:3, "He humbled you, causing you to hunger and then feeding you with manna, which neither you nor your fathers had known, to teach you that man does not live on bread alone but on every word that comes from the mouth of the LORD."

It feels like a bait-and-switch. You came to get one thing and were given another. You thought your needs would be met and now you are getting something different.

But the King's appeal to us includes story after story to buttress our confidence in him. He points, for example, to the apostle Paul. Paul seemed to get what God is trying to tell us. In his letter to Corinth, he wrote about hardships that were far beyond his ability to endure, "so that we despaired even of life" (2 Cor. 1:8). These hardships indicate that God does not always satisfy basic human needs; Paul was not expecting God to spare him from death. But in a phrase that echoes Deuteronomy, Paul writes, "This happened that we might not rely on ourselves but on God, who raises the dead" (2 Cor. 1:9). Paul was delivered from these hardships, but he did not assume that God guaranteed such deliverance in the future.

Did Paul forget Jesus' words about worry? How did he reconcile Jesus' observation about birds that are fed by the Father with his own history of hunger and near-death experiences? Just when you are willing to believe that God will care for your physical needs, you find that he was not speaking literally!

The apostle Paul was not tripped up by this at all because he had access to God's secret wisdom, Jesus himself. Paul viewed the world through the defining event of the kingdom of heaven: Christ and him crucified (1 Cor. 2:2). Jesus Christ was the Word that came from heaven. He was the Bread of Life. When Paul witnessed the King going through hunger, the worst of hardships, and death itself, Paul realized he was witnessing the way of the kingdom. When he was ushered down this path, he welcomed it. What sustained him was spiritual food and drink: "I know what it is to be in need, and I know what it is to have plenty. I have learned the secret of being content in any and every situation, whether well fed or hungry, whether living in plenty or in want. I can do everything through him who gives me strength" (Phil. 4:12–13).

Now is the time to bury the myth that *spiritual* means intangible, something only for the by-and-by. The words of God to which Moses pointed, which was the strength Paul found from Christ alone, are spiritual in the sense that they are eternal. The contrast between earthly and spiritual is not a contrast between the tangible and the intangible; it is between the transitory and the eternal. Earthly is temporary, spiritual is everlasting. When you eat a meal, even if you are so bloated you swear it will be your last, you will be ready for a snack in a few hours. You will be hungry at the next scheduled mealtime. But the food from heaven will leave you satisfied even through lean years.

> When a Samaritan woman came to draw water, Jesus said to her, "Will you give me a drink?" (His disciples had gone into the town to buy food.)
>
> The Samaritan woman said to him, "You are a Jew and I am a Samaritan woman. How can you ask me for a drink?" (For Jews do not associate with Samaritans.)
>
> Jesus answered her, "If you knew the gift of God and who it is that asks you for a drink, you would have asked him and he would have given you living water."
>
> "Sir," the woman said, "you have nothing to draw with and the well is deep. Where can you get this living water? Are you greater than our father Jacob, who gave us the well and drank from it himself, as did also his sons and his flocks and herds?"
>
> Jesus answered, "Everyone who drinks this water will be thirsty again, but whoever drinks the water I give him will never thirst. Indeed, the water I give him will become in him a spring of water welling up to eternal life."
>
> The woman said to him, "Sir, give me this water so that I won't get thirsty and have to keep coming here to draw water."
>
> —JOHN 4:7-15

This was no bait-and-switch, and the Samaritan woman knew it. She would be the first to receive the offer of spiritual food and drink that was foreshadowed by the manna, and there was no way she would refuse. She understood the real intent of the water from the rock and the manna. She received the anti-bait-and-switch. She was lured with something good and given something incomparably better.

Remember that God's stories in Scripture are progressive—they keep getting better. It is as if we are given small doses of reality when we are very young and can't grasp God's sophisticated love and care. When we are older and have witnessed more of God's ways, we are prepared to hear it all. When we were young he gives us manna; when we are old he gives his life. We get *him*.

After Jesus' private invitation to the Samaritan woman, he retold the story of manna again by feeding five thousand people from five barley loaves and two small fish. This becomes the background for his public announcement: The words of God you have anticipated since the days of Moses are now revealed to you in the flesh. Come and eat.

> Jesus answered, "I tell you the truth, you are looking for me, not because you saw miraculous signs but because you ate the loaves and had your fill. Do not work for food that spoils, but for food that endures to eternal life, which the Son of Man will give you. On him God the Father has placed his seal of approval."
>
> —JOHN 6:26–27

Those listening anticipate our own question.

> Then they asked him, "What must we do to do the works God requires?"
> Jesus answered, "The work of God is this: to believe in the one he has sent."
>
> —JOHN 6:28–29

We get food by believing that Jesus is the King sent by the Father. We declare our allegiance to him and acknowledge that we belong to him, not ourselves.

But the crowd anticipates us again, this time with their doubts.

So they asked him, "What miraculous sign then will you give that we may see it and believe you? What will you do? Our forefathers ate the manna in the desert; as it is written: 'He gave them bread from heaven to eat.'"

Jesus said to them, "I tell you the truth, it is not Moses who has given you the bread from heaven, but it is my Father who gives you the true bread from heaven. For the bread of God is he who comes down from heaven and gives life to the world."

"Sir," they said, "from now on give us this bread."

Then Jesus declared, "I am the bread of life. He who comes to me will never go hungry, and he who believes in me will never be thirsty. But as I told you, you have seen me and still you do not believe."

—John 6:30–36

What will you do with Jesus, the better manna? That has been the question all along. Now you are properly reoriented. The focal point is not us and our needs; it is the King, as it should be.

"I am the bread of life. Your forefathers ate the manna in the desert, yet they died. But here is the bread that comes down from heaven, which a man may eat and not die. I am the living bread that came down from heaven. If anyone eats of this bread, he will live forever. This bread is my flesh, which I will give for the life of the world."

Then the Jews began to argue sharply among themselves, "How can this man give us his flesh to eat?"

Jesus said to them, "I tell you the truth, unless you eat the flesh of the Son of Man and drink his blood, you have no life in you. Whoever eats my flesh and drinks my blood has eternal life, and I will raise him up at the last day. For my flesh is real food and my blood is real drink. Whoever eats my flesh and drinks my blood remains in me, and I in him. Just as the living Father sent me and I live because of the Father, so the one who feeds on me will live because of me. This is the bread that came down from heaven. Your forefathers ate manna and died, but he who feeds on this bread will live forever."

—JOHN 6:48–58

The pattern is this: The Father genuinely cares about the daily needs of his children, and he is constantly caring for us, but he wants this to point us to something better. If we don't find our life and strength in Jesus Christ, we will go from one worry to the next.

Do you have any thoughts on how to grow in this? Is a plan emerging? Any plan must include perseverance, talking with others about the King and his trustworthiness, asking for prayer, and regular feeding from Scripture.

THE KINGDOM DOES NOT GIVE US ALL WE WANT

But don't stop considering your own heart. Beneath our questions about God's generosity and his care for our needs is something darker. What we really care about is our *wants*.

God is alert to our daily needs for food and shelter, but that doesn't leave us warm all over. I am persuaded that God will care for my needs if I lose everything I have. My wife and I live amid a generous group of people, and I have seen families in need who have had to ask people to *stop* bringing so many meals. If we were without food, I have no doubt I would end up gaining weight. Clothes? We would be given coupons to our local thrift store and I would be better dressed than I am now. Shelter? We would have our choice among friends who would gladly open their homes to us. We would live like kings. It doesn't take much faith for me to believe that God will care for my needs and the needs of my family.

My wants are what concern me. That's where the battle must be fought. I want:

nice vacations

cars that work

not one guitar, but at least three

gifts for my wife that will impress other people

healthy children who are deeply loved by their spouses

sons-in-law who are lovers of God and never make my daughters cry

health and happiness for my wife

my wife to die *after* me

et cetera, et cetera.

"The kingdom or the possibility of being able to afford your wants? Which do you want?"

"Can't I have both? Could I think this one over for a few days?" (During which time I can make a few last-minute purchases.)

Ugh, how embarrassing. We know it sounds horribly superficial, but, after all, we are only human. Humans want, and then want more. How can we—mere earthlings—be expected to be satisfied by something unearthly? It's against nature. That is true, of course, until we realize that we are God's offspring and Jesus Christ himself shows us the pattern of true humanness. His shorthand version of this entire discussion is simple: "My food is to do the will of him who sent me and to finish his work" (John 4:34).

THE KINGDOM IS GOD'S

What compromises our allegiance and makes us so vulnerable is that our real concern is what *we* get out of the kingdom. Our version of the kingdom looks peculiarly like suburbia, where each one has his or her own half-acre—our own personal domain. But there is no private ownership in the kingdom. All is from God and belongs to God. We are not the owners of our material stuff; we are stewards, but not owners. God is in control and he sits on the throne where he receives glory, honor, and praise.

The kingdom is God's. Not exactly a radical thought, but it is a jolt of reality to hearts that always want more. Then again, it is a wonderful jolt of reality. When you know that the kingdom is God's alone (though he gives it to us), that is the only thing that can lead to peace and rest. Owners are the ones who do all the worrying; stewards simply listen to the owner's desires and work to implement them. Owners are responsible for the outcome; stewards strive to be faithful.

This is starting to sound better until we stumble upon an unpleasant thought: The King can tell us what to do with our money! Now *that* is going too far. My money is sacrosanct. Don't ask my age and don't tell me how to spend my money. No wonder we need so much persuasion to acknowledge Jesus as our only King.

There is no hoarding in God's kingdom. We want to hold everything tightly; God counters by calling us to be generous to those in need. Humility and generosity infuse every aspect of kingdom living. They are unmistakable qualities of the King and, since we have been given the kingdom rather than earned it, humility and generosity *should* be our natural responses.

But life in the kingdom is now officially uncomfortable.

Watch the way Jesus walks through the kingdom. He is always moving toward the marginalized, the physically broken, the oppressed, and the poor. We already know that the rich are reluctant to believe in Jesus because they know it will cost them. Jesus and his followers prefer those who can never help us get a better job or increase the church budget.

Just when your storehouses had enough for tomorrow, you notice some desperate needs around you. The King is close enough to put his hand into your pocketbook and, for most Westerners, that is far too intrusive and impolite. "Go ahead and require public niceness and regular attendance at church, Lord, but remember that my money is my own!"

We get the impression that the Father prefers to keep us on the edge. This is what got us worried in the first place! His plan is to liberate us from our defensive, hoarding, tight-fisted, miserly ways, and to teach us that when we have been given the kingdom—the kingdom!—stinginess is unnatural and unbecoming. We might prefer a different strategy, but if God is molding us to be chips off the old block, his strategy makes sense. It is exactly what we need, because our greatest need is to be what we were intended to be—to be like him.

So, the kingdom is God's and God targets the needs of those who have less than we do. In other words, not only is the kingdom about God, and not me, I don't even come in second! I am to consider others more important than myself in the kingdom. This seems like too much to ask until the King calls us his treasured possession (Ex. 19:5). He is seeking my allegiance with love, not with force and power. The reason we are called to lay up our treasures in heaven is because we are *his* treasure. When you are confident that you are the Father's treasured possession, you are also confident that his loving care will continue forever. Building warehouses is a waste of time and space. His gifts to you become things you want to give him back in gratitude. Then he gives you even more.

A PERSONAL RESPONSE

Life in the kingdom isn't easy, at least not when we want to share the throne. But it really is silly to hold onto things that don't belong to us and aren't that important anyway. I want to say to myself, *Okay, now stop it. Stop holding onto your stuff. Be more generous.* And I *do* say that, but it doesn't really work.

So I confess that I can, at times, be frozen with indecision at the crossroads of the kingdoms. I don't want to be possessed by things that have no longevity. I want to be possessed by Christ. I take small steps of obedience: tithing, serving, and asking others for wisdom about money. (Since there is nothing wrong with a savings account, I don't know where wisdom ends and unbelief begins.) Through it all, I must ask the question, *Why is it about you? You are not the King; you are the servant of the King!* Then I settle back and listen to God's patient and persuasive responses. "He who did not spare his own Son, but gave him up for us all—how will he not also, along with him, graciously give us all things?" (Rom. 8:32).

CHAPTER TWELVE

GRACE FOR TOMORROW

THERE IS A MYTH circulating that Scripture tells us to live for the kingdom today and then tells us about our distant future in heaven, but tells us nothing about the time between now and then. The near future is a complete unknown. God obviously knows the future but we think he keeps it to himself, preferring that we walk around blind while he says, "Trust me."

God certainly has no obligation to tell us anything else, but we would expect fewer secrets from him as our Father. Why doesn't he give us more information? We aren't necessarily looking for stock tips (however nice those might be), but who could argue with some advanced notice of future problems? You would think a loving father would want to give his children a leg up.

Or is this the anxiety talking? Anxiety asks for more information so it can be prepared for the coming apocalypse. It also asks for more information so it can manage the world apart from God.

WE HAVE AN ABUNDANCE OF GRACE

Worry and anxiety *think* that more information will help. The truth, of course, is that it won't. In fact, if you knew what tomorrow would bring, you would probably opt to stay in bed. But put that aside for the moment. The deeper issue is that we still think God is a little stingy. He keeps secrets and plays games with us. He withholds. Can we fully trust someone who does such things? Could you trust a spouse who had secrets? Openness is essential to relationships. And…

Before the questions are even formed, God responds. Once again his holiness is on display. A mere mortal would have had enough of our complaints long ago, but God invites dialogue and displays unlimited patience. His response begins by simply showing us the sheer breadth and depth of Scripture. The Bible is God's revelation of himself. It claims to contain everything we need to know.

That raises the awkward and now unavoidable question: Do you read God's Word? This is God's preparation manual for the future. Do you study it? Do you search it for insights when you are anxious?

Busted.

You have heard people say that reading Scripture is a great antidote for worry. Frankly, that can sound superficial. It seems superficial to me sometimes when I hear it. But don't forget the spiritual warfare that is ongoing in your heart. How could Scripture seem superficial when it has held the attention of scholars since its first word was written? And when will we understand that Scripture is personal? It is God's communication to needy people. *B.I.B.L.E.*

When we actually investigate Scripture, we find that God is not holding back. He reveals himself generously, without reservation, opening his very heart to us. If we think otherwise, if we think he is holding out on us, then we are getting trounced in the spiritual battle.

Jesus said, "I no longer call you servants, because a servant does not know his master's business. Instead, I have called you friends, for everything that I learned from my Father I have made known to you" (John 15:15).

Jesus was the Son who was on his Father's business, so he had to know exactly what the Father wanted. He was privy to the Father's innermost thoughts. We certainly wouldn't expect access to such information, but we have been given it. Suddenly our excuse for anxiety goes right out the window.

The Father must be saying, "What more can I say?" to worriers who feel out in the dark. He has given us everything we need. He has given us what he gave his only Son, and then he poured out his Spirit of wisdom and revelation so that we would know even more.

WE HAVE GRACE FOR TODAY

Much of that knowledge and grace can be summarized like this: As the Father has loved us, so we respond by loving others. We have been given grace to know God's love and to love one another. That sounds a little sketchy at first, but within that simple summary is much more than we realize. It is our navigational guide for today and tomorrow.

When we are paralyzed by fear or anxiety, Scripture gives us our bearings and the Spirit gives us power to take the steps of obedience. Our bearings so far have come out of the question: What is the kingdom? A specific answer is that the kingdom is where the love of the King is our delight, and we search for ways to express that love to others. We fight fear by loving another person, right now.

Sometimes we are anxious about the future because there is no larger agenda that occupies us in the present. Love, however, is an expansive agenda.

WE HAVE GRACE FOR TOMORROW

Now on to the future. Worry and fear are always looking ahead. When the thing we dread is upon us, we usually do well. Anticipation is the killer.

In light of God's generosity and patience and his offer of comfort and wisdom, we should expect him to speak to us about the near future, and he does.

He tells us that <u>there is nothing in the future that can interfere with our kingdom mission.</u> If the difficulty you anticipate comes upon you, you will receive grace to know God's love and grace to love someone else (1 Cor. 10:13). If you get in the car accident you dread, you will have grace to know that God is with you, and you will have grace to bear fruit even in that difficult situation. If your loved one dies before you, you will have grace to know God's comfort and to shine brightly as you reflect your Father's glory. If poverty knocks on your door, you will have grace to trust your King and know that poverty cannot detract from your privilege of being an ambassador who blesses others in his name. As children and stewards who aren't in control but trust the One who is, the assurance of such grace is a blessing.

Were you hoping for more? Well, as you might guess by now, there is more. All you have to do is keep the manna story in mind. Remember that God gave the Israelites grace to trust and obey him when they left Egypt, just as we are given even more grace for faith and obedience when the wilderness is ahead. But they were also given more unexpected grace than they could have predicted or imagined.

Your future includes manna. It *will* come. There is no sense devising future scenarios now because <u>God will do more than you anticipate.</u> When you understand God's plan to give future grace,[1] you have access to what is arguably God's most potent salvo against worry and fear.

JUST SAY "NO" TO FALSE PROPHECIES

There is one bit of data that worriers never factor into their <u>false prophecies.</u> It is this: We will receive grace in the future.

Every once in a while we meet someone who understands this. An eighty-two-year-old widow, who has experienced many losses and tragedies in her life, lets her mind drift toward the coming day and says, "God has been faithful to me today, giving me more than I deserve. He will be faithful tomorrow." She doesn't know in what form the manna will come, but she has gathered it every day for years, and she is quite confident that it will be there tomorrow.

An older pastor, nearing retirement, has counseled more people than he cares to remember who have been victimized by adultery. Amid the pain, however, he has seen that God gives these injured spouses grace when they need it. Each one would have said that they expected to be crushed by such a betrayal and that forgiveness would be impossible. But they hadn't imagined the grace they would be given. As they sought Christ in the midst of the betrayal, they found enough grace to persevere, to find comfort, to have hope, and even to forgive. They could say with the apostle Paul, "We are hard pressed on every side, but not crushed; perplexed, but not in despair" (2 Cor. 4:8).

The pastor saw grace given time and time again, always amazed as he watched his congregants walk by faith in places where he himself couldn't imagine having the grace that they did. Then his wife of thirty years suddenly left with another man, worn down by the years of financial strain and claustrophobic in the role of pastor's wife. The pastor went to his study, where he had counseled so many others, and sat on the opposite side of his desk, where his parishioners would sit. He listened to the years of counsel and called out for grace. His worst nightmare had come to pass, and he had received grace. There would be no reconciliation in his case, but there would be peace, contentment, forgiveness, faith, and love.

TOMORROW'S GRACE DOES NOT SHIELD US FROM HARDSHIPS

You never hear God reasoning this way with anxious people: "What are the odds of that happening? You don't need to worry." "Don't worry; I won't let bad things happen to you." <u>God does not promise grace that removes hardships.</u>

If our child is very sick, we want to believe that grace means that God will heal the child. If we have just been laid off from a job and have no financial cushion, we want to believe that grace means we will be hired tomorrow by an even more stable company, and that the old company will apologize for its egregious mistake with a huge severance package. But that is not the promise. God does not promise that earthly life in his kingdom will be easier than life in our own kingdom. Instead, <u>he indicates that in the kingdom of heaven we will be familiar with the sufferings of Christ. We *will* experience hardships. We will</u> not be spared the difficulties of life. <u>Compared with life outside the kingdom, suffering will be more intense, if only because we love others more deeply.</u>

This seems to take us back where we began. What we fear really *might* overtake us. The bridge really could fall. The plane really could be infiltrated by terrorists. My spouse really could be unfaithful. At first, this would seem to drive us right back to our attempts at controlling our world. Though such attempts might not help, at least we feel like we are doing *something*.

TOMORROW'S GRACE MEANS *MORE*

Then you remember: His grace to you is intended to accomplish *his* kingdom purposes, not your own. Left to yourself, you would bubble-wrap everything valuable to you and invest in armed security. There is nothing inherently wrong in wanting to protect your assets, but we already know that anything that smacks of being tightfisted or self-protective is at odds with the freedom and generosity of the kingdom of God. A withholding lifestyle means that we don't believe that there will be manna tomorrow. We don't believe we will be given enough grace.

And then you remember something else. The story of manna is a story that points to *more*. *More* than you imagine. *More* in a way will surprise you. Our Father is the God of more grace.

So what is this grace? *Grace* is a common word that Jesus Christ has crammed with meaning. Grace was initially associated with loveliness and favor; a fine start. The apostle Paul added *gift* to its meaning, which could include both financial (1 Cor. 16:3; 2 Cor. 8:19) and spiritual gifts (1 Cor. 12:1). This connected grace to our neediness and God's generous provision for our need. Since it implied that we are weak, grace also meant *power*. "My grace is sufficient for you, for my power is made perfect in weakness" (2 Cor. 12:9). If there is any question that the words of God are good news, *grace* should resolve it, because the word has become the summary description of Christianity.

When you think about grace, your world is no longer one of fate, karma or a deistic, passive god. The God of grace is very personal and active. He is especially attentive to those who are needy, and he delights in giving gifts and power to them. Call out in your need and you will be heard. As we saw with the early Hebrews, even if you *don't* call to God in your need, you will be heard, and when God hears, it means that he is already taking action. This is all very personal, even intimate, but there is even more.

When King Jesus ascended into heaven and took his rightful place on the throne, the coronation ceremony was unlike any other. While earthly kings received gifts, Jesus gave gifts. More specifically, he gave *a* gift. He poured out his Spirit on his people. When someone is full of "grace and power" (Acts 6:8), that is the same as saying that the person is full of the Holy Spirit (Acts 6:5). When we receive gifts, they are called either gifts of grace (Eph. 4:7) or gifts of the Spirit (1 Cor. 12:4). When we receive grace, we receive the Spirit of grace (Heb. 10:29). To receive grace is to receive the Spirit; to receive the Spirit is to be given the kingdom of the Spirit; to receive the kingdom of the Spirit is to receive everything imaginable under the reign of King Jesus, including:

Love	Joy	Adoption as God's children
Patience	Gentleness	Power to fight sin

Goodness	Freedom	Power to serve others
Self-control	Faithfulness	Presence of God
Fruitfulness	No condemnation	Promise of future perfection
Peace	Truth	Wisdom
The mind of God	Unity	Life

Among my assorted fears and anxieties is the fear of suffocation, especially through drowning. It doesn't exert itself too often; it usually makes an appearance after news reports of tsunamis, movies such as *Titanic*, and celebratory pileups after a World Cup goal or NFL touchdown on TV. I begin wondering just how many teammates it will take to finally crush the hero on the bottom. What does tomorrow's manna, future grace, have to do with such fears?

It doesn't say that I will be spared suffocation. What it says is that, if I am called to death by asphyxiation, I will have grace when that time comes. What does that mean? I don't know. I can't imagine such grace. I can't imagine anything that would make drowning tolerable. And that is exactly what we should expect: At this moment I don't have grace to drown because I am not drowning! Of course I will worry if I try to envision a drowning scenario. I will project the grace I have received for today onto tomorrow, not comprehending that I will receive grace as needed tomorrow.

We have to go slowly on this one because it is so essential in our battle with worry and fear. Let's say that you are taking a class, and the first thing the instructor does is hand out a test. As you scan it, you know nothing. Little signs and symbols, words you have never seen—your anxiety level rises with each question. You have failed the class before it has even begun!

Then the teacher interrupts, "Did I tell you that this will be your final exam? You don't have to take this now, and you don't know any of this now, but trust me. By the time the class is over you will actually know this. You'll be amazed at how well prepared you will be."

Everyone breathes a sigh of relief. Nothing has really changed. There will be a final exam at the end of the course, and you would fail it if you took it now, but you have no worries. When the time comes to take the test, you will have received the grace that you need to do well.

Are you worried about the future? You are looking at tomorrow as if it was a final exam and you haven't yet taken the class. Of course you panic at the thought. But you haven't considered that you will go through the class before you have to take the final. You will be given all the grace you need when you need it.

What form might that grace take? Be careful here. When we try to imagine grace in some future situations, we might still be resting in ourselves. We want specific confirmation that there will be grace, and we want to calm ourselves not by trusting in the Gracious One but in seeing the future. If I am called to drown, I don't know what grace I will receive. Having never had it, I can't imagine it, and since God gives much more than we ask my prediction no doubt would fall far short. It is enough to know that I *will* receive grace. I will know the presence of the Spirit and I will die, or be rescued, in a way that pleases the Lord.

A PERSONAL RESPONSE

For me, knowing that there is grace for tomorrow has made the most noticeable difference on my own anxieties and fears. The hurdle that was always in front of me was that I couldn't *imagine* that grace, which is another way of saying that I limited God to the size of my own imagination. Now I know that I could never imagine that grace because I have yet to receive it. As a result, I am beginning to look forward to days of final exams rather than dread them.

On a related note, this makes me think about all the times when I *have* received grace, didn't take notice, and didn't thank God for being faithful once again. J. S. Bach began his compositions with "S. D. G." (meaning

Soli Deo Gloria—"solely to the glory of God") and would often insert "J. J." (which stood for *Jesu Juban*—"help me Jesus"). In a similar way, I want to start my day with, "Lord, help me. Please give me grace," and end it with "Thank you."

CHAPTER THIRTEEN

"SEEK MY FACE"

AT THIS POINT, we know that worry and fear are more about us than about the things outside us. They reveal what is valuable to us, and what is valuable to us in turn reveals our kingdom allegiances. We also know that God is patient and compassionate with us, and he gives grace upon grace. Though alert to our divided allegiances, he persists in calling us away from fear and worry, persuades us of the beauty of the kingdom, and gives more than we can imagine.

With this in mind, his words should sound attractive, and we should be more and more inclined to listen. We would still like to abolish anxieties quickly, but we are learning that God values strong foundations and gradual growth, and such foundations are established as we feed on him and his words. As we meditate on Scripture and make it our own, we should anticipate slow but steady change.

Worriers should be experts in a handful of passages. The story in Exodus 16 about manna is the basic framework; the worry passages in Matthew 6 and Luke 12 add essential detail. Although other Scriptures won't change this basic outline, they will dress it up in a way that will bless you. Psalm 27 (with the added headings) is a classic.

PSALM 27

OF DAVID

Confidence

The LORD is my light and my salvation—
   whom shall I fear?
The LORD is the stronghold of my life—
   of whom shall I be afraid?
When evil men advance against me
   to devour my flesh,
when my enemies and my foes attack me,
   they will stumble and fall.
Though an army besiege me,
   my heart will not fear;
though war break out against me,
   even then will I be confident.

One Thing

One thing I ask of the LORD,
   this is what I seek:
that I may dwell in the house of the LORD
   all the days of my life,
to gaze upon the beauty of the LORD
   and to seek him in his temple.
For in the day of trouble
   he will keep me safe in his dwelling;

he will hide me in the shelter of his tabernacle
    and set me high upon a rock.
Then my head will be exalted
    above the enemies who surround me;
at his tabernacle will I sacrifice with shouts of joy;
    I will sing and make music to the LORD.

A Prayer

Hear my voice when I call, O LORD;
    be merciful to me and answer me.
My heart says of you, "Seek his face!"
    Your face, LORD, I will seek.
Do not hide your face from me,
    do not turn your servant away in anger;
    you have been my helper.
Do not reject me or forsake me,
    O God my Savior.
Though my father and mother forsake me,
    the LORD will receive me.
Teach me your way, O LORD;
    lead me in a straight path
    because of my oppressors.
Do not turn me over to the desire of my foes,
    for false witnesses rise up against me,
    breathing out violence.

More Confidence

I am still confident of this:
    I will see the goodness of the LORD
    in the land of the living.

Wait for the LORD;
  be strong and take heart
  and wait for the LORD.

It has been said that the most dishonest time in a church service is during the congregational singing. At that time we say things we have never said to the Lord privately and are not even sure we believe. But if this psalm seems like a stretch, it can still be the cry of your heart without dishonesty. Allow it to be a prayer, a vision. You have been offered the kingdom. How could you not want to know the King? Let the psalm articulate your emerging desire.

The psalm divides naturally into four parts. No threat is minimized. The pattern that has been hard-wired into the psalmist is that the more extreme the threat, the more single-minded he needs to be about his Deliverer.

CONFIDENCE

Before the psalmist prays for help, he makes a public declaration: the Lord is his light, salvation, and stronghold.

Let's say you are playing *Who Wants to Be a Millionaire* and you are stumped by a math question. One of your lifelines is The Math Whiz, so you have no worries. Perhaps you are lost in the Australian Outback, but your traveling companion is Crocodile Dundee. Even if you don't know him, his name brings calm. When you are afraid, you call out to the Lord who is light, deliverance, and strength. Even better, he is "*my* light," "*my* salvation," and "*my* stronghold," and all is well.

Light is always a good thing in Scripture. Bad things lurk in shadows, but the light exposes them and they flee. God's first creative act was to command light to come into the world. When we are fearful or worried, we feel like we are walking in a dark place that is known to be dangerous. Into this vulnerable place comes the God who is light, and the light penetrates everything. Light means life, truth, the banishment of evil. If the psalm stopped here, it would still lead us to comfort.

"My salvation" could also be translated "my victory" or "my deliverance." It recalls the deliverance from Egyptian slavery, but also summarizes all of God's victories, which were consistently against all odds. With Egypt, it was the strongest army on earth on one side and unarmed slaves on the other. People who have been slaves for hundreds of years are not known to be great warriors. With Midian, it was an army "thick as locusts" with literally innumerable camels against 300 unarmed men (Judg. 7:12). God likes his people to be outnumbered because then there is no mistaking that he alone is the Deliverer.

"My stronghold" evokes images of a safe place. While David was on the run from Saul, he had a particular stronghold in the wilderness that was impregnable. When he went there with his men, he was safe. Here he confesses his deeper insight into the nature of strongholds: any safe place is a sign pointing to The Stronghold. His wilderness lair was safe only because God was there.

Armed with this knowledge of God, David could look back and remember times of God-wrought deliverance. He could look forward—with unusual confidence—to the battles he would inevitably face in the future.

Since the psalmist invites us to make this psalm our own, personal reflection is the order of the day. Our anxious tendency is to amass information so that (perhaps) the sheer weight of it would subdue our worries and fears. But the words of God focus us on Jesus Christ. They are words to be savored.

A PERSONAL RESPONSE

1. The psalm is thoroughly God-centered. The focus is not so much on my deliverance but my Deliverer. Only when I know more of God will my faith grow.

2. When we pray we usually jump right in with requests. The homework: to postpone them until you have remembered the character of God.

3. Spend a day with each image: light, salvation, stronghold. A concordance can locate these words in other psalms.

4. Fears about money got us started on all this. If God can be trusted with life-threatening enemies, he can certainly be trusted with your financial future.

5. Center the psalm on Jesus Christ. Note how he is the true Deliverer from our archenemy (Matt. 12:22–29).

ONE THING

The second part of Psalm 27 contains perhaps the most single-minded statement in Scripture. "One thing I ask of the LORD, this is what I seek: that I may dwell in the house of the LORD all the days of my life, to gaze upon the beauty of the LORD and to seek him in his temple." Worry scans the universe looking for more worries to accumulate; it needs to be directed to what is most important. Here, in unequivocal terms, is what is most important.

Seek his face. What is David really asking? He isn't looking for a geographical place because David knew that the entire earth is the Lord's.

> This is what the LORD says:
> "Heaven is my throne,
>   and the earth is my footstool.
> Where is the house you will build for me?
>   Where will my resting place be?
> Has not my hand made all these things,

and so they came into being?" declares the Lord.

"This is the one I esteem:

he who is humble and contrite in spirit,

and trembles at my word."

−Isa. 66:1-2

David was remembering the God of Moses, who promised the Hebrews his Presence and his rest (Ex. 33:14). Moreover, David recalled how God was pleased with Moses and allowed him to be a witness to his glory (Ex. 33:18). David knew that all the beauty of creation pointed to the Creator, and when Moses saw the glory, it was the beauty of God.

While all Israelites knew the presence of God, they also knew that there were degrees of nearness. Most people were kept at a safe distance. Priests were given greater access to God's presence than the people, and the High Priest was given access to the Holy of Holies itself. But only Moses was close enough to witness God's back as his glory passed before him. At the beginning of the New Testament, we find the same pattern. Herod's temple was heavily partitioned, with each wall prohibiting some from going any closer to the Presence: Gentiles were farthest away, then women, men, priests, and the High Priest.

Given the time in which he lived, David was making a bold request. That can happen when you are desperate! He wanted more than God's veiled and safe presence. David was throwing caution to the wind, but only because he had precocious insight into the heart of God. He knew God's forgiving love and he knew that God would not deny needy people access to his throne room.

The image is that you are in the presence of the King. When you are in his presence—in his temple, dwelling, or tabernacle—you are kept safe. Whenever you were invited into an ancient Near East home, the host was responsible for your protection. In the home of a powerful king, you could rest secure. This was more than enough to counterbalance David's fears.

On one side enemies wanted to kill him, on the other was the protective custody of the King. It was no contest.

There is just one catch. When you seek the Lord, it means more than just finding a safe place. It means that you order your life according to the laws of the kingdom. In a few verses, the psalmist will beseech God to "teach me your ways." When you seek the King, you are also seeking the kingdom and its righteousness.

Gaze upon his beauty. In David's day, creation was called beautiful (Job 38:31), women were beautiful, kings could be called beautiful (Is. 33:17), and Jerusalem, the place of God's temple, was beautiful (Ezek. 16:14–15). Only in this psalm is God himself called beautiful. Of course, all beauty exists because it reflects the beauty of God. The reason God is not usually called beautiful is because beauty referred only to those things you could actually see. So when David says that he wants to gaze on the beauty of the Lord, he is saying both that God is truly beautiful and that he wants to be close enough to see it.

We are drawn to the presence of true beauty. Beauty invites and attracts, and inspires us to greater things. In World War II, soldiers fought against Hitler, but it wasn't so much Hitler who inspired their heroism. It was the buddy fighting next to them and the beauty at home whose picture they kept in their pocket.

Beauty is just what worry needs. Worry's magnetic attraction can only be broken by a stronger attraction, and David is saying we can only find that attraction in God himself. If we are to be captivated by the beauty of God once again, we have to think of a long-term study. Anything truly beautiful is more attractive the better you know it. A beautiful painting invites you to explore and find much more depth in it. My wife is much more attractive to me now than when I first met her, which I thought would be impossible. There is no doubt that a search for God's beauty will unveil even more of his beauty.

A PERSONAL RESPONSE

1. Beauty and perfection are nearly identical. To say, "You look perfect" is usually the same as "You look beautiful." Since the references to beauty don't occur that often in Scripture, consider God's perfections instead. He is perfect in his faithfulness (Isa. 25:1), everything he does is perfect (Ps. 18:30), his law is perfect (Ps. 19:7), Jesus' sufferings made him perfect (Heb. 2:10), and by his perfect sacrifice he makes us perfect (Heb. 10:14).

2. We have it much better than David. He could only hope for the opportunity to see God's beauty, but we can witness it on every page of the New Testament in the face of Christ, and the Spirit gives us the presence of Jesus. Be specific: What clarity do we have because we live on this side of the cross?

A PRAYER

It isn't until verse seven that David actually begins talking to the Lord—a worthwhile strategy for us all. Prior to that, he has been talking *about* the Lord and the desires of his heart; now he speaks directly to his God.

Given the confidence David expresses, you would never guess his dire straits. Until now, his psalm has sounded like a hymn of thanks for deliverance, but the reality is that he has not been delivered. Instead, he feels like he is in darkness, and the reason he began by remembering that God is light is because his senses tell him otherwise. It is as if David is flying a plane in a thick fog; when you can't see, you fly by the instruments as any experienced pilot can do. When there is a contradiction between your senses and your instruments, you believe the instruments.

David's senses tell him that God is absent or turned away. The instruments—God's history and promises of faithfulness—tell him that the Lord is the One who loves more dearly than any father or mother.

A PERSONAL RESPONSE

1. There are times to listen to our fears and anxieties because they point us to the things we value. There are times when we don't listen to them because they point us away from God and his truth. David is showing us how *not* to listen to fears and anxieties.

2. Psalm 27 emphasizes the motto, "When in doubt, pray." It seems simple, but we don't. Instead, we worry more and look for ways to gain control of a situation. A goal: to pray with other people. It will aid concentration.

3. David's prayer is less than a quarter of his psalm. Try David's ratio. When fearful, first recount who God is. Remember that he has promised to be found by those who seek him. Review stories of his beauty and perfection until you find yourself confident in him. *Then* pray.

CONFIDENCE

David's actual prayer isn't the last word. Instead, he goes public. He turns to the priests and the people and leads them in a personal response.

I will see the goodness of the Lord. Because of God's promises to Israel, there is confidence that God will again deliver his people. David and his armies will live to fight another day. When they return from battle, they will become the latest story of deliverance, and the events will be tucked away in Israel's history for the comfort of future generations.

Wait. You don't see the deliverance quite yet? *Be strong and take heart*. The words are familiar. They are the words forever linked to Joshua, who heard them from Moses (Deut. 3:28; 31:6–7, 23) and passed them on to the people (Josh. 1:6–7, 9, 18). The historical context is the transition in leadership from Moses to Joshua and the upcoming battles for the Promised Land. The fact that this psalm is composed in Jerusalem—*in* the Promised Land—makes David's confidence unshakable.

Sandwiched around the exhortation to be strong and take heart is the encouragement to wait for the Lord. Wait, wait patiently for the Lord. That is the summary of this psalm of confidence. Once again, we are taken into the mind of God in that, while anxiety prefers immediate deliverance, God might delay it, giving us time to trust him and wait by faith. So the psalmist will wait with confidence, which is to wait by faith. His God is absolutely reliable. While a very reliable human deliverer might encounter accidents and other unforeseen events on his way to our deliverance, God is never waylaid. No one can interfere with his care and deliverance.

A PERSONAL RESPONSE

1. Worry looks for new answers, but it won't find them in this psalm. This psalm offers no novel techniques. But remember that fear and worry don't need something new. Instead, fear and worry need to act on what we already know. Do we pray about those things that cause anxiety? Do we precede our prayers with declarations about God, his character, and his mighty acts, especially as they culminated in Jesus? And do we respond—even out loud, publicly—to the promise that God will be with us and his kingdom will come?

2. Worry is trained to see catastrophe. As a result, when the deliverance of God appears, we miss it. If we do see it, we are already on to the next worry. The kingdom of God is here; therefore, the goodness of the Lord in the land of the living is available for all to see.

What have you seen? How can you train yourself to see? And how can we help each other to see?

3. When David called out to the people and encouraged them to wait on the Lord, make no mistake: He was also speaking to his own heart. Speak this psalm to other people, but overhear what you are saying.

4. When is worry a problem? Whenever it doesn't follow the outline of Psalm 27.

CHAPTER FOURTEEN

WHERE IS MY TREASURE? WHOSE KINGDOM?

EVERYTHING ENDS with either/or. Start anywhere you want—your emotions, your relationships, your job—and you can trace your actions back to kingdom allegiances. You stand either with the true God or the consortium of the Devil, idols, and your own desires. It might sound overly spiritual, but that is the nature of reality.

You begin with your worries and fears.

You can track them to their origin by following the money. Money is not the only way to track our worries, but it is certainly one path every person has followed. For some of us, it is our specialty. As you track your worries to your money, make sure you include cash on hand as well as everything that money can buy.

Bank accounts	Cars	Homes
Schooling	Influence	Relationship

Comfort	Vacations	Help for children
Medical care	Retirement	Independence
Reputation	Toys	Clothes
Furnishings	Hobbies	Dinner out

So far the path is straightforward and easy to see. Now, connect money and your self-oriented desires. Do you remember the standard features of human nature that we can see in very young children? The priority of "mine" is at the top of the list.

For the next step, you need the light of Scripture to mark the way. What is hard to see at first is that our selfish desires are connected to a much larger organization that is "earthly, unspiritual, of the devil" (James 3:15).

Worry (How do you feel?)

Money (What do you value or love?)

Mine (For whose purposes?)

⬇

The earthly kingdom (Which kingdom?)

As you notice specific worries about bills, income, and financial security, make sure that you follow them all the way to the grand, sweeping view of the universe that they reflect. Don't settle for a technique or pill to deal with your worry no matter how helpful it can be in the short term. Hold out for the epic version. Physicists yearn for a grand unifying theory of the cosmos, but we are blessed to have received it as a gift from God. The criteria for an elegant unifying story or theory is that it is simple (e.g., $E = MC^2$), it makes sense, and it is accessible to non-experts. Such is the story of the kingdom.

God's communication to us is clear. The world is marked out by kingdoms. The rightful King has patiently revealed his plan against the Usurper, and it has reached its climax in the death and resurrection of Jesus Christ. That was the event that emptied spiritual prisons and tombs. But as with many other proclamations of victory, there are still battles left to fight. When someone has the advantage in chess, masters will concede a match early. War, however, goes to the bitter end. The D-Day invasion signaled the beginning of the end of Hitler's occupation of Europe, but costly combat remained. Far more decisively, the gospel proclaims the King's victory, but there is much left to do.

Meanwhile, worry reveals our allegiances. Fear and worry are not mere emotions; they are expressions of what we hold dear. They reveal the loyalties of our hearts. If we know Christ and have affirmed our allegiance to him, worry is a sign that we are trying to have it both ways. We certainly don't want to renounce our allegiance to Jesus, but we want to protect what we feel is our own. We are not so sure that the Lord can be trusted with some of these things, so we look for help elsewhere. And if there is no obvious alternate source of help, we worry.

It's easy to tell ourselves that such worry is not a critical kingdom issue. After all, we have not become avowed Satan worshipers. But remember that Satan has forged thousands of covert alliances. Knowing that his conspicuous presence might be too jolting for some, he partners with activities and objects that have lost their shock value. Anything that can be a consuming passion becomes a bridge to his kingdom. Money is a prime example.

The reality is that you can't have dual masters. You can't serve both money and the Lord. It's time to choose sides.

TREASURES ON EARTH

Go back for a minute to Matthew 6, that seminal passage on worry. It actually begins with "therefore": "Therefore I tell you, do not worry about your life, what you will eat or drink." This means it is building on what had just been said, which was clearly either/or. Either the Lord is our master or money is. Either we store up our treasures on earth or we store them in heaven.

> Do not store up for yourselves treasures on earth, where moth and rust destroy, and where thieves break in and steal. But store up for yourselves treasures in heaven, where moth and rust do not destroy, and where thieves do not break in and steal. For where your treasure is, there your heart will be also. . . . No one can serve two masters. Either he will hate the one and love the other, or he will be devoted to the one and despise the other. You cannot serve both God and Money. Therefore I tell you, do not worry.
>
> —Matt. 6:19–21, 24–25

We live across the street from the first house we bought. During the years the bank owned it and gave us the privilege of living there at a whopping seventeen percent interest rate, we spent hundreds of hours painting and landscaping. I was particularly proud of a small white fence in front of the house. When we restored it, it was the finishing touch to a long project.

We were attached to the house, but it was getting small for our two children. When the larger house across the street came up for sale, we jumped at it. We particularly enjoyed the large picture window in the front. It made the interior much lighter.

The problems began within a week of moving in. While enjoying our picture window we noticed that the buyer of our old house was inspecting the fence. A discriminating person of refined taste, no doubt. But within a half hour, the fence had been pulled out. Every post and rail had been sledge-hammered, and the splintered remains were at the curb for the next day's trash pickup. That began a long lesson in the temporal nature of our earthly possessions.

What does it mean to store up treasures on earth? It doesn't mean that IRAs are wrong, or the recommendation that we save ten percent of our income is unspiritual. It means that anything labeled "mine" is already rusting. If our hope rests in our IRA or our savings, then we have reason to worry, because it never seems to be safe enough or large enough.

Worry, therefore, is not simply an emotion that erodes our quality of life or a pain to be alleviated. It is a misdirected love that should be confessed. It is trying to manage our world apart from God. It is making life about *our* needs, desires, and wants.

TREASURES IN HEAVEN

Can't you just hear Jesus say, "How would you like a place where nothing rusted, nothing wore out, and investments were guaranteed to pay double-digit interest?"

"Count me in!" Like the Samaritan woman, we couldn't refuse such an offer.

"You can begin," he says, "by turning away from investments that promise emptiness and nothing more. You can begin by turning away from yourself and turning to me."

Start with confession. Any journey back to the kingdom of God must go through confession. Anxiety is a string around our finger reminding us that money has become our refuge. Find anxiety about finances and you find sin; it is as simple as that. Confession acknowledges that we still invest in both kingdoms, hoping to minimize our risk. The rule of kingdom investment, however, is all or nothing. All hedged bets are deposited in the earthly kingdom—the one with "mine" written all over it. Everything must go into one account or the other.

This doesn't mean that every penny must go into the offering basket. You might be a world-class giver, at least on your 1040 form, but you still fret about finances. You are not confessing what percentage you give and keep; you are confessing how money has been your hope, security, and confidence. The problems, at root, are relational, and the way to deal with relational problems is to actually confess them to the Lord.

Have you ever known that you had wronged another person and, instead of confessing it, you just tried to be extra nice? It doesn't work. For one thing, you never know for how long you must be overly nice. For another, you are always wondering if the other person noticed the offense and if he is thinking about it. Confession is the only way to deal with relational wrongs.

Confession changes everything. When we confess to God that our worry is a sin against him, we turn away from the kingdom of earth. We burn our bridges and say with Peter, "Lord, to whom shall we go? You have the words of eternal life" (John 6:68). We are now in a position to see the attractiveness and worthiness of the kingdom and to take part in it.

LET THE KINGDOM ATTRACT YOU

> The kingdom of heaven is like treasure hidden in a field. When a man found it, he hid it again, and then in his joy went and sold all he had and bought that field. Again, the kingdom of heaven is like a merchant looking for fine pearls. When he found one of great value, he went away and sold everything he had and bought it.
>
> —MATT. 13:44–46

There are different ways to enter the kingdom. Some people stumble upon it, some search for it. Whatever way we find it, we are hooked once we do. One man was working in the fields, found something of inestimable worth, buried it again, and gave up everything he had to buy the field. The other man had been looking for one precious pearl his entire life. When he found it, of course he gave up everything else for it. Both men happily gave up everything they owned to have something much better.

You can't imagine either of them second-guessing themselves. There is no wavering, no regret. Notice the joy of the man who found the treasure. The kingdom was announced as a kingdom of joy (Luke 2:10); those who are brought into it can know a joy that can never be taken away (John 16:22). Such joy can sound like the impossible dream and, indeed, it might be a long way off. But like everything else in Scripture that seems too good to be true, let it arouse and inspire you. Don't write it off as impossible. Let it be a vision and hope that invades your prayers.

The words of missionary Jim Elliot are beginning to make sense: "He is no fool who gives what he cannot keep to gain what he cannot lose."

Storing up treasures in heaven. How do we actually amass these treasures? The obvious answer is that we walk by faith. We live in the name of Jesus rather than in our own name. Our life is because of him and for him. We love others as he loved us. That is all true. But through this walk of faith, our attention is riveted to the Author of our faith more than the daily successes and failures of our spiritual walk.

Life in the kingdom is about a person. It is about a person. We all know that joy is connected to relationships. People are much more important than things. Even the most miserly and wealthy will begrudgingly admit this basic human reality. The greatest human joy can be found in loving and being loved.

With this in mind, even the most jaded person can't be disappointed when Jesus Christ is his true treasure. Jesus is the pearl of great price, the water that leaves us forever quenched, the eternally satisfying bread. We belong to him, and he belongs to us. The refrain from Song of Solomon captures it, "I am my lover's and my lover is mine" (Song 6:3).

The relationship, however, is lopsided. Jesus loves more. He makes the first move toward us. In other words, if God is to be our treasured possession, we can expect that he has first made us *his* treasured possession.

Then Moses went up to God, and the LORD called to him from the mountain and said, "This is what you are to say to the house of Jacob and what you are to tell the people of Israel: 'You yourselves have seen what I did to Egypt, and how I carried you on eagles' wings and brought you to myself. Now if you obey me fully and keep my covenant, then out of all nations you will be *my treasured possession.* Although the whole earth is mine, you will be for me a kingdom of priests and a holy nation.'"

—Ex. 19:3–6, *author's emphasis*

For you are a people holy to the LORD your God. The LORD your God has chosen you out of all the peoples on the face of the earth to be his people, *his treasured possession.* The LORD did not set his affection on you and choose you because you were more numerous than other peoples, for you were the fewest of all peoples. But it was because the LORD loved you and kept the oath he swore to your forefathers that he brought you out with a mighty hand and redeemed you from the land of slavery, from the power of Pharaoh king of Egypt. Know therefore that the LORD your God is God; he is the faithful God, keeping his covenant of love to a thousand generations of those who love him and keep his commands.

—Deut. 7:6–9

And the LORD has declared this day that you are his people, *his treasured possession as he promised,* and that you are to keep all his commands.

—Deut. 26:18

It is hard not to reciprocate when someone immensely attractive says "I love you" first. Even better, you don't have to be concerned that you somehow misled him with a one-time display of grace and beauty. If he ever woke up next to you or saw you at your worst, you don't have to worry that he would renege on his declaration of "treasured possession." His commitment and love go deeper than his response to anything in you. Instead, he loves you because that is the way *he* is: He is a lover, a faithful, extravagant lover. He was not initially drawn to your greatness, and he won't run away when your less attractive side is revealed.

And there is more. He is the King, and when he brings you to himself he offers you everything that is his. He doesn't say, "Up to one-half of my kingdom." He says he is pleased to give us the kingdom. Why worry about a stolen bike when, by faith, you have received the kingdom of heaven, and you can never lose it?

> Praise be to the God and Father of our Lord Jesus Christ! In his great mercy he has given us new birth into a living hope through the resurrection of Jesus Christ from the dead, and into an inheritance that can never perish, spoil or fade—kept in heaven for you, who through faith are shielded by God's power until the coming of the salvation that is ready to be revealed in the last time.
>
> —1 PETER 1:3–5

How can we store up treasures when we already have everything? We live as people of the kingdom. We love him as he has first loved us. We change the story of our lives. The basic themes were lust and aloneness: We wanted more and more, and we were persuaded that we were alone in the universe. But in the kingdom, lust is silly. It is wanting *less* than what we already have. It is replacing eternal joys with temporary highs.

Our new emotion is gratitude. We have been given a gift of inestimable worth. Each day, as we understand more of its value, we are increasingly humbled and thankful. Our fingers gradually loosen from their ossified, clenched grasp. We begin to learn words other than "MINE." In our gratitude, we want to love the One who has given such a costly gift, and the way we love him is to imitate him or obey his commands.

Faith expressing itself in love (Gal. 5:6) is the way we store up treasures that last. Whenever our old hoarding instincts kick in, we pursue the greater treasure. "The wisdom that comes from heaven is first of all pure; then peace-loving, considerate, submissive, full of mercy and good fruit, impartial and sincere" (James 3:17).

A PERSONAL RESPONSE

Confession gets a bad rap. We tend to place it in the same category as a public scolding. But confession is the way to true wisdom and knowledge. While worry and fear live in the dark and are ignorant of what is going on around them, confession brings light. The kingdom is not for the smart but for the contrite. I can't gloss over confession.

Psalm 73:25 can be my guide. "Whom have I in heaven but you? And earth has nothing I desire besides you." The psalmist is an explorer who has been to places we want to go.

GOD SPEAKS

on people and

their judgments

ONE WAY to track fears and worries is to follow the money. Another is to follow them back to other people's possible judgments of us. What will people do to me? What will they say about me? What will they think about me? Will they love me? When we call it peer pressure, it sounds like a recent, teenage phenomenon, but being controlled by the opinions of others is as old as recorded history. Expect this route to follow the same spiritual map that money did: It's not about you and your kingdom; it is about the kingdom of heaven.

CHAPTER FIFTEEN

DO NOT TRUST IN MAN

WE SO DESPERATELY need each other's approval.

I was told that a professor who taught in my area of interest had a thirty-two-page resumé and was only thirty-five years old.

Thirty-two pages of accomplishments in thirty-five years. Double-space a few entries and he could become the sole member of the 35/35 club: thirty-five pages of achievements at thirty-five years old. That has to be a record! All I could think was that this guy had a *lot* of accomplishments.

That was immediately followed by the thought that I will never have a thirty-two-page resumé, even if I pad it with every instance when my wife or children said I was the best father or best husband in the world. They usually say this on birthdays and Father's Days with only a little prodding such as, "Who's the best dad in the world?"

What a failure I am.

Do you see the connection with fear and worry? Keep the fear/need connection in mind. Whatever you think you need will control you. If you need something from other people—love, acceptance, approval—they hold the keys to something very valuable to you. You will live in fear that they might not deliver. You will fear those who are the gatekeepers to the fulfillment of your needs.

Why do adults fear a little extra weight? Health is rarely the issue. The real issue is what you will think of me. Why do so many people fear public speaking more than death? The opinions of other human beings are by far the scariest things on the planet.

Money is one fear that Scripture highlights. People are another. Like our concerns about money, the fear of other people is so common that it can be assumed; it sits in the background of all of our lives.

FEAR OF MAN IN SCRIPTURE

If misery loves company, people who fear people can live in ecstasy because this fear is everywhere. It's been that way for a long time.

In the Old Testament, one watershed event was the divine liberation of the Israelites from Egypt. This event so thoroughly revealed the character of God and the true nature of people that the rest of Scripture builds on this foundational story. You hear echoes of it in every story of deliverance; the provision of manna is a paradigm of God's response to human need; and our tendency towards idolatry is first seen with the golden calf fiasco. If there is something important to be said about God or ourselves, the seeds can be found in the events that unfolded when God heard the cries of his oppressed people in Egypt.

Fear of man was apparent before the exodus, but Scripture really exposes this universal struggle when the spies of Israel are sent on a reconnoitering mission into the Promised Land.

At the end of forty days they returned from exploring the land. . . . They gave Moses this account: "We went into the land to which you sent us, and it does flow with milk and honey! Here is its fruit. But the people who live there are powerful, and the cities are fortified and very large. . . ."

Then Caleb silenced the people before Moses and said, "We should go up and take possession of the land, for we can certainly do it."

But the men who had gone up with him said, "We can't attack those people; they are stronger than we are." And they spread among the Israelites a bad report about the land they had explored. They said, "The land we explored devours those living in it. All the people we saw there are of great size. . . . We seemed like grasshoppers in our own eyes, and we looked the same to them."

That night all the people of the community raised their voices and wept aloud. . . ."If only we had died in Egypt! Or in this desert! Why is the LORD bringing us to this land only to let us fall by the sword?". . . And they said to each other, "We should choose a leader and go back to Egypt."

Then Moses and Aaron fell facedown in front of the whole Israelite assembly gathered there. Joshua son of Nun and Caleb son of Jephunneh, who were among those who had explored the land, tore their clothes and said to the entire Israelite assembly, "The land we passed through and explored is exceedingly good. If the LORD is pleased with us, he will lead us into that land, a land flowing with milk and honey, and will give it to us. Only do not rebel against the LORD. And *do not be afraid of the people of the land,* because we will swallow them up. Their protection is gone, but the LORD is with us. Do not be afraid of them."

But the whole assembly talked about stoning them. Then the glory of the LORD appeared at the Tent of Meeting to all the Israelites. The LORD said to Moses, "How long will these people treat me with contempt? How long will they refuse to believe in me, in spite of all the miraculous signs I have performed among them?"

—NUMBERS 13:25, 27, 30–14:11, *author's emphasis*

This incident was the reason why the people, who were on the verge of possessing the land God had promised them, wandered for forty years in the desert until an entire generation of doubters died. The problem was not that they overestimated their foe. No doubt there *would* be intense fighting ahead, and the enemy can certainly be intimidating. The problem was that they underestimated the Lord. Even though they had just witnessed his power over Egypt, they didn't believe their God could defeat much lesser nations.

Israel shows us that we can fear people to the point where we disobey God. In this case, the people feared the inhabitants of Canaan and said no to God's command to take the land. The problem wasn't so much that they experienced fear. The problem was that they turned away from God when they were afraid.

Once again, life is structured in terms of either/or. In the Sermon on the Mount, the choice was between money and God, but nearly anything can stand similarly opposed to God in our lives: work, hobbies, reputation, the opinions of others, and so on. And anything that is opposed to God in our lives is actually one of the many gods of the kingdom of earth. You will always be running scared if you worship other gods, because idols can't deliver on their promises.

In the Old Testament, the choice before us was typically stated in two different ways. One was idols or God; the other was people or God.

This is what the LORD says:
"Cursed is the one who trusts in man,
　　who depends on flesh for his strength
　　and whose heart turns away from the LORD.

He will be like a bush in the wastelands;
　　he will not see prosperity when it comes.
He will dwell in the parched places of the desert,
　　in a salt land where no one lives.

But blessed is the man who trusts in the LORD,
  whose confidence is in him.

He will be like a tree planted by the water
  that sends out its roots by the stream.
It does not fear when heat comes;
  its leaves are always green.
It has no worries in a year of drought
  and never fails to bear fruit."

—JER. 17:5–8

Why are we afraid? Because people have something we want and we are not sure we can get it. In some Old Testament situations the people simply wanted to stay alive, for which we can hardly blame them. We too can encounter enemies that threaten our lives, but more often our enemies are those who threaten things as important to us as life itself. They have the power to both give and take away our reputation, acceptance, prestige, and love.

When Jesus sent out his disciples to proclaim the coming of the kingdom, he warned them, "Do not be afraid of those who kill the body but cannot kill the soul. Rather, be afraid of the One who can destroy both soul and body in hell" (Matt. 10:28). It was unlikely that they were going to be killed on this particular mission. They might be threatened, but not killed. Jesus was concerned enough to warn them because, in the face of disapproval by kinfolk, they might waffle in their allegiance to Jesus and his message. Perhaps they would water it down when they met resistance, or they would say nothing at all if they were going to a village where they could be rejected by family and relatives.

The Pharisees certainly didn't heed Jesus' exhortations. They feared confessing their faith "for they loved praise from men more than praise from God" (John 12:43; also 5:44). Although some of them believed that Jesus was the King, they were more concerned about how a public demonstration of their allegiance would affect their reputation.

The real poster boy for the fear of man, however, was not one of the Pharisees. It was the apostle Peter, perhaps the most revered person in the history of the church. In the face of possible rejection, he denied any knowledge of Jesus. He succumbed to this before Jesus' death and resurrection when he was intimidated by the questions of a servant girl. He fell victim to it again even after the Spirit was given when he acted one way with Jews and another with Gentiles. He reminds us that people have not changed that much since the days of the Hebrew spies.

FEAR OF MAN IN OURSELVES

Perhaps the most peculiar feature of the kingdom of heaven is that its residents are occasionally embarrassed to admit that they belong to it. Have you ever heard of a Muslim who was afraid to speak of Allah? Most Muslims seem proud of who they are, despite the negative news regarding some adherents. And while there are Christians who wear evangelistic T-shirts and have Jesus bumper stickers, it is common knowledge that every Christian, at some time, has been ashamed of the gospel. There are many reasons for this, but the primary reason is that we are cut from the same cloth as Peter. We worry about the opinions of others. At the first sign of rejection we opt for whatever we think will win us the approval, prestige, or love we desire.

There is nothing wrong with wanting to be loved or wanting a good reputation. We should want both. It would be inhuman not to. As citizens of the kingdom, our good reputation honors the King and, having been loved by the King, we certainly delight in being loved. The problem comes when we want these things too much, when we want them for our own glory rather than God's.

Notice how human desires go topsy-turvy when we stray outside God's kingdom. As kingdom residents, we have been loved with an everlasting love and we have the privilege of loving others as we have been loved. We stand in the shadow of Jesus, who revealed what human life was intended to be: He loved others even when he wasn't loved. Jesus shows us that to be truly human means that our desire to love others outdistances our desire to be loved ourselves. True humanness is found more in a sacrificial love for our enemies than in being the object of another person's affections. Yet we often live as though the opposite were true. Without adequate human love, we feel paralyzed to love. We want to be filled with the love of others *before* we move out in love towards others. This is normal for us, but normal does not mean that it is either right or true. At root, our yearning for love and acceptance *from* other people (when it is more important than loving and accepting others) is evidence of allegiances to ourselves. We prefer to be the king rather than serve the King.

But if we serve the King, our desire to be loved could not outdistance our commitment to love others in his name. Our own approbation would seem almost meaningless, irrelevant. Rejection would hurt, but it wouldn't sidetrack us from our mission of love.

It is an odd thing. We can be dominated by the opinions, and even the perceived opinions, of other people. The problem can become so severe that we can be mortified by what people *might* think about us, even if we don't know them and will never see them again. If you want to see this in neon lights, look at teenagers.

The girl who cried because she thought her haircut was ugly.

The boy who cried because he thought his haircut was ugly.

The girl who wouldn't go shopping with friends because she didn't own the right boots.

The crisis over a pimple.

The teen who couldn't stand being ordinary.

The teen who couldn't stand being different.

The need for designer label clothes, which look like everything else apart from the actual label.

In adults, you find the same thing and more.

Plastic surgery.

Concerns about status. One reason money is the cause of such pervasive fear is that it can enhance popularity, at least for men.

Success of children to enhance our own status.

Low self-esteem. This isn't so much that I feel bad about myself, as it is that I feel bad about myself because I think you feel bad about me.

Sometimes life can feel like we are always going to a high-school reunion where everyone else looks better and has done more. Fear comes in many forms.

A PERSONAL RESPONSE

What do I need from other people? What is most important to me? Where do I value people and what they can give me above God? How do I actually put my trust in others?

The questions could go on and on. Although I am in good company, that doesn't help. I thought I would grow out of this when I turned twenty. Then I thought I would grow out of it when my age made me less cool. But it still feels as though there are giants in the land.

There's that question again that undergirds so much worry: Why am I so concerned about *me*?

CHAPTER SIXTEEN

LOVE MORE THAN NEED

SPIDERS, SNAKES, SHARKS, and huge needles are palpable fears for most of us. The heart races, we let out a scream. There is nothing subtle about it. Our worries about people's opinions, on the other hand, aren't accompanied by massive adrenaline dumps. They are ordinary, everyday experiences. When the causes of these worries fade, what remains is a residue of low self-esteem or a vague sense that something isn't right.

If only one kind of fear could be eradicated, we would gladly keep our phobias in order to lose our fear of man. The question, of course, is how it can be done.

This problem has received a great deal of attention in our society in the past few decades. Those deemed experts have offered a few basic strategies.

1. Avoid people who are unhealthy for you, like those who tear you down rather than build you up.
2. Love yourself more.

3. Rest in God's love so you don't have to rely on the affection and admiration of other people.

Since these strategies have had only marginal success, let's go back to the drawing board. This is a universal problem. Scripture certainly discusses it. We should expect a simple, clear way out.

WANTS AND NEEDS

We've seen that there are words that cluster together: fear, worry, anxiety, trust, treasure, control, need. Fear and worry reveal what we treasure. They show where we want control but lack it. They expose allegiances. To use everyday language, they point to what we think we need. We worry when our perceived needs are threatened.

So, what do we need from other people? For a quick refresher, there is love, sex, admiration, appreciation, protection, respect, attention, to be remembered for at least one year after we die. We all can check off items on that list and add many more. We can also see the connection between these perceived needs and worry. Now what?

A Buddhist approach has some appeal. If we could only neutralize passion and get to the point where we needed nothing! Many Christians have walked this path, especially after being deeply hurt in a relationship. "I will never let myself be vulnerable in a relationship ever again." They try to kill desire and passion. There are times when we wish we didn't have to feel. This approach, however, is just another way to try to make life work apart from God. It is another variation on trusting in ourselves, and it is doomed to failure.

A solution that seems more biblical is to rely on God's love more than the opinions of other people. This makes sense but, having tried that approach myself over the years, I would say that it, too, is less effective than it seems. No matter how much I try, God's love in itself doesn't quite deliver me from desiring psychological trinkets from others. For me, God's love can sometimes feel like the love of a wonderful human parent: It is an immense blessing, but it's not powerful enough to erase my desire for love, respect, and admiration from my wife and others.

Certainly, the knowledge of God's love can invade every nook and cranny in our lives, so I am not trying to minimize its power. The question isn't about God's love; it is about our desires and perceived needs. For example, if I believe that I need a Ferrari, God's love does not intend to satisfy that need. That doesn't diminish the love of Christ for us. The question is what I really need.

We tend to give our needs very little scrutiny. But for me to say that I need a Ferrari suggests that the word *need* is elastic, stretching all the way from food and shelter to personal lusts. Where along that spectrum will I find my desire for the good opinions of others?

Desires and needs, of course, are moving targets. In the span of a minute or two I can move from wanting my wife to love me, to needing my wife to love me, to demanding that my wife love me, and then back to simply wanting love. I can find the same pattern with other perceived needs such as sex, respect, admiration, and my need to be right.

At one end of the continuum, these desires are normal and appropriate. Call them mere or simple desires. Without them you are not human. At the other, they are complicated desires, self-serving demands that are guaranteed to damage relationships. As you drift from desire to demand, the boundary is fuzzy but the distinction is critical. If I simply want love from my wife, expressed according to my own idiosyncratic definition, our relationship is not in any particular danger. But if I say I need that love, I will be angry if I don't get it.

One reason the boundary between these two is hard to identify is because our *demand* is relabeled as *need*. Most everyone knows that to demand love from others is overtly self-serving. Need, however, isn't accompanied by warning bells from our consciences. Instead, it seems so right, so human.

Yet veiled beneath our use of the word *need* are the things we treasure, even worship.

Can you see how this intersects with fear? When the thing you treasure is in jeopardy, life feels very uncertain. If you slide toward the need/demand end of the continuum, you will notice free-floating anxiety and a lifestyle that is always trying to protect and defend your psychological vulnerability.

Our task is to somehow monitor our psychological desires so that they don't keep slipping into psychological needs. Given that we live on an incline, that won't be easy.

WHAT I NEED VERSUS WHAT I GIVE

What can we do? God made us this way, didn't he? He created us with the need for love. Without love we feel less than human. Love is the *sine qua non* of life. But there are at least two different loves. One love is what we receive; the other is what we give.

When we talk about our need for love, we are usually referring to the love we receive. Our unstated goal is to balance these two loves so that we both receive love and give it. Take marriage, for example. Marriage books say that marriage and close relationships should be 50–50, or 100–100. Each person gives the same amount. There are no books that say marriage is a 60–40 proposition. That is a recipe for either unhappiness or divorce.

In reality, however, the balance is almost impossible to achieve. Inequities are the rule: 49–51, 70–30. We don't concern ourselves too much with the person who is giving less but receiving more. At least we don't get concerned about his or her psychological state. The problem lies with the one who is giving more but receiving less. We consider this situation to be unhealthy or damaging. Continue this lopsided relationship and there will be a cost.

Which do we really need—to give love or receive it? We resist the question because we want to say both.

Yet Scripture seems to favor the imbalance. Not that we aspire to have our friend or spouse love us less, but that "in humility [we] consider others better than [our]selves" (Phil. 2:3). When the kingdom of God is ruling our hearts, we aspire more to serve than be served, honor more than be honored, and love more than be loved. This doesn't mean that we don't care about being loved; it simply means that we always want to outdo others in love.

Do we run the risk of a lopsided relationship? Absolutely. That is the relationship we have with God—he always loves first and most. We are the runaway bunnies whose mother always pursues us. Throughout Scripture God is the one who loves more than he is loved. He always makes the first move. He advertises his extravagant affection for us even when we are indifferent or opposed to him.

When Jesus Christ, God incarnate, walked the earth, the pattern continued. Throughout his life Jesus was rejected by his people and misunderstood by his disciples. At the most difficult point of his life, he was betrayed, denied, and abandoned. But through it all his love was unwavering. In this, he established the pattern for true humanness. This is the way we were intended to be.

This is life in the kingdom. It wants love, but it wants even more to love others deeply. Its treasure is to grow in the fruits of the Spirit, foremost of which is to love others.

TO LOVE MORE THAN TO BE LOVED

One way to deal with the fear of others is to keep our desires in check. When our desire for love becomes a need or a demand, we have become controlled by others. A better path is to seek to love others more. Always strive to have an imbalance in your heart where the desire to love outdistances the desire to be loved: "This is the message you heard from the beginning: We should love one another. . . . This is how we know what love is: Jesus Christ laid down his life for us. And we ought to lay down our lives for our brothers" (1 John 3:11, 16).

The foundation for our entire life is that we were loved first by God. While we were his enemies, we were pursued by him. When we see that our relationship with God began with the most extreme imbalance, in which God loved us totally while we hated him, we approach the small imbalances we encounter in daily life in a completely different way.

Let's say a wife wants to love her distant husband. As she does, her anger over his neglect gives way to hurt, but her hurt is hedged by her commitment to love him. When he is cruel, she doesn't bring out his slippers and ask how else she can serve him. Love is concerned about her husband; if she dismisses his cruelty, she is not loving him. Instead she asks, "Honey, how should I take your abusive speech? Is it directed at me, or did I misunderstand? As it is, what you said was very hurtful."

This wife is neither nag nor doormat. Her questions don't take great cleverness and they aren't intended as a manipulative trap for her spouse. But through them the wife, though hurt and living in a very difficult situation, can live in freedom, without fear. If she is continually recalibrating the gauge of love so that she is loving more than she is needing love, she will walk in freedom. But as soon as her need for love overwhelms her commitment to love, she will live again in fear. At that point she will be forever monitoring her husband's moods anxiously. Everything she says and does will be done with the goal of earning his love. When she doesn't receive it she will be crushed, angry, or both. A woman who feels like a doormat is not the one who loves more and needs less; she is the one whose need for love consistently exceeds her desire to love.

HOW TO DO THE IMPOSSIBLE

This rebalancing act makes sense. The problem, of course, is that we are not very good at it. To be truly human is to be imitators of the King, and we are still unskilled at mirroring our King and Father.

Scan your relationships. You can probably find one where you are controlled by another person because you want something from him or her that you aren't getting. You may intuitively grasp the spiritual logic of loving more than being loved, and you may be inspired to try it immediately. If so, wonderful! Do it. Do it now, but remember that the love offensive might not go as well as you envision.

"Honey, how should I take your abusive speech? I . . ."

"You should take it to heart, that's what you should do."

We can work up the motivation to approach someone in love, but when we are rebuffed we might find that our goal was not so much to love as to find a different strategy to help us *be* loved. Persistence in rebalancing demands the impossible. It demands the work of the Spirit of love.

How can we have more of the Spirit? There is no mystery to how the Spirit works. The Spirit comes as we fix our minds on Jesus. So we meditate on the love Jesus Christ has shown to us.

> Dear friends, let us love one another, for love comes from God. Everyone who loves has been born of God and knows God. Whoever does not love does not know God, because God is love. This is how God showed his love among us: He sent his one and only Son into the world that we might live through him. *This is love: not that we loved God, but that he loved us* and sent his Son as an atoning sacrifice for our sins.
>
> —1 JOHN 4:7-10, *author's emphasis*

The task is to look at the True Human so we can be truly human.

It isn't about me. Before setting out to love others deeply, we need more than good intentions. The light is beginning to shine on our psychological needs. For the most part, they are, at root, desires run amok. They began as normal desires for love and mutated into something very different. This happened because we made the world about us and our desires. We want to be admired, respected, and important. We want fame, as long as it doesn't interfere with our comfort. We want . . . glory, glory for ourselves.

What we really need is a changed heart.

There is it again: Whose kingdom? Where is our treasure? Our treasure is the admiration of others; our kingdoms are our own. The way out begins with what Scripture calls repentance. In shorthand form, this means that we confess that we had made it all about us. We were building our own kingdoms, and we now recognize and state before God that we were wrong.

Who am I? If I am not the king, then who am I? I am a child of the King and my goal is to bring honor to my Father. I am a servant of the King and my purpose is to make *him* famous. "You are not your own; you were bought at a price" (1 Cor. 6:19–20).

When my kingdom is at stake—my reputation, my quest for being loved—there is much to lose. Out of fear I commit myself to self-protection. Does this sound familiar? When the things we value are threatened, we protect them. In this case it is the same as protecting ourselves. The alternative is to lose my kingdom and be a simple servant of the Most High God. His kingdom is never threatened because he is all-powerful and he doesn't need anything from us. He calls us to love and worship him, but he doesn't need it in the sense that we talk about needing love and affirmation.

This should sound liberating to those who are in bondage to the fear of other people. When we see ourselves as kings who need affection, we are highly vulnerable. But as children and servants, we owe a debt of love to others. We were loved by God more than we loved him; there will always be that imbalance in our relationship. The only appropriate and healthy response is to treat others the way God has treated us. The result? People's (perceived) opinions don't have the same power to crush us anymore. Instead, we are less concerned about how we are treated and more concerned with how we treat others. Rejection may still hurt, but it won't control us.

A PERSONAL RESPONSE

I wasn't expecting to be led back to the question, *Why am I so concerned about me?* I expected anger to lead me there, but I thought fear and worry would be different. But I shouldn't be too surprised. So many personal struggles keep circling back to a motto that has served me well: When in doubt, repent. Life is certainly much easier when I am less concerned about myself and more interested in the King. Contrary to the rumor that it destroys self-esteem, such a perspective leads me down a path that feels quite human. It feels like the way I was intended to be.

The most immediate applications for me are in marriage and evangelism. In marriage I don't want to be dominated by the fear of rejection. I want nothing to keep me from loving my spouse. But when I am putting my trust in her more than in Christ, when I value her love and acceptance more than I desire to love her, when I fear her disapproval more than I fear God, I need to rebalance myself according to kingdom priorities. I want to talk with her instead of retreating and punishing her in silent anger. I want to be free from fear so I can do the obvious things love would do.

"Sheri, are you angry about something?"

"Did I do something to upset you?"

"Are things okay between us? It seems like you were a little testy just then."

"Ouch. Let's talk."

When we rebalance the scales of love, it doesn't mean that rejection or a lack of love doesn't matter anymore, but it does mean that rejection, real or perceived, doesn't control us. When we feel rejected we can still ask the question, *How can I love this person?*

When it comes to talking to others about Jesus Christ, I don't want to be controlled by the other person's possible rejection. If my first concern is to be seen as intelligent, I will certainly be vulnerable when I talk about Jesus, because the cross and the resurrection seem foolish to many. But as a child of the kingdom, I want my love and interest in others to outweigh my desire to be liked.

Now, how do *you* apply this?

CHAPTER SEVENTEEN

FIGHT FEAR WITH FEAR

I HAD A TOOTH pulled recently. Afterwards, the dentist indicated that there might be problems with the bone that held the tooth—not a good thing. A legitimate cause for mild worry, wouldn't you say? About an hour after I came home, I received a call from a very good friend. He was calling from the doctor's office because they would not allow him to come home. His MRI showed a tumor and they had him scheduled for emergency surgery the next day. My dental woes, of course, were no longer a concern.

That's the way it works with fear. Sometimes the only thing that can dislodge it is a greater fear. A woman with a fear of water will lose that fear if her child is in danger of drowning. A man who fears a small investment is going sour quickly forgets about the possible loss when he hears that his company might have to lay him off.

Remember Jesus' parting words to his itinerant disciples? "Do not be afraid of those who kill the body but cannot kill the soul. Rather, be afraid of the One who can destroy both soul and body in hell" (Matt. 10:28). In other words, when you fear the Lord, there is not much else to fear.

Let me put it more positively, because the fear of the Lord can be a delight to us, as it was to Jesus himself. If you have preached before thousands, you aren't going to be anxious about leading family devotions. If you are trained in medicine and have parented five children, you aren't going to worry when your neighbor asks you to watch her ten-year-old for twenty minutes. If you really want to fight fear, learn to fear Someone who captures your attention in such a way that your other fears suddenly seem pedestrian and unimportant.

A BETTER FEAR

To fear the Lord is one way we are instructed to respond to God. There are many ways God calls us to respond to him, such as with love, obedience, honor, and trust. Yet the call to fear the Lord is the most frequently commanded and central response. Why, then, isn't it more popular? We barely need to ask. Our goal in life is to get rid of fear, not accumulate more of it. The fear of the Lord seems like a step backward. But in Scripture, the fear of the Lord summarizes a very rich response to God. All other responses to him emphasize certain aspects of it.

The "fear" in "the fear of the Lord" has a much broader meaning than we normally assign it. It can mean obedient reverence and awe. It is a great joy, a prized possession (Isa. 33:6), a fountain of life (Prov. 14:27). It is the foundation for all wisdom and knowledge. For our children it is essential (Proverbs; Ps. 34:11). God's goodness is stored up for those who fear him (Ps. 31:19). The angel of the Lord encamps around those who fear him (Ps. 34:7). The eyes of the Lord are on those who fear him (Ps. 33:18). (And don't think that the psalmist is talking about terror; when he elaborates on this fear, it includes our hope in his unfailing love.)

Looking for comfort? "He who fears the LORD has a secure fortress, and for his children it will be a refuge" (Prov. 14:26). Scripture certainly makes the fear of the Lord look inviting.

But make no mistake; there still is a certain fear in the fear of the Lord. Notice, for example, what people do when they know they are in the presence of God. Job said, "I am unworthy—how can I reply to you? I put my hand over my mouth" (Job 40:4). "My ears had heard of you but now my eyes have seen you. Therefore I despise myself and repent in dust and ashes" (Job 42:5).

Isaiah cried out, "Woe to me! . . . I am ruined! For I am a man of unclean lips, and I live among a people of unclean lips, and my eyes have seen the King, the LORD Almighty" (Isa. 6:5). Ezekiel fell facedown (Ezek. 1:8). The disciples, after witnessing that Jesus was also the Creator God who could calm the sea with a word, were terrified: "Who is this? Even the wind and the waves obey him!" (Mark 4:41).

Lest we think that such behavior is spiritually primitive, unable to comprehend the grace of God in the gospel of Jesus Christ, consider the apostle John. If anyone knew the love of God, he did. He even wrote, "There is no fear in love. But perfect love drives out fear, because fear has to do with punishment. The one who fears is not made perfect in love" (1 John 4:18). But when he was unexpectedly ushered into heaven's throne room, he sounded just like Isaiah: "When I saw him, I fell at his feet as though dead" (Rev. 1:17).

Each of these men knew the love of God, and each one was shown it in these encounters. Those who were mute spoke. Those who were on the ground and near dead arose and were sent on missions by the King. God said to them, "Do not be afraid" (Rev. 1:17). But they all understood that one of the proper postures in the presence of God is to be bowed low, very low.

C. S. Lewis teaches about the fear of the Lord through the lion Aslan, who was good but not tame. The apostle Paul says, "Consider [both] the kindness and sternness of God" (Rom. 11:22). He is both our Father and our Lord; he is not to be trifled with.

God is holy. Life in the kingdom of heaven is always responsive. Our God initiates and makes himself known to us and we respond. The fear of the Lord is, of course, a response to God. What are we responding to? We are responding to his holiness.

You have probably heard definitions of *holy* such as "consecrated," "set apart," and "pure." But it is difficult to find a synonym that does it justice. That's because *holy* is not so much an attribute of God as it is a way to talk about his essential nature. In other words, no matter what God reveals about himself, he is revealing his holiness. His love is holy, his kindness is holy, his sternness is holy. The reason the fear of the Lord is such a robust response to God is because it is a response to his holiness, and his holiness pervades every one of his attributes.

Think about God's holiness this way: it means he is incomparable. God cannot be compared to anything in creation. "Your ways, O God, are holy. What god is so great as our God?" (Ps. 77:13).

Your challenge is to clear your mind of all human references. For example, if you have ever been angry with God, it is because you thought, *I would never allow such a thing to happen,* and you examined (and judged) God according to human criteria. The truth is that his justice and love is greater than—different from—our own; and with that knowledge, all we can do is walk humbly before him. Unless we learn what fear means from God's character alone, we will either neutralize the fear in the fear of the Lord or we will overemphasize it. There is no human being who can perfectly blend kindness and sternness, justice and mercy, love and strength, compassion and anger. So reject any human face that comes to mind.

God is holy in his love. Let's start with the forgiveness of sins. No doubt you have wronged other people in your life and they have forgiven you. That is certainly an expression of the grace of God. But don't use the experience of human forgiveness to understand the forgiveness of God. Remember: we have been enemies of God. We still find the seeds of rebellion in our hearts every day; we didn't even seek God and beg his forgiveness, yet he is pleased to forgive.

One common feature of all world religions, except for the religion revealed in the Old and New Testaments, is that the gods demand some kind of human penance when they are wronged. Human beings must pay the gods back by giving more money, adhering to proper rituals, going through some form of self-punishment, or practicing some means of works righteousness. When religions are shaped by the way people treat one another, such a system is unavoidable. The psalmist knows this. He knows that all other gods keep records of who has been naughty and who has been nice. But God is holy, and his forgiveness is holy. Nothing can compare to it. As a result the psalmist says, "If you, O LORD, kept a record of sins, O Lord, who could stand? But with you there is forgiveness; therefore you are feared" (Ps. 130:3–4).

Do you ever think that your sins are *too* bad, and that forgiveness for those sins requires you to get your act together first? If so, you don't fear God. You are minimizing his forgiveness. You are acting as though his forgiveness is ordinary, just like that of any person or make-believe god. If you think like that, you don't believe he is holy. In contrast, the fear of the Lord leads us to believe that when God makes promises too good to be true, they are indeed true.

God is holy in his sternness. Now consider the opposite problem— and most of us do have both. Let's say that we are occasionally unmoved by God's forgiveness of our sins. We believe it and are basically pleased, but not exactly wowed. It doesn't surprise us because we have all forgiven others at one point or another.

As a teenager I once went on a double date with a good friend, only to find that my good friend asked *my* date out the very next day. (And she accepted, which is another story.) I was absolutely indignant and didn't talk to him for a year. But time heals many wounds, and by the time high-school graduation came around, I was sitting near him in the ceremonies and we had a very pleasant reunion. I considered my past anger much ado about nothing. Apparently, I had forgiven him.

So maybe forgiveness is not that big of a deal. We all do it. Therefore, when God forgives we can take it all in stride. Here again the fear of the Lord is exactly what we need.

God's holiness should startle us. When (to our minds) forgiveness for our sins seems impossible, we are not startled by the self-sacrificial love of Jesus Christ. We minimize it to conform to our assumption that such forgiveness is impossible. Similarly, when forgiveness of sins seems ordinary to us, we are not startled by the holy righteousness of God that leads to his holy hatred of sin. Instead, we minimize both his righteousness and the seriousness of our own sin.

We need to listen again. All disobedience is personal. Our sin is not just against God's law; it is against God. Any time we stray away from the kingdom of God, whether by following our own desires, following other gods, or imitating the Father of Lies, we provoke the jealous God to anger. His anger will accept only death as the appropriate penalty for treason (Deut. 6:14–15).

When we complain, we hold him in contempt. The white lies we tell are against the God of truth. The anger we display is murderous toward others and stands in judgment of God himself. And it is not just what we do that is so serious; it is also what we don't do. We don't love God and neighbor with our whole heart. In our spiritual indifference we can go for days thinking that our personal interests are paramount; that is, we forget God. When there is persistent sin, there is no fear of God (Rom. 3:18).

For all this, the wrath of God is poured out. It will fall on us, if we insist on living in the anti-God kingdom and trust in ourselves, or it falls on Jesus. Either way, the wages of sin is death.

Can you see how the focus of our attention is shifting from worries to things that are even more important?

God's holiness is summed up in the holy gospel. As the fear of the Lord surfaces in your heart, notice how mercy and justice hold each other in a system of checks and balances. Love and mercy never become sentimental; justice and sternness don't veer off into wrath that abandons all offenders.

"Righteousness and peace kiss each other" (Ps. 85:10) in the death and resurrection of Jesus Christ. That is the gospel.

The holiness of God, expressed in both his love and justice, finds its zenith in the gospel of Jesus Christ. The gospel announces the liberation found in the death and resurrection of Jesus Christ. In that death we find the seriousness of sin: The Son of Man was crushed instead of us; Jesus himself drank the cup of God's wrath in our place. God's anger and righteousness are truly holy. Yet in the gospel we also find unprecedented mercy, love, and forgiveness. The penalty our sins deserve is redirected so that all we receive is grace.

THE FEAR OF THE LORD

The fear of the Lord is not for specialists who focus on one attribute of God to the exclusion of others. It is prized throughout Scripture because it is such a mature response to God. It comes when we know that God is King, Lord, and Father. He is the High and Exalted One as well as the Suffering Servant. He both hates sin and delights in forgiving sinners.

How can we define it? The fear of the Lord results from knowing that I always live *coram deo*—I live before the face of the Holy God. His holiness leaves me amazed at both the magnitude of his forgiveness and the seriousness of my own sins. Because he is holy I want to obey him wholeheartedly. "The fear of God will be with you to keep you from sinning" (Ex. 20:20).

The great blessing in the fear of the Lord is that it gives us a heart to flee from sin and run toward obedience.

> And now, O Israel, what does the LORD your God ask of you but to fear the LORD your God, to walk in all his ways, to love him, to serve the LORD your God with all your heart and with all your soul.
> —DEUT. 10:12

Come, my children, listen to me; I will teach you the fear of the LORD.
Whoever of you loves life and desires to see many good days,
keep your tongue from evil and your lips from speaking lies.
Turn from evil and do good; seek peace and pursue it.

–Ps. 34:11–14

My flesh trembles in fear of you; I stand in awe of your laws.

–Ps. 119:120

Blessed are all who fear the LORD, who walk in his ways.

–Ps. 128:1

To fear the LORD is to hate evil.

–Prov. 8:13

Through love and faithfulness sin is atoned for; through the fear of the
LORD a man avoids evil.

–Prov. 16:6

Since we have these promises, dear friends, let us purify ourselves from
everything that contaminates body and spirit, perfecting holiness out
of reverence [fear] for God.

–2 Cor. 7:1

HOW FEAR DISPLACES FEAR

What does all this have to do with fears and anxieties? It displaces them.
They topple from their lofty perch and are replaced by what is more important. Whatever is most important is the thing that rules us.

Can you hear the echo of the Sermon on the Mount? After Jesus reasoned with us about our worries and anxieties, he gave us the premier anti-anxiety treatment: "Seek first his kingdom and his righteousness" (Matt. 6:33). You treat worries by pursuing what is even more important.

Fear still reveals our allegiances, this time in a positive way. If we have a mature fear of the Lord, it means that we value and revere him above all else. That's how we fight fear with fear.

Do you worry about money? What you love and value is showing. You are living in the future, where what you love is in jeopardy. Come back to the present and ask the simple questions, What does it mean to follow Christ today? How can I be obedient now?

Do the opinions of other people control you? What you love and value is showing. You love reputation, love, respect, adoration. Ask yourself, Why am I so concerned about myself? Then consider what God asks of you. What he requires is that you walk humbly with him, showing love and mercy as you have received love and mercy.

A PERSONAL RESPONSE

My world must be very small for me to be preoccupied with the opinions of others. What a relief to be offered something bigger, something more important than the anxieties that keep me awake at night.

The challenge now is to grow in the fear of the Lord. We begin by asking for it. This is a gift God wants to give us, so we can be sure that when we ask for it, we are praying according to God's will. Then we meditate on the mighty acts of God.

> For the LORD your God dried up the Jordan before you until you had
> crossed over. The LORD your God did to the Jordan just what he had done
> to the Red Sea when he dried it up before us until we had crossed over. He

did this so that all the peoples of the earth might know that the hand of the
LORD is powerful and so that you might always fear the LORD your God.

—JOSH. 4:23–24

I can grow in the fear of the Lord by diligently reading Scripture, truly listening to sermons, participating in worship, and asking friends how they have been learning more of the mighty acts of God. All these means will help me fight back when fear attacks.

Then I want to speak about these mighty acts to others. Have you noticed that when you actually put what you believe into speech, it encourages your confidence in God? We can fight fear by proclaiming God's greatness to others. "He put a new song in my mouth, a hymn of praise to our God. Many will see and fear and put their trust in the LORD" (Ps. 40:3).

Am I talking about my fears and worry here? Absolutely. With the fear of the Lord I am headed down a path of safety. When I fear the Lord, I fear nothing else. "The fear of the LORD leads to life: Then one rests content, untouched by trouble" (Prov. 19:23).

Do you want more? Read Psalm 34 and make it your psalm.

GOD SPEAKS

on death, pain,
and punishment

MONEY and people are insignificant threats compared to the specter of death that hangs over us all. Death is truly the last enemy. No matter how we may try to avoid or euphemize it, death haunts us more than we think. The following section tries to look death in the face. Since God clearly wants to speak deeply to our fears and worries, we can be sure that he will speak to our fear of death.

CHAPTER EIGHTEEN

FEAR OF DEATH

One cannot look directly at the sun or death.
—LA ROCHEFOUCAULD, 1665

ANIMALS HAVE NO burial rituals. William Butler Yeats writes, "Nor dread nor hope attend a dying animal; a man awaits his end dreading and hoping all...man has created death."[1] Every living thing dies, but only humans die with ceremony. Unlike the rest of creation, we see the horror of death and we alone have hope that there is more to life than death.

You have to face death. You don't have to stare at it until you are cross-eyed, but you have to face it. If there are critical matters that you either postpone or relegate to the margins of your life until a more opportune time, those matters won't wait. Postpone your look at death and the reality of death will express itself in hypochondria and close attention to all things medical; in the avoidance of important conversations with friends and family; in background anxiety; and, according to some, a missed opportunity to know hope and joy.[2] There are no thoughtful people, Christian or not, who prescribe denial.

Some authors, like Ernest Becker, might put you between a rock and a hard place. On the one hand, they say you have to face death; on the other, they remind you of the possible side effects, such as the risk of running stark raving mad in the streets.[3] But the consensus is that the risk is worth it.

Is this making too big a deal out of death? If you follow cultural trends, you might think so. Funeral homes advertise "life celebrations." Sentimentalists say that death is a natural part of life. Modernists suggest that there is no life after physical death, so get over your romantic attachment to immortality. In this they follow the old Epicurean view of death that says, "Death is nothing to us." Others are fatigued with the pain and meaninglessness of life and either welcome death, at least in theory, or seem numb in the face of it. Camus represents this group when he writes in *The Stranger*, "Today mother is dead. Or maybe yesterday; it doesn't matter."

Avoid the horror of death if you like, but at root there is something anti-human about that avoidance. Indifference lasts only until your mother actually dies. Although some remain adamant atheists when they face death, the norm is that a sudden interest in the supernatural kicks in once we hear the news that our disease is terminal.[4] Death no longer seems natural when you receive a diagnosis of a chronic, debilitating disease. It only seems natural when we fade away in our sleep after a full, rich, and pain-free life, surrounded by loved ones. And even then, death is only natural because it is universal.

FEARS OF DEATH

It is more accurate to say that we have *fears*—plural—of death. Some are more common than others, and we usually have more than one. So the place to begin is to specify our fears.

Fears of eternity. Children usually begin to come alive to numbers at around age six or seven. At first, the challenge is to count to one hundred, but once they get there the sky is the limit. They have learned the pattern that can potentially keep them counting forever.

I remember the first time I heard about the number *google* long before it was made popular by the Internet. It immediately trumped the highest number any of us knew and silenced all number boasting—until we started "google and one," "google and two."

Google was fun. What came next was not. Without warning, just as we were exhausting all the possibilities of google, someone yelled out "infinity," which left us in stunned silence and immediately ended all number games. It was the end because there is no such thing as "infinity and one," and we all knew it. Even more telling was that the concept of infinity hurt our minds. We didn't like it. We didn't want to talk about it. We didn't want to think about it. So we retreated to baseball and its more manageable numbers.

Ask around and you will find that fears of infinity continue unabated. The idea of living for eternity, whether it is good or bad, is enough to freak out otherwise rational people. The most effective way to deal with it? Denial, and I am only partially kidding. If the actual length of eternity is too much for you, you are right: A finite mind can't truly grasp the infinite, so stick with things you *can* understand. In addition, you are violating one of the rules of "How to deal with worry." You are imagining the future rather than living wisely in the present. You are forgetting that whatever challenges are up ahead, we will be given grace for them when they come, but not before.

Fears of the way you might die. This is an even more common fear. With technology that can extend the amount of time we are sick, the actual way we die is an increasing fear.

A spiritually mature woman, full of faith, was paralyzed by news of possible abnormalities discovered by her routine mammogram. If she had heard the same news three years earlier, she would have simply arranged for a follow-up appointment and gone about her daily activities. But two years earlier, her neighbor had a similar mammogram that turned out to be cancerous. For an entire year she helped her friend as the cancer and its treatments ravaged her body. Her friend eventually lost the battle and died in severe pain.

It is one thing to be courageous in the face of the unknown. It is something else again to face the known.

Grace for tomorrow. Future grace. Manna when you need it. If you fear the way you might die, you must become an expert in foretelling the future. Your forecast must be, "I have no idea how God will do it, but through your prayers I believe that God will give me the grace I need when I need it." Or, in the words of a king of Israel, "We do not know what to do, but our eyes are upon you" (2 Chron. 20:12).

You can't trust in technology, because technology is one of the problems. You can't trust in pain management, because medications don't always cut through the pain. There are no other options. Your God has fenced you in so that your only option is to trust that he will give you grace.

What has this grace looked like with others?

Grace to believe that God is good.
Grace to have joy even while the body is wasting away.
Grace to cry out and be certain that God hears.
Grace to know that you are not alone.
Grace to trust rather than fear.
Grace to know that death is not the end.

Fears of hardship for loved ones. If he will give grace to you, he will also give grace to your family, but it is hard not to fear the hardships they might experience. When pastors speak with dying congregants, they usually offer words of comfort about life after death, and these indeed are comforting. But the prospect of death often focuses the mind on very practical matters. When people with dependents first hear that death is near, their initial thought is not necessarily about the afterlife, it is about their insurance policy.

Will insurance cover the bills? Does the spouse or children know where to find the will? Will my wife have to work? Does my husband know where the recipes are? Who will do the taxes? Who will feed the dog? It is a toss-up. Should you call your pastor or your accountant?

If your finances aren't in order, by all means get them in order. If you are underinsured, purchase more. If you don't have a will, make one. These are practical and spiritual ways of loving others.

Once these are out of the way, you get to the next layer of worry. Will your loved ones grieve? Will they be okay? Will they be taken care of? All your financial planning won't touch these worries.

Go back to the manna principles. God acted in response to the cries of his people. The people of Israel weren't especially righteous; they weren't even crying out to the Lord, yet he heard them. This means that God will certainly hear you. So don't be anxious; pray. It is one of the many purposes God gives to those who know that death is near. Pray for those you love. Pray that they would receive the kingdom. Pray for specific features of the kingdom you know God wants to give. When people ask how they can pray for you (and they will), ask them to pray for your family. Develop a group of friends who will commit themselves to pray for your family. Set up times with them when you can do so together. Don't worry. Pray.

Fear of the unknown. You are going into seventh grade. Your family has just moved to a new school district and you don't know a soul. When you wake up for that first day of class, you *will* be anxious. You don't think you are going to be murdered on the way to school, you just don't know what to expect. You don't know the teachers. You don't know the students. You don't even know how to get to your homeroom, let alone how to navigate to a new classroom each period. If you had an older sibling who had attended the school, it would have helped. He or she could have told you about the teachers, given you a heads up on where to eat lunch, and sketched a map of the building.

Heaven is a fine place. That much we know, or at least we hope. But no sibling has gone before you to give you some inside information, and God himself is mum on the details. Theologians who study these things still wrangle about the few things Scripture mentions, largely because heaven is usually described in metaphoric language.

"Absent from the body, . . . present with the Lord" (2 Cor. 5:8, KJV) is the sum of it. If that is not enough to assuage our fears, it is probably because we are concerned about judgment.

Fear of judgment. Chicken Little thought the sky was falling. He had no special revelation, he just *felt* like the sky was going to fall. He sensed impending doom. He didn't know when it would happen, but he was confident that it would.

We think Chicken Little foolish because skies don't fall, but Chicken Little was the children's version of the thousands of doomsday prophets who have predicted that the end is near and it won't be pretty. Chicken Little is also the poster chicken for everyone who senses worry and anxiety but can't quite locate its source.

It is as if we have done something wrong and Mom says, "Wait until your father gets home."

> Since the children have flesh and blood, he too shared in their humanity so that by his death he might destroy him who holds the power of death—that is, the devil—and free those who *all their lives were held in slavery by their fear of death.*
>
> —HEB. 2:14–15, *author's emphasis*

Here our view of the cosmos opens again. The kingdom of the earth is the kingdom of Satan. As the anti-kingdom, Satan's domain is a prison where everyone has the sentence of death. In other words, the reality is much worse than the sky falling. Try not to think too deeply on this, or you will suddenly have the peculiar sense that your sentence has been passed while you are left guessing as to the execution date. It could be in the next few minutes, it could be years from now, but it will happen. That is why anxiety free-floats through the human race.

Not that anyone actually wants to talk about the fear. No, give a rendition of Hebrews 2 in the public square and you will be ignored.

> This is the verdict: Light has come into the world, but men loved darkness instead of light because their deeds were evil. Everyone who does evil hates the light, and will not come into the light for fear that his deeds will be exposed.
>
> —JOHN 3:19–20

These deeper spiritual realities tend to be suppressed and denied. We suppress them because we prefer the illusion of independence to living under the reign of Christ with its moral obligations. But suppression doesn't stop the steady stream of art, literature, and movies from expressing our fears of death and possible judgment. Something that powerful will express itself in some way.

For those who have declared their allegiance to Christ, such fears should be relieved. Scripture is unequivocal that Jesus came to release captives and destroy the despotic ways of Satan. "There is now no condemnation for those who are in Christ Jesus" (Rom. 8:1). Yet there are many Christians who live with the fear of judgment. We know that the apostle Paul certainly looked forward to being with Christ. We know that Scripture points to a wedding feast on the other side of death, and we will no longer see Christ as if through a veil but we will see him face-to-face. But that minor detail of being judged for our works leaves us with nagging anxieties.

PERSONAL RESPONSE

Thinking about death is becoming a way of life for me. That's not because I like it. It's because I and those I love will die, and there are times when it scares me. Yet I can be scared with hope. I am persuaded that one way I can glorify God is to trust him even in the face of death. So I invite you to identify your own fears of death and stick with them until hope is firmly planted in their place.

Talk about these things with others and learn how they are finding grace.

CHAPTER NINETEEN

FEAR OF JUDGMENT

Man is destined to die once, and after that to face judgment.
—HEB. 9:27

If we deliberately keep on sinning after we have received the knowledge of the truth, no sacrifice for sins is left, but only a fearful expectation of judgment and of raging fire that will consume the enemies of God.

—HEB. 10:26–27

For we must all appear before the judgment seat of Christ, that each one may receive what is due him for the things done while in the body, whether good or bad.

—2 COR. 5:10

You, then, why do you judge your brother? Or why do you look down on your brother? For we will all stand before God's judgment seat.

—ROM. 14:10

For the Son of Man is going to come in his Father's glory with his angels, and then he will reward each person according to what he has done.

—MATT. 16:27

This is why we feel like the sky is falling. On the other side of death there is a judgment, and everyone will appear before the bar. Whatever this judgment seat is, a courtroom has never been a place where people were celebrated. Instead, it was where your life was in the balance. People didn't enter smiling.

For those who have put their trust in Jesus Christ, this is not what you signed up for. You understood that the judgment for your sin fell on Jesus instead of yourself, and you have been spared the gauntlet. But then you encounter those passages about everyone being judged—and judged for their works!

Yet the Judge will make distinctions. The final judgment is when the kingdom of heaven and the kingdom of the earth are fully separated (Matt. 13:25–30). This distinction should come as no surprise in that some people follow Jesus and others don't, but it is still controversial. We live in an era when such distinctions are occasions for pride and prejudice, but this distinction is a result of God's judgment, not our own. Any dismissal of charges against us is a gift, so there is no reason for one group to lord it over another. This is only reason for thankfulness and humility.

FOR UNBELIEVERS

For those who have preferred to live outside the bounds of the kingdom of Christ, the King will offer neither protection nor amnesty. While he constantly invites and even pleads with people to come to him while they live on earth, the judgment seat is final. At that time, those who avoided Jesus Christ will see reality much more clearly. Right now, their rejection of Christ might not seem personal. Teaching about Jesus just seems to them like one of many philosophies of life. Maybe the disciples got it wrong and

Jesus never really claimed to be God. And where is Jesus anyway? No one has seen him recently, so how can you center your whole life around someone you have never actually met? On the surface, it can seem more like intellectual doubts than personal rejection.

These seem like reasonable excuses now but at the judgment seat, what passed as casual indifference on earth will be exposed more accurately. The indifference is ultimately anti-Christ.

An affair can seem innocent until the adulterer is caught. Then he or she stands ashamed and without excuse. The clarity of the judgment seat will not surprise those who don't follow Jesus, but it will devastate them.

> Jesus turned and said to them, "Daughters of Jerusalem, do not weep for me; weep for yourselves and for your children. For the time will come when you will say, 'Blessed are the barren women, the wombs that never bore and the breasts that never nursed! Then 'they will say to the mountains, "Fall on us!" and to the hills, "Cover us!"'"
>
> —LUKE 23:28–30

Jesus is saying that when he is finally revealed as the Judge of all (John 5:27), those who rejected him will prefer the mountains to fall on them than to be naked, ashamed, and condemned before him. In other words, if you reject the King or are a mere dabbler in the kingdom, then your present fear and anxiety are a blessing. They serve the same function as pain receptors, in that they tell you when you are in physical danger. People without pain receptors gradually lose body parts because they don't realize that they have their hand on the stove or are walking with a piece of glass in their foot. Such people know it is folly to numb those receptors when they are functioning well.

> I tell you, my friends, do not be afraid of those who kill the body and after that can do no more. But I will show you whom you should fear:

Fear him who, after the killing of the body, has power to throw you into hell. Yes, I tell you, fear him.

—LUKE 12:4-5

Listen to fear; don't run from it. If it feels as if you live under a bad sign, your interpretation might be askew but your fear isn't. Don't try to numb yourself. Let your fear and worry speak loud and clear. Then listen again to the claims of the King. Let him woo you to a place of real peace and rest. He never tires of inviting you, no matter how many times you have rejected him so far.

FOR BELIEVERS

On the surface, the situation doesn't seem that much better for followers of Christ. We too have to pass through a judgment before we know the blessings of perfect fellowship with God and each other. We are assured that there is ultimately no condemnation (Rom. 8:1), but the evaluation of our works takes some of the joy out of that pronouncement, and it adds a dash of fear.

Judgment and believers. What do we do with these passages that say we will be judged by our works? There are a couple of possibilities.

One is that this "judgment" will be an awards ceremony. Using fire imagery, the apostle Peter suggests that bad works—those not done out of faith in Jesus—will be burnt to ashes. They were empty before, and at judgment their emptiness will be manifest. They will come to nothing. But good works done in faith will result in "praise, glory and honor when Jesus Christ is revealed" (1 Peter 1:7).

Everything we do now has eternal implications, of that we can be sure. It would be odd, however, if the righteous Judge remembered only the good (which was the work of his Spirit in us anyway) and passed over all the bad. More likely, the praise, glory, and honor will be given to King

Jesus, who is the author and perfecter of our faith (Heb. 12:2). A variation on this picture is that we will be given crowns in the end times, and we will lay those crowns before the throne (Rev. 4:10).

So far so good.

Another possibility is that this judgment will be a judgment of our kingdom allegiances. How can you judge allegiances? By looking at the way someone lives. If a man says he loves his wife and is committed to her, you look for the evidence in his actions. If he is truly committed, he will not be a perfect husband, but he will be circumspect in his relationships with other women, he will guard his heart so lust isn't given free rein, he will show kindness and affection to his wife, and he will ask forgiveness when he doesn't. Genuine commitment is verifiable. It can be witnessed by God and others.

Did you hear "not perfect"? Keep the marriage analogy in mind. No spouse is perfect, but there are many spouses who are faithful and make good faith efforts to love.

Mere words, of course, don't tell the whole story. If a husband says that he is committed to his wife but is devoted to Internet porn, has been sexually unfaithful, hides money for his own purposes, or is abusively angry, then you believe what he *does* more than what he says. It should be no surprise to him when he is told that he neither loves his wife nor is committed to her. When stated allegiances are accompanied by treasonous actions, you judge allegiances based on deeds.

> Do you not know that the wicked will not inherit the kingdom of God? Do not be deceived: Neither the sexually immoral nor idolaters nor adulterers nor male prostitutes nor homosexual offenders nor thieves nor the greedy nor drunkards nor slanderers nor swindlers will inherit the kingdom of God.
>
> —1 Cor. 6:9–10

The acts of the sinful nature are obvious: sexual immorality, impurity and debauchery; idolatry and witchcraft; hatred, discord, jealousy, fits of rage, selfish ambition, dissensions, factions and envy; drunkenness, orgies, and the like. I warn you, as I did before, that those who live like this will not inherit the kingdom of God.

—GAL. 5:19-21

The problem is that every Christian with an intact conscience can acknowledge that he or she has broken and continues to break every command. Selfish ambition, language that tears down rather than builds up, and an imperfect love for God and other people reside in the heart of every believer. At issue for us, however, is not perfection (1 John 1:8). That can only be given to us by Christ alone, and it awaits eternity. The issue can be put this way: Which direction do you face? Is your face turned toward Christ or away from him? To use the marriage analogy, my wife is not expecting sinlessness but faithfulness. She will not divorce me because of my many sins and weaknesses. Divorce, the sign of broken commitments, would only come after my face has clearly turned away from her and toward someone else.

Getting nervous? Remember, the assurance that we belong to God is a big deal in Scripture. There is no reason that you should be kept guessing. If you are a member of a church that takes allegiance to Christ seriously, then you have, in a sense, already appeared in court with witnesses who testify that you are a follower of Christ. The pastors and leaders of your church know you are not perfect, but they have evidence that you turn to Christ when you see your sins. Does your church practice discipline of those who claim to follow Christ but persist in their own sin? If so, the fact that you are known but not excommunicated is an earthly sign of a heavenly reality (Matt. 16:19; 18:18).

The seared conscience. We have reason to be sobered, perhaps, but not afraid. If final judgment examines our spiritual allegiances, there should be nothing to worry about. As followers of Christ, we live for him rather than ourselves. When we see sin, we turn from it. Since we know we can be blind to our sin, we live among a community that can help us see.

But if our life in the kingdom is no different from the way we lived when we were outside the kingdom, there *is* cause for alarm. If we are reluctant to forgive, why would we think that we have been forgiven (Matt. 6:15)? If we hate others, why would we think that we follow the King who has loved his enemies? "The man who says, 'I know him,' but does not do what he commands is a liar, and the truth is not in him" (1 John 2:4).

Will we be perfect forgivers, perfect lovers? Certainly not. We will be forgivers and lovers who confess our sin and turn to Jesus for mercy and grace to forgive and love more and more deeply.

> God "will give to each person according to what he has done." To those who by persistence in doing good seek glory, honor and immortality, he will give eternal life. But for those who are self-seeking and who reject the truth and follow evil, there will be wrath and anger.
>
> —ROM. 2:6–8

Check your conscience. Ask others if they see obedience to Christ in your life. Consider what others would see if your private behaviors were public. Remember that confession of sin is not the threat to self-esteem that people think. Confession and repentance are some of the most Godlike things we can do. They elevate and liberate us. So take time to consider your life. Where are you living for yourself and your own desires? Ask the Spirit to give you grace to walk in the light rather than the darkness.

The scrupulous conscience. Those with inactive or seared consciences don't fret about eternal matters. Their fear still seeps through, but it's veiled. It appears as low self-esteem, a lingering sense of not measuring up, and defensiveness. Meanwhile, those with more scrupulous consciences are always thinking about eternal matters and final judgment.

If this is your experience, be careful in the way you think about the judgment seat. You already feel condemned, so your interpretation of the judgment seat only confirms it. But be suspicious about your fears. Doesn't it make sense that, if you are *that* concerned about your citizenship in the kingdom, this interest has been sparked by the Spirit himself? Read through the Gospel of John and notice how many were completely oblivious to the identity of Christ. Any interest anyone has in Jesus Christ is not natural to us. It is stirred by God himself. Does it make sense that God would arouse such an interest in the kingdom but exclude you from it? There is absolutely no warrant for this in Scripture. God constantly invites and doesn't refuse those who come. *We* are the ones who refuse to come (Matt. 22:2–3); he is the one who holds out his hands and beseeches us to come (Matt. 11:28). Don't think that God is like a human being.

If condemnation and fears of judgment haunt you, it is time to consider the possibility that the issue might be neither your own sin nor God's displeasure. You know that Satan rushes in at any mention of legal matters. Although expelled from the courtroom (Rev. 12:10), he knows that we still waver at the thought of judgment and are easy targets. After all, whatever the accusation might be, there are probably kernels of truth to it.

Murder? Yes, you got me. I have not always wanted the best for others and I have certainly stood in judgment (Matt. 5:21–22).

Adultery? Ouch. Yes, I am familiar with lust (Matt. 5:28).

And so it goes. There is no defense. If the conversation never gets to Jesus and the righteousness he gives us as part of our new citizenship, we are silenced. And condemned.

Now notice where you are. Since this mock courtroom never directed all eyes to Jesus, you should suspect that you aren't even in the *real* courtroom. Satan is no longer allowed there. The cross of Christ exiled him and his lying ways (Rev. 12:10).

When you belong to the King, how can you discern the difference between the Devil's condemnation and the Spirit's conviction? How can you determine if you are in the bogus courtroom or the real one?

In the real courtroom:

- you know your good deeds are not enough
- your hope is in Christ alone for your deliverance
- when convicted of sins, you are pointed past your sins and on to Christ
- the last word is always hope.

In the Devil's counterfeit:

- the attention is all on your sins
- you stand and fall on your own behavior
- you are alone without an advocate
- questions are raised about the extent of God's forgiveness.

Christ alone, Christ alone—that is your defense. When you are feeling weak, ask for the Spirit to teach you more about how righteousness is not inherent to you but has been given to you by the righteous acts of Jesus (Rom. 5:15–21). We are given this when we put our faith in Jesus rather than ourselves. How can you know when you are trusting in yourself? When you think that your good deeds will outweigh your bad.

A scrupulous conscience, however, always has a retort that keeps it from rest. "If my righteousness comes from relying on Christ by faith, how do I know I have enough faith?" There again, get suspicious. Like a moral boomerang you keep coming back to yourself. Consider faith this way: It means that we give up. Faith says, *I need Jesus.* It is not a work, it is an act of desperation, and you are certainly familiar with that!

As if this isn't enough to bring relief, we are also given other people. Rest in the judgments made by your pastors or elders. Rest in how you are a member in good standing of your church. You are thinking in terms of perfection; think in terms of faithfulness. The normal Christian life is a race of repentance. The very fact that you are convicted of sin is a work of the Spirit (John 16:8), so you can accept conviction with a smile on your face, knowing that it is just one more evidence that you belong to Christ. Now allow the Spirit to "convict" you of the righteousness you are given by Christ.

Don't think that God is preparing for a sneak attack at judgment day, like an adversarial lawyer who tries to take us by surprise while we are on the witness stand. God delights in leading his people into the light. He speaks openly with us. Also, remember how God tests his people? These tests are intended to show us our own hearts. In other words, you don't have to embark on a monastic, introspective tour of your life. When God tests you and reveals your mixed allegiances, simply turn to him.

The only surprises in heaven will be for those who think they are particularly righteous or good, which certainly does not include those with scrupulous consciences (e.g., Matt. 7:21–23). The Heidelberg Catechism mentions the qualifications for taking the Lord's Supper, which can be a torturous time for those who aren't skilled in turning quickly to Christ with their sin. Interestingly, the Catechism says that the Lord's Supper is for those who are "displeased" with themselves.

> 81. Q. Who are to come to the table of the Lord?
>
> A. Those who are truly displeased with themselves because of their sins and yet trust that these are forgiven them and that their remaining weakness is covered by the suffering and death of Christ, and who also desire more and more to strengthen their faith and amend their life. But hypocrites and those who do not repent eat and drink judgment upon themselves.[1]

Keep the basic rhythm of Scripture in mind: For every one look at your own sins, take ten looks at Christ. He takes the initiative; we respond.

We know that we live in him and he in us, because he has given us of his Spirit. And we have seen and testify that the Father has sent his Son to be the Savior of the world. If anyone acknowledges that Jesus is the Son of God, God lives in him and he in God. And so we know and rely on the love God has for us.

God is love. Whoever lives in love lives in God, and God in him. In this way, love is made complete among us so that we will have confidence on the day of judgment, because in this world we are like him. There is no fear in love. But perfect love drives out fear, because fear has to do with punishment. The one who fears is not made perfect in love.

We love because he first loved us.

–1 John 4:13-19

A life of love and a race of repentance. The scrupulous conscience— a.k.a. obsessive-compulsive disorder in modern discussions—has misunderstood life in the kingdom. It assumed that we would be relatively sinless and, when those few leftover sins appeared, we would simply say no and be done with them.

The reality is that the Spirit convicts of sin. One piece of evidence of kingdom life is that you will see *more* sin, not less. Outside the kingdom of heaven, there is no concern about sin. That doesn't mean that unbelievers are so bad; it means that they are indifferent to the fact that their sin is against God. They hide the more shameful sins, but they don't do battle with them. When you are brought into the kingdom of light, you both see sin and, for the first time, get in a battle with it. The battle means you are alive.

The rules of engagement are simple. When you see sin, you confess it as ultimately being against God. You respond in gratitude for the forgiveness he already gave you because of Jesus' death, which was the payment for sins. Then, knowing that you have been given the Spirit so you can do battle with sin, you attack. You ask for the power to love. You ask others to pray for you and counsel you. You adopt a zero-tolerance policy with sin. When you fall in defeat, you learn from it and get right back into the battle.

You will see more and more sin, but you will also notice that the Spirit is changing you. There have been times when you responded in humility rather than arrogance, love rather than indifference or even hatred. The change will be gradual but noticeable. Keep your eyes open. How are you different because of what Jesus has done? When you see it, the apostle John says that you can allow that evidence to assure you that you truly belong to God.

A PERSONAL RESPONSE

I rest in Christ alone. That is the only foundation secure enough to uphold me in the last day. I want to say that more often. I want to remember it every morning. Then I want Christ alone to inspire and empower me because I am no longer my own.

But I still have this lingering sense of judgment. I can see evidence in me of both the seared conscience and the scrupulous one. For the seared conscience, my prescription is a daily habit of confession. For my scrupulous conscience, I still want to rid myself of the vague sense that God is a heavenly predator, quick to exploit my weaknesses and sins. Nothing could be further from the truth! In reality, he is quick to mercy and slow to anger. He himself has assigned the Spirit to take up my case, and I am praying that the Spirit would assure me of the truth.

How do you respond? Don't gloss over this one. The Spirit delights in giving you assurance that Christ has done it all, and what is Christ's is yours through faith. Stay with this until you notice inklings of joy and rest.

CHAPTER TWENTY

A GLIMPSE OF HEAVEN

LET'S SAY YOU have said "Christ alone." You are engaging in the battle with sin. Yet you still have times when you are haunted by thoughts of judgment. Then what?

Peace is a big deal to God, so you can be sure that he will keep speaking words of truth and encouragement until you "get it." Of course, you will finally get it when you see the Prince of Peace face-to-face, but you can bring him honor by knowing peace even before then.

We have absolutely no evidence that God ever throws up his hands and says, "You are driving me crazy! What more can I say?" If he says "Do not be afraid" hundreds of times, there is no reason to think that he will be silent during your struggles. How strange it would be for God to say, "Okay, you persuaded me. You aren't my child." How backwards! He is the One who persuades us.

Listen, and give God the last word. Here are some more ways he speaks to those who confess faith in Jesus but still struggle with feelings of condemnation.

CONFESS SECRET SIN

If you are immune to the message of hope and deliverance, there are obvious questions begging to be asked.

Is there a reason why you feel so condemned? What have you done that deserves judgment? What are you doing that you want to hide? Are there sins you are reluctant to tell anyone?

If these questions apply to you, don't be too surprised that fear and low-grade paranoia are always within reach.

Past sin. Perhaps you struggle with the memory of past sin. An old sexual relationship still haunts you from time to time. Past theft, lies, cheating, or other hidden sin replay in your mind and you are too ashamed to say anything about it. Send out reconnaissance for any hint of, *I can't believe God would forgive me for that.*

If you try to avoid these past sins, you will always be looking over your shoulder. You will choke out spiritual growth. You must do something with them.

Start by being surprised at how much God says to you about such things. All of Scripture points to the forgiveness of sins through Jesus Christ. "All the prophets testify about him that everyone who believes in him receives forgiveness of sins through his name" (Acts 10:43). Your avoidance and hiding suggest that you think God remains silent until you completely reform—and you haven't. The reality is that God is never silent. He always speaks to you with words of invitation.

Now remember. Listen. God does not forgive you based on the quality of your confession or your resolve to be a better person. But you keep thinking otherwise. Your standard is what *you* would do to someone like yourself, and chances are that you would not let the incident pass quickly. God, however, forgives for his own name's sake. "I, even I, am he who blots out your transgressions, for my own sake, and remembers your sins no more" (Isa. 43:25). There may be no finer words in Scripture. God bases his forgiveness on himself and his forgiving character, not on the quality of your confession.

So confess your sin to God in faith. By that I mean you confess sin, believing that God is exactly who he says he is. You confess while you give God all authority to interpret reality, instead of giving your personal feelings authority. Your feelings will say condemnation, but God says he doesn't treat you as your sins deserve. God must win in this interpretive battle.

Here is a way to test your progress: Confess your past sin to another person. This isn't essential for forgiveness, but it can be wise. Let's say that you notice a breakthrough in the way you understand God's forgiveness. Let's say that you even notice inklings of joy. Now, what would it be like if someone else knew your past sin?

If you shudder at the thought, your liberation is incomplete. After all, if we are persuaded that we have been forgiven by the divine Judge, why would we cower at the judgments of people who are no different from ourselves? Yes, people can reject us if we tell them certain sins, but that reveals more about them than about us. If they do, we can move toward them, confronting them if necessary, and aim for reconciliation and unity.

At least talk with your pastor about these things. The rule of thumb is that when we find ourselves stuck, we enlarge the circle and include others who can help. This is a way of relying on God and following his means of growth and change.

Confession to another person is not a way to artificially unload guilt. The one who hears your confession is not a priest who will grant absolution. The reason you confess something private is to test your own heart. It is also a way to close the door to one of Satan's condemnatory devices. Satan delights in keeping all things in the dark, where they can accumulate more condemnation, but we can do battle by keeping our lives in the light.

Sin hidden to ourselves. We are still trying to listen to fear. Sometimes it points back to past sins that have never been confessed; sometimes we think that forgiveness can't extend to the really bad sins of our past.

At other times, fear hints of guilt and condemnation that we can't tie to anything in particular.

Whether or not there is a definitive connection between your fear and a specific sin, you can't go wrong if you echo the psalmist's plea, "Search me, O God, and know my heart; test me and know my anxious thoughts. See if there is any offensive way in me, and lead me in the way everlasting" (Ps. 139:23–24).

You can't lose with this approach to fear. If you are reluctant to say this to God, perhaps because you feel condemned enough already, then you have exposed something significant going on in your heart. You do not have a clear conscience before the Lord and you don't live with a keen sense of God's ever-present mercies. If you say it and the Spirit reveals sin to you, then you are blessed. The Father is teaching you how to be more and more like him, and confessing and turning away from sin are central to our transformation.

Please don't think that God is playing games with you. "I see sin in your life; now you are going to have to guess what it is." If games are being played, we are the players. We are the ones who avoid the light. Seeing sin does not demand unusual intelligence or insight, it just takes a willing heart.

What have I seen in my own heart? Typically it comes down to my attempts to establish my own kingdom rather than say that God is God and I trust him. I have a hard time believing words that seem too good to be true.

Present sin. Condemnation might also point to present sins that are known to you but hidden to others. Check your conscience. Is it clear? If your life were truly known by others, would you feel exposed and ashamed? Are there secret sins currently in your life that you don't want to confess? Are there sins that, when you confess them, you are already planning on doing again? If these questions reveal hidden sins, be overjoyed that you feel guilty. If you didn't, you would have reason to doubt God's patience and endurance with you. Be on guard here. The alternative to confession is denial and trying to sear your conscience. And here is something to fear: with practice, these strategies are effective. They can numb you spiritually. Then you would lose your warning system that activates when you are straying outside kingdom boundaries.

Look especially for where you might hate others. "We know that we have passed from death to life, because we love our brothers. Anyone who does not love remains in death" (1 John 3:14).

REST IN THE GRACE TO BE GIVEN

One of the principles God gives to those who worry is that we should focus on today and trust him to give us the grace to handle tomorrow. Today you collect manna and walk humbly with your God in faith and obedience. Tomorrow he will be faithful to his promises. He will give you the grace you need, which might come in the form of manna, food from a friendly neighbor, or some other means.

This principle can also be applied to worry about judgment. Focus on following Christ and living in the kingdom *today*. That will be more than enough. When tomorrow comes (which in this case is the judgment seat), trust him to give you the grace you need. Such trust pleases him.

In most situations we don't know the specific way God will give us grace, but we do know some of the specific ways we will receive grace at the judgment seat. For example, when we see Jesus face-to-face, we will be perfect, without sin. This means that you will love God perfectly, worship him completely, and trust him and his judgment without reservation. You will think the way God thinks, at least as much as creatures can think like their Creator.

You will also know the love of God. Right now you cannot understand how God can have an unwavering love toward you, because you see your own heart and how quickly it can turn toward your own desires. But when you see Jesus you will truly know love.

Even the most doubt-ridden believer must acknowledge that God has chosen to reveal his sacrificial love as the fullest expression of his being. All Scripture is fulfilled in the gospel, the death and resurrection of Jesus Christ. Everything points to this event. It was the moment when kingdoms were re-aligned and human life changed. In the gospel God revealed himself as the Servant of humanity. The Father did what Abraham didn't; he sacrificed his only Son. That sacrifice effectively put an end to the entire sacrificial system.

You can't doubt that God loves at the cross. And, as God himself argues, if he demonstrated sacrificial love then, how could you think he would leave you on your own now (Rom. 8:32)? In most universities today, the hard part is getting admitted. Once admitted, the university will do everything possible to help you graduate. In a similar way, God argues that he did not deliver us so that we could be left to ourselves. He delivered us so that we would belong to him and receive all the benefits of being brought into God's family (Rom. 8:32).

When you are perfect, you will know his perfect love.

KNOW THE GOD WHO DELIGHTS IN HIS PEOPLE

Consider this image of heaven. God sings with enthusiasm because he delights in his people. It isn't exactly cool, because kings, dignitaries, and other cool people don't get too excited, but it is true. God says it about himself.

We have hints of this when we read that God is pleased to give us the kingdom (Luke 12:32). That isn't too surprising when we remember that he chooses to be sacrificial toward us. More accurately, since it is part of his nature, he *delights* in his sacrificial love toward us. His delight is more exuberant than we think.

> Sing, O Daughter of Zion; shout aloud, O Israel! Be glad and rejoice with all your heart, O Daughter of Jerusalem! The LORD has taken

away your punishment, he has turned back your enemy. The LORD, the King of Israel, is with you; never again will you fear any harm. On that day they will say to Jerusalem, "Do not fear, O Zion; do not let your hands hang limp. The LORD your God is with you, he is mighty to save. He will take great delight in you, he will quiet you with his love, he will rejoice over you with singing."

—ZEPH. 3:14–17

Nothing delightful about yourself? Nothing to sing about? That is the point. This is not about you, it's about God. He is the One who takes away our punishment. He is the One who gives us new hearts. His singing comes from the work he has done in us.

All we do is bring nothing. No righteousness in ourselves. No ability to pay him back for our sins. No boasting that we were better than other people. God simply asks us to come with nothing.

Too good to be true? If that is how it seems, then we are on track. Even our confession of sin is a delight to him.

Now the tax collectors and "sinners" were all gathering around to hear him. But the Pharisees and the teachers of the law muttered, "This man welcomes sinners and eats with them."

Then Jesus told them this parable: "Suppose one of you has a hundred sheep and loses one of them. Does he not leave the ninety-nine in the open country and go after the lost sheep until he finds it? And when he finds it, he joyfully puts it on his shoulders and goes home. Then he calls his friends and neighbors together and says, 'Rejoice with me; I have found my lost sheep.' I tell you that in the same way there will be more rejoicing in heaven over one sinner who repents than over ninety-nine righteous persons who do not need to repent."

—LUKE 15:1–7

It's enough to make you pleased to see yourself as the black sheep of the family.

Here is another way to look at it. Do you believe that the Father loved the Son? There is absolutely no question about that. Now notice what happened when you acknowledged that Christ alone was your Deliverer. At that time you were brought into the kingdom of Christ. When you come into the kingdom, you don't come as a slave but as a royal child. You receive all the benefits of the King's family. Included in those benefits is the love of the Father. Everything the Son has is yours. The Son has the exuberant love of the Father, so you have that love too.

PREPARE FOR A WEDDING FEAST

How does delight fit into a courtroom picture? A judge who sings? It actually fits better than we think. The Old Testament provides the background for New Testament judgment, and the saints of old were excited by the prospects of God's judgment.

> May the nations be glad and sing for joy,
>> for you rule the peoples justly
>> and guide the nations of the earth.
>> —Ps. 67:4

> Say among the nations, "The LORD reigns."
>> The world is firmly established, it cannot be moved;
>> he will judge the peoples with equity.
> Let the heavens rejoice, let the earth be glad;
>> let the sea resound, and all that is in it;
>> let the fields be jubilant, and everything in them.
> Then all the trees of the forest will sing for joy;

they will sing before the LORD, for he comes,
he comes to judge the earth.
He will judge the world in righteousness
and the peoples in his truth.

–Ps. 96:10–13

Awake, and rise to my defense!
Contend for me, my God and Lord.
Vindicate me in your righteousness, O LORD my God.

–Ps. 35:23–24

The picture in their minds is something akin to our civil courts (cf. Luke 18:1–5) where the judge would make matters right. Injustice has been a plague throughout human history and a just world is certainly something to look forward to. The little person, the poor, the marginalized will all be heard. When we consider God's judgment from a corporate perspective more than an individual one, we can see how it is an occasion for praise and rejoicing. No longer will oppression be tolerated or the voices of the weak ignored. Instead, all will be as God intended it.

As pleasant as that sounds, there is another image of the end times that is at least as attractive. Scripture provides more than one picture of life after death; a judgment seat isn't the only one. Equally prominent in Scripture, if not more so, is the wedding banquet: "Then he said to his servants, 'The wedding banquet is ready, but those I invited did not deserve to come. Go to the street corners and invite to the banquet anyone you find.' So the servants went out into the streets and gathered all the people they could find, both good and bad, and the wedding hall was filled with guests" (Matt. 22:8–10; also Luke 14:14–24).

If you feel at times like a spiritual street person, destitute and homeless, then you are invited. If you are spiritually superior, smug, or indifferent, then be warned. It is the outcasts and those who come as needy children who eat at the banquet table.

How can this be? Outcasts and those with a glaring sense of their own spiritual neediness can only put their trust in someone other than themselves. This is what God requires—that we <u>trust in him alone. Otherwise, we are trying to accumulate capital for our own glory, our own kingdom.</u>

Our trust in Christ is never perfect, but it is one sign that we belong to Christ and that the work of the cross is applied to us. In part this means we are cleansed. Robes that were once blemished and hands that were bloody because of our murderous ways are washed. They are white, and white is the color of a bride beautifully dressed for her husband (Rev. 21:2). We are intended to be the bride of Christ, and when we belong to him we are intended to hear, "As a bridegroom rejoices over his bride, so will your God rejoice over you" (Isa. 62:5).

Always the bridesmaid and never the bride? We all know what that feels like. But the bridegroom calls us to himself because he is the One who made us clean and beautiful. How do you qualify to be a bride? Simply acknowledge that you need cleansing and beauty from Christ.

A PERSONAL RESPONSE

It is all free. Whatever blurriness there is in our vision of eternity, we know that God invites us and he gives us life for free. With free admission, there are no worries at the door.

> The Spirit and the bride say, "Come!" And let him who hears say, "Come!" Whoever is thirsty, let him come; and whoever wishes, let him take the free gift of the water of life.
>
> —REV. 22:17

CHAPTER TWENTY-ONE

ALREADY DEAD

JANIS JOPLIN was right, at least in part. In "Me and Bobby McGee," she sang, "Freedom's just another word for nothing left to lose." Hold tight onto the things of this world and you will be anxious. Let go—die to the world—and (here's where we part company with Janis) you will be liberated, alive, and unafraid.

The stuff I am accumulating? I once thought a relatively expensive guitar was stolen and I had a mini-panic. Either the guitar was lost or my wife moved it; they were the only possibilities. I was both scared and peeved—until I found it, wonderfully hidden in an impossible-to-find spot, right where I left it.

At those times I wonder what it would be like to lose everything. What if a fire consumed all my belongings and only spared my wife and me? Like those who have actually experienced such a disaster, I would think first about the family pictures; then I would wonder if my computer files had been backed up at work. No doubt I would forget a few commitments without an appointment calendar. At some point I would wonder about the cat.

Then I think I would begin to notice something that feels like freedom. I have just lost everything. I am dead to my possessions, and they are dead to me. It isn't as bad as I imagined. Now there is nothing left to lose. There is nothing to clutch and possess.

Have you seen any of the many movies in which the hero should have died but didn't? Along with his sense of survivor's guilt, especially if he was in a train wreck and most other passengers died, a common response is a certain recklessness. His present life feels like a freebie. He already died in a way and, having faced his worst fear, he isn't afraid of anything anymore.

C. S. Lewis cites an unknown writer, "He who has God and everything else has no more than he who has God only."[1]

WE DIED

There is something anticlimactic about death. That is neither to minimize the wonder of being perfect and seeing Jesus Christ face-to-face or the grief of death and loss. But in light of the cataclysm that has already taken place at the cross, death has been robbed of some of its drama.

The wedding days of my two daughters were very significant days, but in many ways they seemed like normal days. The big days were when they met their prospective spouses, when they realized that they loved them, when they decided to marry, and, of course, when my future sons-in-law ran the gauntlet I set up to winnow out the weak and unworthy.

If we are fixated on things that surround our future death, we don't understand that most of the important stuff has already happened. We have already died with Christ. There is no more penalty for sin that must be paid—Jesus was the perfect sacrifice. Our liberation from the kingdom of darkness has been secured. No change could be more significant. Eternity will be beautiful, but it will just add color to the life we already have in Christ.

Our entire earthly life consists of understanding more and more of what happened to us when we were converted. To us, it might have been a lightning-bolt moment when the Spirit of God opened our eyes to the truth. It might have happened over a period of time, before which we didn't believe but after which we did. Or we might have always had knowledge of the truth and never had a time when we doubted. However God brought us to himself, our public declaration that Jesus is Lord and our conviction that Jesus died and was raised from the dead are tangible evidence of a Copernican revolution of the soul.

Also crammed into that event is our own death.

> What shall we say, then? Shall we go on sinning so that grace may increase? By no means! We died to sin; how can we live in it any longer? Or don't you know that all of us who were baptized into Christ Jesus were baptized into his death? We were therefore buried with him through baptism into death in order that, just as Christ was raised from the dead through the glory of the Father, we too may live a new life.
>
> If we have been united with him like this in his death, we will certainly also be united with him in his resurrection. For we know that our old self was crucified with him so that the body of sin might be done away with, that we should no longer be slaves to sin—because anyone who has died has been freed from sin.
>
> —Rom 6:1–7

You have to understand something about the Hebrew culture. A Hebrew was always part of a larger group, and life was one for all and all for one. What happened to the patriarch of the clan happened to you. You were united with him. If he suffered shame, so did you. If he won a victory, it was on your behalf. It would be as if you yourself had won.

In a similar but even more profound way, Christ is our new Patriarch or King. Our previous head was Adam (Rom. 5:12–21). His death was our own. All the good things we could possibly do were not enough to loose us from his legacy of condemnation. Only a new head, who demonstrated a new obedience and who died but could not be held down by death, could give us a death that leads to life.

What Jesus experienced, we too experience. If he is honored, we are honored. If he dies, we die. Therefore, the apostle Paul can say that we died. We died to our old master. We died to the reign of sin. We died to the way of life of the old kingdom. "I have been crucified with Christ and I no longer live, but Christ lives in me. The life I live in the body, I live by faith in the Son of God, who loved me and gave himself for me" (Gal. 2:20).

If you have a hard time looking forward with joy, look backward and see what has already happened. You can't die twice. If you have died with Christ, the second death has no power over you: "Blessed and holy are those who have part in the first resurrection. The second death has no power over them, but they will be priests of God and of Christ and will reign with him for a thousand years" (Rev. 20:6).

Not good enough for heaven? You're right. But notice how Satan keeps us in fear and how we can respond to him. "God is angry at you," he whispers. "His movie of your life isn't going to be pretty."

"You're right," we answer. "All disobedience against God deserves judgment, even death. And I certainly have been disobedient. But I already died. I can echo what the apostle Paul said, 'I have been crucified with Christ and I no longer live, but Christ lives in me.'"

> But we see Jesus, who was made a little lower than the angels, now crowned with glory and honor because he suffered death, so that by the grace of God he might taste death for everyone. . . .
>
> Since the children have flesh and blood, he too shared in their humanity so that by his death he might destroy him who holds the power of death—that is, the devil—and free those who all their lives were held in slavery by their fear of death.
>
> —HEB. 2:9, 14–15

Do you see it? We are back in the courtroom again. We have violated the law and stand condemned. But "the law has authority over a man only as long as he lives" (Rom. 7:1). All judgments are dropped if the accused dies. "For you died, and your life is now hidden with Christ in God" (Col. 3:3).

DYING FOR DUMMIES

Now let's make it practical. What difference does it make that you have already been crucified with Christ?

No condemnation. We are joined with Christ by faith, not by the quality of our works. And don't think that faith is a kind of work; it is resting in another when we can't save ourselves. It is stating to others that Jesus is your Lord and King. Once joined with Christ, we find that much more happened than we realize. In the same way that "I do" at the altar means much more than we understand at that moment, so everything changes when we put our faith in Jesus.

Do you feel like you aren't yet good enough? You have been united with Jesus. What is his is now your own, and he has given you his righteousness.

Do you fear the judgment of God? Jesus died for sin, and you already died with him. The law has no more power over you. The death you died with Jesus overshadows any future death. The judgment that fell on him overshadows any future judgment.

But do you still *feel* condemned? Don't forget that feelings can lie. They demand that they are right even when they aren't.

No shame. The real heart of having died is that there is no condemnation before God. If we have already died with Christ, then our worst vision of final judgment will be nothing in comparison. But the implications of our dying cannot be contained in our relationship with God alone. Such central spiritual matters touch everything in our lives, including our relationships. No longer do we have to protect our reputation. Instead, we can die to it and concern ourselves with more important matters, such as how to love others.

No longer do we have to be consumed with how we are treated. Dead people aren't concerned about personal glory.

No worries. Now let's look at the other things we have tried to hold onto, even after we have died with Christ. What do you have to lose? What is so important to you that you are self-protective or anxious? Cars, houses, jobs, IRAs, health, personal appearance, financial security? Our death has implications for all these.

We are stewards of our possessions. Contrary to the hopes of all the Pharaohs who stuffed their graves with enough gold to get them through eternity, we can't take our stuff with us.

Death has changed our relationship with everything in earthly life. We continue to appreciate health and prosperity when we have them, but they aren't the cherished possessions they once were.

What about spouses and children? Isn't it right and loving to be concerned about their health and physical safety? Absolutely. But when those fears come, we will never allow fear to have the last word. Instead we will say, "When I am afraid, I will trust in you. In God, whose word I praise, in God I trust; I will not be afraid. What can mortal man do to me?" (Ps. 56:3–4)

Can we say that we die to our children? Yes, in a sense, but it isn't exactly our children. We die to our notions that God doesn't care about them. We die to the fear that no one is in control. We die to our belief that God is not always good. We die to the grasping that says, "My children are mine and mine alone."

PUT TO DEATH

When we say we have died with Christ, it is shorthand for saying we have both died and risen to life with him. As we live with him, we no longer live for ourselves; we live for him who died for us (2 Cor. 5:15). This opens the door to the possibility of bold obedience.

What does this have to do with fear? Fear paralyzes. Sometimes you run away, at other times you freeze. But when you have died, you are bold. Nothing can be taken from you that is of any value. The things of greatest worth are assured us in Jesus Christ. The result? We are ready to do whatever God calls us to do.

> Now if we died with Christ, we believe that we will also live with him. For we know that since Christ was raised from the dead, he cannot die again; death no longer has mastery over him. The death he died, he died to sin once for all; but the life he lives, he lives to God.
>
> In the same way, count yourselves dead to sin but alive to God in Christ Jesus. Therefore do not let sin reign in your mortal body so that you obey its evil desires. Do not offer the parts of your body to sin, as instruments of wickedness, but rather offer yourselves to God, as those who have been brought from death to life; and offer the parts of your body to him as instruments of righteousness. For sin shall not be your master, because you are not under law, but under grace.
>
> —Rom. 6:8–14

If you have read *The Lord of the Rings* or seen the movies, you cannot forget Gimli, the surly yet lovable dwarf. With Frodo in grave danger, Aragorn suggests the diversionary tactic of attacking the enemy's front door, the Black Gate of Mordor. When Aragorn asks if his friends are willing to join him, Gimli, ever the man's man, immediately responds, "Certainty of death? Small chance of success? What are we waiting for?!"

When you erode the fear of death with the knowledge that you already died, you will find yourself moving toward a simple, bold obedience. It's as if fear needs to be replaced in our lives, and it is replaced with the simple question, What does my Father, the King, want me to do now?

Since, then, you have been raised with Christ, set your hearts on things above, where Christ is seated at the right hand of God. Set your minds on things above, not on earthly things. For you died, and your life is now hidden with Christ in God.

—COL. 3:1-3

"Things above"—that's something on which we can meditate. What are they? They certainly include the details of earthly life, but those details are now seen with the knowledge that God is with us and that he will give us manna tomorrow. As a result, there is a wholeheartedness in what we do. We aren't always compromised by our concerns about the future. We can give all our attention to the way our faith can express itself in love right now.

THE STING OF DEATH

No one can be indifferent in the face of death: it would be unnatural for human beings who were intended to live eternally with God. It brings heart-wrenching loss that isn't what God originally intended for people who love each other. But the real sting of death has been taken away.

"Where, O death, is your victory? Where, O death, is your sting?" The sting of death is sin, and the power of sin is the law. But thanks be to God! He gives us the victory through our Lord Jesus Christ.

Therefore, my dear brothers, stand firm. Let nothing move you. Always give yourselves fully to the work of the Lord, because you know that your labor in the Lord is not in vain.

—1 COR. 15:55-58

Take judgment out of death and it loses its fangs.

A PERSONAL RESPONSE

It is hard to grasp being dead *and* being alive. But it's true, and it may be one of our most powerful assaults against the fear of death and judgment. I find great hope when I begin to understand this reality. It can even bring an audible sigh of relief. Then, before the next breath, I notice the stirrings of freedom. The old shell of self-protection and self-preservation falls off—at least for a while—and my thoughts move toward the reckless, not in the sense of dangerous or foolish but in the sense of being less self-conscious and self-focused.

Lord, that's what I want—a bold obedience.

So what are we waiting for? We belong to another and we are on a mission.

GOD SPEAKS

peace be with you

IF WE still feel slow to really grasp what God says to fearful and anxious people, we can take heart. As he has already shown us in the Sermon on the Mount, when he exhorted us not to worry, God is patient and willing to walk slowly with us, all the while speaking even more persuasive words to our fearful hearts. What follows is not new, but it enhances everything that God has already said.

CHAPTER TWENTY-TWO

"I WILL BE WITH YOU"

LET'S SAY YOU still have lingering doubts. Does God really care? Past hurts still have a hold on you. You feel like you have been fooled once and you won't be fooled again, so this time you are going to trust yourself and try to control your world better than before. Or perhaps you simply believe that what God says is too good to be true. You feel unworthy of his care and protection. Life becomes a spiritual stalemate and no one is budging.

But God, of course, is moving toward you. When you doubt, he reveals more of himself. When you think he is too good to be true, he reveals that he is so good that he *must* be speaking the truth, because no one could make up anything so glorious.

He speaks about the cross. The cross of Christ proves his love and faithfulness. What more can he say than that? When you allow your own history of abuse or disappointment or betrayal to challenge the love of God, the cross continues to stand as the conclusive proof of his care. No, it doesn't answer all your questions, but the truth it conveys about God and his love is irrefutable. Your task is to open your eyes, remember that God's love is more sophisticated than you realize, and look for the goodness of the Lord. When you see it, tell someone.

If you believe that judgment *still* looms, then consider repentance. Not repentance for your many sins (most likely you have done that numerous times), but repentance for believing that God is like a human being. You are reasoning like this: if a human being knew your heart, why would he or she forgive you? You wouldn't forgive yourself. You certainly wouldn't *delight* in someone like yourself. If *you* wouldn't, why would God?

What you are forgetting is that when God calls himself holy, he is saying that he is not like people. His entire history of dealing with his people is a demonstration that he does the unexpected when it comes to mercy and grace. If God seems too good to be true, you are beginning to know him. He does not treat you the way a human being would. Instead, he wants his love to stand out in bold relief from the mediocrity of human relationships. He wants to be seen as incomparable.

Whatever has seemed extraordinary up to this point is now going to be intensified. If you think God has already said a lot to you and your worries, raise that by a power of ten. What follows will not add much that is new—all the basic themes were marked out when he gave manna—but it should *sound* new, like the difference between hearing a CD and sitting on the front row of a live concert. You know the songs but the live experience makes every song more memorable.

THE GOD WHO REPEATS HIMSELF

You know that God says "Do not be afraid" over and over again. His repetition is assuring and comforting when we listen closely, but repetition usually tends to be an occasion when we shut down and ignore what someone is saying. Parents tell teens to call after 10:30 P.M.; if it is the thousandth time, teens will roll their eyes, decide that their parents are overprotective, and be offended that their parents take them for fools who don't know the routine. In modern culture we want novelty. If you say the same thing in the same way, fewer and fewer people will listen.

The oral culture of Scripture, however, interpreted repetition in a different way. Important days in history were reenacted yearly. When you wanted to dramatize the importance of what you were saying, you repeated it. Only those things that were critical deserved repeating. The more it was repeated, the more important it was.

So don't think of Scripture's repetition in terms of "Take your vitamins." Think of it in terms of "I love you." If spouses say it once a year, you wonder if they really mean it. But if they say it every day and back it up with their actions, their partners are blessed by their love.

When God repeats himself, listen carefully. As a way to punctuate "Do not be afraid," God adds the critical reason why: "I will be with you." And he is happy to repeat himself.

THE HISTORY OF "I WILL BE WITH YOU"

God's assurance of his presence spans all Scripture. With Adam, he is not the distant, unapproachable God; he comes near. He walks with him and clothes him when Adam's sin reveals his own nakedness. With Noah, he promises to never again cut off all life from the earth, which is another way of saying that he will be with his creatures. He promises Abraham to be his God and the God of his offspring. By the time we get to Abraham's son Isaac, the connection between our fear and God's promise of his presence is well established. From here on out, "I will be with you" will become like a motto—a memorable saying—that will precede some of the most significant events of biblical history. When God says it, he evokes a flood of memories.

Isaac. Isaac was having a rough go of it. A famine forced him to be a nomad. He first went to Philistine country, which was not the most hospitable. After a falling out with the king, he was harassed by other shepherds who wanted pastureland for themselves. To force him out, these shepherds filled Isaac's wells with dirt. For a herdsman, this was the most perilous of times.

It was then that God assuaged Isaac's fears by saying that he would be with him.

"I am the God of your father Abraham. Do not be afraid, for I am with you; I will bless you and will increase the number of your descendants for the sake of my servant Abraham" (Gen. 26:24).

Already we find the basic outline of God's strategy: He allows his children to have their backs to the wall so that when deliverance comes, it will obviously be from God alone. Then he speaks words of comfort, promises his presence, asks for our allegiance, and reveals his deliverance. Immediately after God's comforting words to Isaac, Isaac responds in faith and erects an altar as a memorial of God's visitation. After he has a feast in the presence of his enemies, thus making peace, his servants find a new well.

Moses. Moses was a rare man who truly knew God. After the golden calf debacle, God told him to lead the people to another place and said that his angel would go with them. To a normal person, this would sound good. An angel is a representative of God and, since God was already angry with the people, this seemed like a safe alternative to the actual presence of God himself.

Yet Moses knew better. There was much to fear—a rebellious people, an angry God, an inhospitable wilderness. An angel would never do.

> Moses said to the LORD, "You have been telling me, 'Lead these people,' but you have not let me know whom you will send with me. You have said, 'I know you by name and you have found favor with me.' If you are pleased with me, teach me your ways so I may know you and continue to find favor with you. Remember that this nation is your people."

The LORD replied, "My Presence will go with you, and I will give you rest."

Then Moses said to him, "If your Presence does not go with us, do not send us up from here. How will anyone know that you are pleased with me and with your people unless you go with us? What else will distinguish me and your people from all the other people on the face of the earth?"

And the LORD said to Moses, "I will do the very thing you have asked, because I am pleased with you and I know you by name."

–Ex. 33:12–17

The only real treatment for fear was God's presence. Moses was willing to argue his point and God was pleased to give his presence.

Years later, at the end of Moses' final speech before his death, he offered the people the same comfort he himself had received. He wanted to end with the things that were most important: "Be strong and courageous. Do not be afraid or terrified because of them, for the LORD your God goes with you; he will never leave you nor forsake you" (Deut. 31:6).

The psalmists. The main criterion for psalmists was that they know God. As such, they were disciples of Moses, who knew that God would be present with his fearful people because he had promised to do so. That is why David wrote in Psalm 23:4, "Even though I walk through the valley of the shadow of death, I will fear no evil, for you are with me; your rod and your staff, they comfort me." In Psalm 118:6–7, the psalmist affirmed, "The LORD is with me; I will not be afraid. What can man do to me? The LORD is with me; he is my helper. I will look in triumph on my enemies."

Isaiah was not technically a psalmist, but his prophecies, with their glorious pictures of God written with beauty and elegance, made him an honorary member. After warning Israel and even predicting judgment, he always ended with hope because he knew God and his promises. His hope rested on God's faithfulness to his oath: He will not forsake his people. "But Zion said, 'The LORD has forsaken me, the Lord has forgotten me.' 'Can a mother forget the baby at her breast and have no compassion on the child she has borne? Though she may forget, I will not forget you!'" (Isa. 49:14–15).

Notice that Isaiah understands our tendency to compare God to people. Such a God will never comfort. Instead, Isaiah takes the closest of human relationships and says that God's faithfulness and presence is even more certain.

The apostle Paul and a poorly placed verse. "Do not be anxious about anything," wrote the apostle Paul, "but in everything, by prayer and petition, with thanksgiving, present your requests to God" (Phil. 4:6). He echoes the Sermon on the Mount but his passage is much more succinct and, frankly, seems somewhat sterile. In the Sermon on the Mount, Jesus surrounds his exhortation with the assurance that our Father in heaven sees us—we are in his presence. We would expect Paul to say something similar, but maybe you can't say everything in a short letter. Perhaps Paul just had time to rattle off a few staccato commands before he closed his letter.

Yet that doesn't seem like a satisfactory explanation. Relief from anxiety and the promise of God's presence are so intimately linked by this point, we are surprised that a reference to God's nearness wouldn't be automatic for the apostle. Look at the tradition he follows: "'But now be strong, O Zerubbabel,' declares the LORD. 'Be strong, O Joshua son of Jehozadak, the high priest. Be strong, all you people of the land,' declares the LORD, 'and work. For I am with you,' declares the LORD Almighty. 'This is what I covenanted with you when you came out of Egypt. And my Spirit remains among you. Do not fear'" (Hag. 2:4–5).

Then we discover that a poorly placed verse is what has thrown us off. Later organizers of Scripture bundled Paul's reference to God's presence with the preceding verse: "Let your gentleness be evident to all. The Lord is near" (Phil. 4:5).

There is the line we anticipated. By the time we get to Philippians we have biblical precedent to confidently insert God's presence into every scriptural encouragement not to be anxious, but this is too important to the apostle Paul to leave it to us to insert. For him and for us, it doesn't make any sense for God to tell us not to be anxious unless he also promises to be with us.

Jesus and the Spirit. Do you want to know what is important to someone? Listen to him pray. We have that opportunity with Jesus just before his crucifixion.

> "My prayer is not for them [the disciples] alone. I pray also for those who will believe in me through their message, that all of them may be one, Father, just as you are in me and I am in you. *May they also be in us* so that the world may believe that you have sent me. *I have given them the glory that you gave me,* that they may be one as we are one: *I in them and you in me.* May they be brought to complete unity to let the world know that you sent me and have loved them even as you have loved me.
>
> "Father, *I want those you have given me to be with me where I am,* and *to see my glory,* the glory you have given me because you loved me before the creation of the world."
>
> —JOHN 17:20–24, *author's emphasis*

It is very familiar now—still amazing but familiar. Jesus prayed that we would be in him and he in us. This is turbo-charged closeness. Jesus prayed that we would be in his presence, and then he went to the cross to make it happen.

Everything depends on this. Without his presence we cannot be like him; we cannot be empowered to contribute to a growing kingdom; we cannot know security or comfort. So he prays that we would be with him. In a relationship, presence is essential.

When Jesus prays that we would be with him, he is emphasizing that we will live in his presence forever. He is praying that our death would not separate us from him and his love. But we don't have to wait for such an intimate presence.

> "And I will ask the Father, and he will give you another Counselor to be with you forever—the Spirit of truth. The world cannot accept him, because it neither sees him nor knows him. But you know him, for he lives with you and will be in you. I will not leave you as orphans; I will come to you."
>
> —JOHN 14:16–18

The Spirit is the presence of Jesus to us.

Listen to prayers, and listen to final words. When a loved one is going away for a long time, you hang on every word as the time to leave gets closer. If you are the one leaving, your words pick up more and more gravity. Jesus' last words to us are, "And surely I am with you always, to the very end of the age" (Matt. 28:20).

A PERSONAL RESPONSE

Yes, when I am anxious I feel alone. I don't want to necessarily *feel* God's presence—my feelings are too unstable to serve as a barometer for something so important. Instead, I want to *believe* what God says in a way that no human threat could cause me to doubt that his name is Immanuel, God with us.

Do you notice a recurring theme? When emotions are strong, they want to tell us what is true. Everyone has experienced that. It happens every day. But the fact that this experience is common shouldn't numb us to the fact that it is a pivotal spiritual battle.

Who is in charge? God and what he says or me and how I feel?

CHAPTER TWENTY-THREE

"I PROMISE"

A TRUSTED FRIEND makes you an outrageously good offer: an all-expense paid trip to Hawaii, the car you always had your eyes on but knew you could never afford, front row seats at that sold-out event. Chances are you won't simply say, "Oh, thank you." Even as your hopes run high, you will be incredulous.

"Are you kidding?"

"No, I'm not kidding."

"Really?"

"Yes, really."

"No."

"Yes."

"Promise?"

"Yes, I promise."

"Do you swear?"

"I swear."

When telemarketers make offers that are too good to be true, you assume that's the case, ask for documentation, and read the fine print. You don't ask follow-up questions like, "Do you swear?" If they took a solemn oath that what they were saying was true, that would only make you more suspicious. But when a good friend makes such an offer, you ask questions, and each time you get an affirmative response, your smile gets a little broader. By the time you hear "I swear," there is nothing else to ask. You are certain that your friend really will do it, and you are throwing your arms around the person, alternately kissing and thanking him.

This is how God responds to our doubts. He repeats, "Do not be afraid," because he has given us good reason not to be afraid. But that is only the beginning. Although you would expect the King to speak in edicts and forbid questions, this is a King who actually invites us to voice our doubts. When we do, he will go so far as to make his word a public, legal oath that is witnessed by others. He uses the strongest language possible to assure us of his truthfulness and reliability.

When Jesus spoke things that would raise a few eyebrows, he began by saying, "Verily" or "Truly." In the Gospel of John, which is the Gospel that is especially interested in truth, witnesses, and accurate testimony, John records Jesus' words as "Verily, verily." Jesus emphasizes his truthfulness and faithfulness by saying it twice! In other words, Jesus is saying, "In contrast to the false promises, inaccurate prophecies, and empty words you have heard so often from your leaders, what I am about to say is true. I can be trusted. Yes, believe me, because I am the Truth."

Jesus is inviting careful legal scrutiny of his words. This is not empty rhetoric that is meant to flatter or temporarily appease and comfort. Instead, Jesus is placing himself in the line of the prophets who spoke the words of God. And these words are designed to speak meaningfully to fearful people.

THE COVENANT-MAKING GOD

You will not find in any religious record a story in which a god takes the initiative and binds himself to a legal agreement with human beings. The triune God, however, makes promises to fearful people, seals them with an oath, reminds us of them, and then makes more promises.

> Men swear by someone greater than themselves, and the oath confirms what is said and puts an end to all argument. Because God wanted to make the unchanging nature of his purpose very clear to the heirs of what was promised, he confirmed it with an oath. God did this so that, by two unchangeable things in which it is impossible for God to lie, we who have fled to take hold of the hope offered to us may be greatly encouraged.
>
> —Heb. 6:16–18

Noah. Noah was one of the first to witness this amazing display of grace. In the midst of rebellion on earth, God pursued Noah and his family and gave an oath that he would save them. "But I will establish my covenant with you, and you will enter the ark—you and your sons and your wife and your sons' wives with you" (Gen. 6:18). A covenant, in this case, is a promise that goes to the greatest lengths possible to assure its outcome. It would be analogous to "I swear on my mother's grave," or two boys who swap blood as a way to seal an oath. In court, people are put under oath and swear to tell the truth with their hand on a Bible. In the legal climate of the day, a covenant was an inviolable promise.

What is peculiar about God's covenant is that it doesn't benefit him. Some covenants were made between equals, in which case they were intended to establish fairness. Other covenants were made between a powerful country and a neighboring, less powerful country. If the more powerful king initiated the covenant, it would go something like this: "I won't annihilate you if you give me fifty percent of your crops, wives of my choosing, and all your young men for my army." A covenant was intended to make the rich richer. But God has nothing to gain.

When you are the one making all the promises and the other person keeps doubting you, at some point you want to forget it. You have nothing to lose; you are only trying to help the other person, and he or she keeps making it difficult. There are many such reasons why God shouldn't make covenants, but he did and he does.

After the flood, God made another covenant. The context was fear and worry. Noah and his family had just witnessed global catastrophe. What do you think would be going through their minds at the first sighting of a distant cloud? As a way to make his promise as comforting as possible, God made *another* covenant.

> "I now establish my covenant with you and with your descendants after you and with every living creature that was with you—the birds, the livestock and all the wild animals, all those that came out of the ark with you—every living creature on earth. I establish my covenant with you: Never again will all life be cut off by the waters of a flood; never again will there be a flood to destroy the earth."
>
> And God said, "This is the sign of the covenant I am making between me and you and every living creature with you, a covenant for all generations to come: I have set my rainbow in the clouds, and it will be the sign of the covenant between me and the earth. Whenever I bring clouds over the earth and the rainbow appears in the clouds, I will remember my covenant between me and you and all living creatures of every kind. Never again will the waters become a flood to destroy all life. Whenever the rainbow appears in the clouds, I will see it and remember the everlasting covenant between God and all living creatures of every kind on the earth."
>
> —Gen. 9:9–16

Abraham. Abraham was told to leave his family and travel to a new land. In the ancient Near East, this was not done. Abraham was forsaking an inheritance and a community. But during this most uncertain time, God made an oath to Abraham: "I will make you into a great nation and I will bless you; I will make your name great, and you will be a blessing. I will bless those who bless you, and whoever curses you I will curse; and all peoples on earth will be blessed through you" (Gen. 12:2–3).

God is under no compulsion to make a covenant. He receives no benefit from it. He is simply revealing who he is: the God who comes close, makes promises, and punctuates them with an oath when times are particularly uncertain.

When Abraham and Sarai were old and there was no human reason to think they would have children, God needed to say nothing at all. He had already made a promise that was legally binding. There was nothing new to say. But given Abraham's concerns about his age, God reaffirmed his covenant, this time in even more profound terms.

In an ancient version of "cross my heart and hope to die," God again promised both an heir and land. He swore on his own life and essentially said that he would bring judgment on himself if his word did not come to pass (Gen. 15).

When Abraham was ninety-nine God again confirmed the covenant. Uncertainty, of course, was the occasion. Abraham thought, *Maybe Ishmael could be the child of the promise*, because he did not see any way his wife would bear children. But God not only reaffirmed what he'd said before, he got more specific, saying that Isaac would be born within a year. He even allowed Abraham to participate in the covenant arrangement through his obedience and allegiance to God (Gen. 17). For a daily reminder, God renamed Sarai and she became Sarah, which indicated that she would be the mother of royalty.

Isaac's life was less eventful. He was given a wife and, without delay, he had two sons. He received both heirs and land. He could see them with his eyes.

20 year delay! see Gen. 25:20-21, 26

Without times of fear or uncertainty, there was no need for God to reaffirm his promises. But his son Jacob was another story. When Jacob essentially stole his older brother's rights as firstborn, he went on the run. The very first evening under the stars, God came to him and renewed his vows.

> I am the LORD, the God of your father Abraham and the God of Isaac. I will give you and your descendants the land on which you are lying. Your descendants will be like the dust of the earth, and you will spread out to the west and to the east, to the north and to the south. All peoples on earth will be blessed through you and your offspring. I am with you and will watch over you wherever you go, and I will bring you back to this land. I will not leave you until I have done what I have promised you.
>
> —GEN. 28:13–15

You could misinterpret other renewal times as God searching out good people to make a pact with them, but Jacob makes it clear that God takes the initiative toward all kinds of people, even usurpers and connivers like Jacob. God makes promises because that is what he does. It is an extension of his extravagant mercy and grace. It is not because he is recruiting the best of the best.

JESUS IS THE FINAL GUARANTEE

All roads in Scripture lead to Jesus. All the oaths God makes eventually have their guarantee and fulfillment in him (Heb. 7:22). He is the One who writes the last will and testament and willingly dies so that the promises can have their full effect. He is the High Priest who makes the final sacrifice for sin so that another sacrifice never has to be made. The sacrifice, of course, is himself. His blood puts an end to the sacrificial system and ushers in an ever-better series of promises.

"The time is coming," declares the LORD,
    "when I will make a new covenant
with the house of Israel
    and with the house of Judah.
It will not be like the covenant
    I made with their forefathers
when I took them by the hand
    to lead them out of Egypt,
because they broke my covenant,
    though I was a husband to them,"
    declares the LORD.
"This is the covenant I will make with the house of Israel
    after that time," declares the LORD.
"I will put my law in their minds
    and write it on their hearts.
I will be their God,
    and they will be my people.
No longer will a man teach his neighbor,
    or a man his brother, saying, 'Know the LORD,'
because they will all know me,
    from the least of them to the greatest,"
    declares the LORD.
"For I will forgive their wickedness
    and will remember their sins no more."

                —JER. 31:31–34

This is the covenant of peace that he secured by his own death. This is his assurance that he will never leave us (Ezek. 37:26–28).

All this is unprecedented. When someone makes a promise to you, it is often because he did something wrong.

"I promise, Mom, I swear, I will never again come in after curfew. Please let me go out tonight."

But God makes promises to us because *we* did something wrong, and we cannot believe we could ever receive such mercy and grace.

The apostle Paul put it this way: "For no matter how many promises God has made, they are 'Yes' in Christ" (2 Cor. 1:20). Forgiveness of sins is one of the premiere promises (Heb. 8:12).

A PERSONAL RESPONSE

Yes, Lord, I trust you. Please give me the gift of a deeper trust.

Do you notice that there is work involved in trust and faith? Since we are children in a relationship and not computer hard drives that receive periodic downloads, we are meant to hear, wrestle with, and respond to what God says. "Isn't that nice!" is not enough. With fear and anxiety a response is even more important because these emotions prefer to either run or freeze.

In any relationship, listening takes work.

CHAPTER TWENTY-FOUR

"PRAY"

PRAYER IS HARDER than we think. On the surface, it seems so easy that we gloss over it as a way out of worry. Who *can't* talk to God and say, "Help, I am afraid"? But our natural instinct is to trust in ourselves and take control when life is out of control. To actually stop and pray is contrary to our sense that we must *do* something—and do it quickly.

By contrast, there is Martin Luther's strategy. On especially busy, worrisome days, he woke up earlier to pray *more*. Meanwhile, the rest of us are having a fitful night's sleep, mulling over the answers we will be giving to our interrogators, waiting for first light so we can get up and get to work.

Prayer is counterintuitive. It is the opposite of what we would normally think or do. Therefore, we are compelled to call out, "Lord, teach us to pray" (Luke 11:1). Fear and anxiety are *always* occasions for us to mature as people who pray.

WHY PRAY?

"Cast all your anxiety on him because he cares for you" (1 Peter 5:7). Some people have scribbled their various worries on pieces of paper and then thrown them in the trash as a way to dramatize Peter's teaching. But don't miss the holiness that infuses Peter's words about God.

Peter is writing to people who are in real trouble. They have made a stand for Christ on the front lines of the battle against the kingdom of earth, and the war is raging. They have many reasons to worry. They have lost friends, jobs, and social status. They have seen brothers and sisters tortured and even martyred because of their faith in Christ. And then, of course, they have their own internal troubles within the church.

Through all these difficulties Peter exhorts Christians to be submissive and humble. Do good to those who are bad to you. Don't retaliate. Follow the example of Christ, who subverted the world order through his humble obedience in life and death.

Such humility before other people is possible only as we walk humbly before God. This is where we pick up the passage about casting our anxieties on the Lord: "Humble yourselves, therefore, under God's mighty hand, that he may lift you up in due time. Cast all your anxiety on him because he cares for you" (1 Peter 5:6–7).

God's mighty hand. Once again we find that anything related to "Do not worry" is surrounded by reasons why we don't have to worry—why we can cast our anxieties on God. In this case, Peter begins by reminding us that we are under God's mighty hand when our backs are against the wall.

Are images coming to your mind? God's mighty hand made its appearance in biblical history during the exodus. It was this mighty hand that delivered the people from Egypt.

But I know that the king of Egypt will not let you go unless a mighty hand compels him. So I will stretch out my hand and strike the Egyptians with all the wonders that I will perform among them.

—Ex. 3:19–20

Then the LORD said to Moses, "Now you will see what I will do to Pharaoh: Because of my mighty hand he will let them go; because of my mighty hand he will drive them out of his country."

—Ex. 6:1

Then Moses said to the people, "Commemorate this day, the day you came out of Egypt, out of the land of slavery, because the LORD brought you out of it with a mighty hand."

—Ex. 13:3

Peter is telling us that we are the new people of God, and God is taking us through the wilderness by way of his mighty hand. But it is different for us. Along with having the Spirit of God with us, we know how the story goes. We know that any mention of God's mighty hand means that there will be a mighty deliverance (cf. Deut. 9:26, 29; 26:8; Jer. 21:5; Ezek. 20:33–34; Luke 1:66; Acts 4:28; 11:21; 13:11). To humble ourselves before God means that we acknowledge his kingship and sovereign power. It means that we trust in him as the Deliverer. We pray, and we wait for him.

Cast your anxieties. One lesson we learn from the original wilderness experience is that the people never really called out to the Lord. In one sense they did; they spoke to him with contempt because of their grumbling, but that certainly wasn't a prayer. When they complained, it was either to no one in particular or to Moses and Aaron. "They do not cry out to me from their hearts but wail upon their beds" (Hos. 7:14) was God's indictment against them and many who followed.

So there is historical precedent against calling out to the Lord when we have trouble. Once again, we are reminded that prayer is not natural to us. Complaining and grumbling are, but not prayer. Yet along with this historical precedent is a growing tradition that gains ground every day: The people of the kingdom are calling out to the King. Peter is imploring us to be part of that tradition.

His teaching is familiar—don't worry, pray—but his imagery is unique. It is only used one other time in the New Testament, when the disciples cast or threw their cloaks on a donkey so Jesus could sit on it (Luke 19:35). The basic idea is that we are carrying burdens we were never intended to carry alone. Our natural tendency is to go it alone, or, if the load is too heavy, to call a friend to help. But Peter paints a different picture. In an act that could never have been conceived by a human being, the King comes and beseeches us to lay our burden on him.

Keep this in your mind: He is the God who comes to serve rather than be served (Matt. 20:28). Don't expect to understand it, because we have no analogy for this in all of human life, but believe it. There is nothing begrudging in his service. It is his choice, and he has sworn himself to it.

Just like Jesus' persuasive appeal not to worry, Peter is doing his best to persuade us to be a new people who call out to the Lord. Let Peter persuade you. He begins by exhorting us to know that our God is the Creator God. He holds history in his hand. He delivers with a mighty hand, the grandest display being the death and resurrection of Jesus Christ. That was the act that subdued enemy forces and conquered death itself. If he really did this, don't we see that his greatest act was a self-sacrificial act of service? In keeping with his character, he continues to serve; he invites us to cast our burdens on him as we would cast burdens on an ox. Granted, it isn't easy to say you need help. It is humbling—and that is the point. In one of the amazing paradoxes of the kingdom, when God takes our burdens and takes the position of a servant, he reveals our inability and his sufficiency. As such, he is exalted as the God of the mighty hand.

He cares. We know he cares. "Do not be afraid, little flock" (Luke 12:32). "Look at the birds of the air; they do not sow or reap or store away in barns, and yet your heavenly Father feeds them. Are you not much more valuable than they?" (Matt. 6:26). When it comes to anxiety, Scripture is happy to repeat this encouragement. And it is repeated because it is so hard for us to believe.

I know that there are many people who are willing to carry my burdens, but I don't immediately call them all when I have trouble. First I talk to my wife. I know that she cares. She has never once seemed sleepy or indifferent—well, maybe sleepy with very slow blinks—when I have expressed my concerns. She shares in them. She has even rebuked me when I have carried burdens and not shared them with her. Even if she can't do anything about my worries, it makes a huge difference to have her share them.

If it is this way with a spouse or good friend, how much more with God! He rebukes us when we don't speak of our burdens. He is delighted when we cast them on him. And he alone can do something about them.

Why would we ever be slow to speak with him? According to this passage, it is because of our pride. The passage is about humility, and casting our cares on the Lord is an expression of humility. Prayer is evidence of humility. Prayerlessness means that we neither believe him, which is pride, nor turn to him because we prefer to trust in ourselves.

Like everything else in the Christian life, all change and growth must travel first through Jesus Christ, and then through our response of humility before him.

HOW TO PRAY

We pray because God cares for us, but even the disciples, who certainly knew something about prayer, asked Jesus *how* to pray (Luke 11:1). Here is where prayer *really* goes against our instincts.

If the Christian community is in agreement on anything, it agrees that petitions are best kept for last. The best known acronym for prayer is ACTS: adoration, confession, thanksgiving, and supplication. It is devised to restrain us from making prayer a laundry list of requests. Throughout church history wise men and women have preached that prayer is more than petitions, and no doubt wise people will continue to preach it because we are so slow to learn.

The Lord's Prayer. They take their cue, of course, from Scripture: "When you pray, say: *'Father, hallowed be your name, your kingdom come.* Give us each day our daily bread. Forgive us our sins, for we also forgive everyone who sins against us. And lead us not into temptation'" (Luke 11:2–4, author's emphasis).

Jesus' template for prayer is clearly intended to be a basic outline. It is good to repeat it together on Sunday mornings, but we are filling in the details the rest of the week. The apostle Paul said that the only thing he preached was Christ and him crucified (1 Cor. 2:2), but he could preach for hours at a time without repeating himself. In a similar way, Jesus gave us this outline for prayer but his prayer time would typically last the entire night.

Our task is to be an expert in "hallowed be your name" and "your kingdom come." "Hallowed" means to be known and declared as holy. Our first desire is that God would be known as he truly is, the Holy One. Implicit in his name being hallowed is that his glory or fame would cover the earth.

This takes us out of ourselves immediately. Now our first concern is God's renown. Somehow, we want God's glory to be increasingly apparent through the church today. If you need specifics, keep your eyes peeled for the names God reveals to us. For example, we can pray that he would be known as the Mighty God, the Burden-Bearer, and the God who cares.

"Your kingdom come" overlaps with our desire for his fame and renown. It is not so much that we are praying that Jesus would return quickly, though such a prayer is certainly one of the ways we pray. Instead, it is for God's kingdom to continue its progress toward world dominion. The kingdom has already come and, as stewards of the kingdom for this generation, we want it to grow and flourish.

The kingdom of heaven is about everything Jesus taught: love for neighbors and even enemies, humility in judgment, not coveting, blessing rather than cursing, meekness, peacemaking, and, yes, trusting instead of worrying. It is a matter of "righteousness, peace and joy in the Holy Spirit" (Rom. 14:17).

Paul's prayers. If you read Paul's letters carefully, you will notice that he is always praying or asking for prayer. His letter to the Ephesians is best understood as an extended prayer with a few interruptions for some teaching. After the initial greetings, he writes, "I keep asking that the God of our Lord Jesus Christ, the glorious Father, may give you the Spirit of wisdom and revelation, so that you may know him better" (Eph. 1:17).

Paul prays that we would know God better. In other words, he wants God's name to be hallowed. The exaltation of his name can happen no other way.

Next, notice how he prays that the kingdom would come.

> I pray that out of his glorious riches he may strengthen you with power through his Spirit in your inner being, so that Christ may dwell in your hearts through faith. And I pray that you, being rooted and established in love, may have power, together with all the saints, to grasp how wide and long and high and deep is the love of Christ, and to know this love that surpasses knowledge—that you may be filled to the measure of all the fullness of God.
>
> Now to him who is able to do immeasurably more than all we ask or imagine, according to his power that is at work within us, to him be glory in the church and in Christ Jesus throughout all generations, for ever and ever! Amen.
>
> —Eph. 3:16–21

Paul prays that Christ would dwell richly in our hearts, thus transforming us into kingdom citizens. God's kingdom expands as Christ takes root in our heart and we become his imitators and followers.

His advice to anxious people on how to pray? "The Lord is near. Do not be anxious about anything, but in everything, by prayer and petition, with thanksgiving, present your requests to God" (Phil. 4:5–6). In contrast to the grumbling in the original wilderness story, we are to retell it in a way that honors the deliverance we have received. When you call out in your need, do it with thanksgiving. You can include those things you see with a naked eye, such as God's daily provision, but give thanks too for his gifts that transcend our daily needs. Thank him for his physical and spiritual care, his patience toward us, his unfailing love, his quickness to forgive, his nail-pierced hands and feet.

A PERSONAL RESPONSE

If I know that prayer isn't going to be easy, I am better prepared to deal with my excuses. For example, too often I will begin to pray, then gravitate to the things that worry me, start trying to solve them, realize I am not really praying, and then decide to attend to the urgent matters and pray later. When I know that prayer is not natural, I realize that I shouldn't wait for prayer to feel easy. If it seems hard, I am on the right path.

Now let's do some praying.

CHAPTER TWENTY-FIVE

BRING ON THE WORST

WHEN WE GET distracted during prayer, we need help. One strategy is to pray with other people. That includes flesh-and-blood friends as well as saints of the church who have left us their written prayers. Among those written prayers, the Psalms are the favorites.

You could open to any psalm at random and it would be edifying and relevant. Some, however, are more precise in the way they put a voice to your personal struggles. If you are familiar with fear, Psalm 46 is a surgical strike on the soul. And, considering how you would like to get in the habit of postponing requests until you have remembered who your God really is, this psalm is ideal because it doesn't even contain a request!

THE APOCALYPSE

The situation couldn't be more frightening. Don't think for a moment that the psalm doesn't quite understand your dire circumstances. Yeats' poem, "The Second Coming," comes to mind. "Things fall apart; the centre cannot hold;

Mere anarchy is loosed upon the world." It is as if the world is being un-created. But even in the midst of this terrifying scene, the psalmist begins with God.

> God is our refuge and strength,
>> an ever-present help in trouble.
> Therefore we will not fear, though the earth give way
>> and the mountains fall into the heart of the sea,
> though its waters roar and foam
>> and the mountains quake with their surging.
>
> —PSALM 46:1–3

Yes, the psalm is a stretch for us, not because of the potential brutality of the situation, but because of the psalmist's radical trust in God. So let it stretch you. Let the psalmist take you places you could never go on your own. Let him be your guide through perilous times. He, after all, is a person like you. The faith he had can be your own and more, because you live on the side of history where the Spirit of God has been poured out on you. The Spirit gives you the knowledge of God.

"God is our refuge and strength, an ever-present help in trouble." A good friend was in the hospital with surgical pain so severe he couldn't think, and he assumed he was going to die. The only words he could say were these words. That's what we are aiming for. We want these words to be automatic when trouble comes knocking.

What do they mean? That God can be found when we need him. Don't forget that he was found by Israelites who were not even looking. How much more will he be found by those who call out to him in their desperation.

Here is the challenge. When you call out, you might *feel* like he isn't present or easily found. That is the nature of pain. The worse it is, the more alone you feel. But this is a time when the words of God must override your feelings. There are times when we listen to our feelings and times when we don't. This is a time when we don't. Instead, whenever there is a clash between our sensory experience and the promises of God, the promises of God win. The one who says "Verily, verily" can be trusted. Call out and he will be found when you need him.

And you *will* need him. The scene in front of you is terrifying, especially if you have ever experienced or seen video of a hurricane. Swimming prowess is irrelevant in the face of roaring seas; Herculean strength is no match for falling mountains. But—if you can imagine this—the scene for the original readers was even worse. Their frame of reference was the great flood, when the seas ignored their boundary lines. The result was not a twenty-four-hour storm followed by clear skies; the result was the destruction of humanity with the exception of one family that was miraculously saved.

The psalmist is painting the worst of situations, and he is saying, "I'm ready. I have a refuge in the Creator, and his word is stronger than your brute force."

I AM WITH YOU

Worriers obsess over worst case scenarios, so here is an ideal occasion for obsession and "See, I told you so. The sky is, in fact, falling." Before you know it, skilled worriers have run with this description of chaos and elaborated on it in exquisite detail, but the psalmist interrupts the worrier's prophecies.

The psalmist knows that creation is no match for the Creator, so the heart of the psalm is a reflection on the place of God's presence. God's presence on Mt. Sinai and the Holy of Holies in the Jerusalem temple are what come to his mind. For us, our residence, the kingdom of heaven, is being pictured.

There is a river whose streams make glad the city of God,
    the holy place where the Most High dwells.
God is within her, she will not fall;

God will help her at break of day.
Nations are in uproar, kingdoms fall;
he lifts his voice, the earth melts.
The LORD Almighty is with us;
the God of Jacob is our fortress.

—PSALM 46:4–7

In contrast to destructive seas, irrigating streams make the city of God fruitful. In contrast with toppling mountains and nations, the city of God will never fall. While the chaos of creation and the power of nations are temporary, the kingdom of God is eternal.

The theme is familiar. Psalm 46 is speaking of the upheaval of creation, especially as expressed in the unjust power of nations. The New Testament uses similar language, but it says that God is our refuge when there is looming financial catastrophe.

Do not store up for yourselves treasures on earth, where moth and rust destroy, and where thieves break in and steal. But store up for yourselves treasures in heaven, where moth and rust do not destroy, and where thieves do not break in and steal. For where your treasure is, there your heart will be also.

—MATT. 6:19–21

God is also our refuge when we face physical catastrophe.

Therefore we do not lose heart. Though outwardly we are wasting away, yet inwardly we are being renewed day by day. For our light and momentary troubles are achieving for us an eternal glory that far outweighs them all. So we fix our eyes not on what is seen, but on what is unseen. For what is seen is temporary, but what is unseen is eternal. Now we know that if the earthly tent we live in is destroyed, we have a building from God, an eternal house in heaven, not built by human hands.

—2 COR. 4:16–5:1

How do we do such things? How do we live secure? It is no secret. We trust in Christ and live like the children we were created to be.

Since, then, you have been raised with Christ, set your hearts on things above, where Christ is seated at the right hand of God. Set your minds on things above, not on earthly things. . . . Put to death, therefore, whatever belongs to your earthly nature: sexual immorality, impurity, lust, evil desires and greed, which is idolatry.

—COL. 3:1–2, 5

Get the picture firmly in your mind. On one side you have the worrisome events. Go ahead and even exaggerate them, but don't spend too much time doing it. On the other side is an unshakable kingdom that makes all the commotion look like a tempest in a teapot, a de-clawed tabby up against the king of the jungle. And don't think that God is ignoring the commotion. As the ever-present help, he quickly comes to his people at the break of day, when battles are usually fought. Contrary to our feelings, he is already on the move. It's enough to make you break out into a chorus, "The LORD Almighty is with us; the God of Jacob is our fortress."

BEHOLD, YOU NATIONS

Throughout the Psalms you will notice that we don't keep our thoughts to ourselves. These are not simply private audiences with the King. After we have learned more about him, we proclaim his mighty works to the world.

This is exactly what we need as fearful people. Too often we settle for the simple knowledge of facts. Once we know the facts, we move on to other facts we hope will ease some of our anxiety. What we need is to know the facts, meditate on them, say amen to them, put our trust in the King, and then talk about it to others. Don't trust yourself if you just nod in agreement with the truth. There is a difference between nodding and speaking.

I recently taught a seminar that was thirty hours of classroom teaching in five days. During breaks, students would ask if I was tired. I replied that it is a lot easier—and more blessed—to speak for a week than to listen. For better or worse, they seemed to believe me, especially by Friday.

The reason I can get energized over the course of a week is the same reason preachers like to preach: When I speak the truth, I am built up in my faith. I demonstrate my certainty in the promises of God. In short, I see that I really believe what God says.

> Come and see the works of the LORD,
>> the desolations he has brought on the earth.
> He makes wars cease to the ends of the earth;
>> he breaks the bow and shatters the spear,
>> he burns the shields with fire.
> "Be still, and know that I am God;
>> I will be exalted among the nations,
>> I will be exalted in the earth."
> The LORD Almighty is with us;
>> the God of Jacob is our fortress.
>
> —PSALM 46:8–11

There is nothing tame about this proclamation. God is the Divine Warrior whose power and authority are absolute. Neither the unleashed creation nor the terrible destructive force of hostile nations can compare to the desolation he brings on those who oppose him and his kingdom.

His authoritative command, "Be still," was echoed by Jesus when he issued an edict to the raging seas. "He got up, rebuked the wind and said to the waves, 'Quiet! Be still!' Then the wind died down and it was completely calm" (Mark 4:39). When God says stop, the nations will stop.

The eyes of the universe will then be glued to the Lord. He will be the Redeemer and Deliverer or he will be the Judge of those who oppose him. Either way, he will be exalted and he will bring peace.

Anxieties and fears need an alternative. They need something bigger and better that will make the provoking events seem insignificant in comparison. Here is something bigger. Here is a conclusion that leads us into the fear of the Lord. While it might look like the other forces are winning, they are not. God will be exalted, and we will be amazed.

With that, the psalmist concludes by repeating the chorus, "The LORD Almighty is with us; the God of Jacob is our fortress." But it isn't a mere repetition. Each stanza has given us more reason to trust God. The second stanza, where we were brought into the city of God, taught us that God is indeed our fortress. The last stanza proclaimed that he is the Lord Almighty. He leaves us at peace in his citadel while he goes out conquering.

A PERSONAL RESPONSE

I have to keep remembering that this psalm is both present and future. I wait for future, complete deliverance, but the kingdom *has* come with Jesus Christ. The Divine Warrior is Jesus; and he reigns now. No doubt there are perils ahead, as there were for the Israelites when they entered the land promised to them. But the Lord leads into battle, and at times he wins battles without our participation.

> Therefore, since we are receiving a kingdom that cannot be shaken, let us be thankful, and so worship God acceptably with reverence and awe, for our "God is a consuming fire."
>
> —HEB. 12:28–29

CHAPTER TWENTY-SIX

"PEACE BE WITH YOU"

EVERYONE KNOWS at least one Hebrew word, the word *shalom*. Like the Hawaiian word *aloha*, you hear it in greetings, partings, and blessings. It is usually translated as *peace*, but it means much more.

Jammed into this one word is everything good.

peace	harmony	contentment
freedom	completeness	well-being
prosperity	health	safety
love		

Nothing that blesses a life is missing. This is shalom. This has been our quest.

Ma sh'lom'cha is a Hebrew equivalent of the English "How are you?" Literally translated it asks, "What is your peace or well-being?"

"Grace and peace to you" begins nearly every letter in the New Testament.

"Now may the Lord of peace himself give you peace at all times and in every way. The Lord be with all of you" (2 Thess. 3:16). This is what the apostle Paul prays. This is what we need.

This peace—shalom—is the polar opposite of fear and anxiety. We know we *don't* want fear, worry, and anxiety—at least the unnecessary ones. But that goal is so elusive that we rarely consider what it is we really *want*. What we want is shalom. We want everything to be right in the world.

Try to be anxious when there is real shalom. You can't do it. You sleep like a baby. Everything is right. What is there to worry about? Children are safe, loved ones are healthy, racism is a fleeting memory, judges are just, and there are no wars or economic threats. All is well.

Believe it or not, peace is the way God intended it. Danger and reasons for worry are intrusions. Shalom was God's original intent for all creation. He is, after all, the God of peace (Rom. 15:33). Jesus is the Prince of Peace, and he is remaking all things in the direction of shalom. How could it be any other way, given that all creation is designed to reflect him?

THE BREACH OF SHALOM

You know the story. There were no threats in Eden. There was peace among animals, peace between humans, and peace with God. There was even peace within the actual garden as weeds didn't threaten to choke out or overrun God's plantings. The breach in shalom occurred when we disobeyed God.

We are accustomed to thinking about a spiritual sector to our lives. We know we are spiritual beings, but we prefer to keep a "balance," since we are also physical, emotional, and so on. But if "spiritual" is shorthand for our relationship with God, it is not a component of life; it is the very essence of life. Everything is connected to our relationship with God. If you disagree, you have discovered why you are just a bit cantankerous as you read this book.

The connection between our relationship with God and everything else is especially apparent in Genesis, when humans breached the peace God had established in Eden. Everything was as it should be until human beings disobeyed God. The fracture in that relationship changed everything. The damage could not be contained, but it affected everything, first our relationship with each other, then our relationship with animals and our work.

It all seems a bit cataclysmic for just a piece of fruit. But think about it in terms of kingdom allegiances. In that one act of disobedience, Adam and Eve decided to investigate the other possibilities. They wanted to try life apart from God in a kingdom where they could ascend one more rung. They didn't think it through, but if asked, they might have assumed that everything would be the same except for a bit more autonomy. But there is no life apart from the Author of life. There is no peace apart from the Prince of Peace. Opt for another kingdom and everything is scented with death.

The breach in shalom came as a result of our sin.

MEMORIES AND REMINDERS OF SHALOM

Having been created for the kingdom of God, our desire for peace is innate. When we notice relics of it, we welcome them. We appreciate news stories of noble self-sacrifice. We feel blessed with good health, especially after we have experienced sickness. It perks up our entire day if a clerk says we overpaid for an item that just went on sale. A good love story appeals to us all, even to children who complain about the kissing scenes. We catch ourselves staring at our kids when they are playing well together. We are amazed when a boss thinks about the needs of employees over her own. We will always stop for beauty, in whatever form it takes.

These arouse old memories of how God intended it to be. It is true that we can become accustomed to everything being out of kilter. Children can come to believe that parental violence or abusive discipline is normal, but they still have hope for something else. We recognize the vestiges of what is right in our world, and we intuitively know when something isn't. We might not know how to make it right, but we know the things that disrupt peace.

Of course, what is wrong is rarely if ever ourselves or our fault. It is always our government, our bosses, our parents, our spouses, or our genetic code. Rarely does anyone answer the question, "What is wrong with the world?" with "I am."

That, in fact, is part of the disruption of God's peace: We blame-shift, judge, and find fault in others while we pardon ourselves. When we see such arrogant behavior in others, we are outraged. But in ourselves, it somehow seems like we are doing justice. We have been wronged and we are trying to make it right, by yelling, belittling, ignoring—by hating. Justice is essential to peace, and such biased judgments wreak havoc on our modern world.

When we are quick to judge others rather than look at our own hearts, we are electing to live outside of the kingdom of heaven, and outside the kingdom there are only false hopes of peace. Apart from repentance, any dabbling in the kingdom of the earth constitutes treason against God and bondage to Satan.

What does this have to do with our own fears and worries? When we trace the history of fear, it goes back to humankind's disobedience against God. All fear dates back to that moment. The sin-fear connection is inescapable. Therefore, when confronted with worries and fears, we should encourage our instincts to look at our own sin so that we can be people who make peace rather than break it.

THE RESTORATION OF SHALOM

Before thinking more specifically about how to be peacemakers, we must know that such things are possible. It is always a good idea to contribute to God's peace in whatever way we can, but if we live in an era where it simply won't make any difference, we will be less motivated to pursue God and his peace.

The peace of God, however, is on the move. Never underestimate what happened when Jesus died on a cross.

During his earthly ministry, Jesus clearly thought something was wrong. He confronted a wicked and adulterous generation who did not have ears to hear his message of the kingdom (Matt. 16:4). Other prophets confronted specific issues, such as Baal worship and the belief that the temple itself might save them rather than the Lord. Jesus cut to the chase. Israel and the entire world had been taken hostage by the Evil One.

The stories of Scripture are about conflict and wars. The exodus, Joshua's battle for the Promised Land, the Hebrew judges' stand against idolatrous nations—there was no peace. The war was even waged *within* Israel as she always had her share of renegades who didn't follow the Lord.

All this says that the true God was not ruling the world in the way he intended. An alien power held sway, and that power was more enduring than Baal or Rome. If the kingdom of heaven was going to come with power, the old order would have to be terminated. This was the essence of Jesus' mission.

Not surprisingly, Jesus' ministry began with a confrontation with Satan. Where Israel had failed in the wilderness, being reluctant kingdom representatives and pursuing other gods instead, Jesus went into the wilderness on Israel's behalf and withstood satanic temptations (Matt. 4; Luke 4). Armed with humility and trust in the Father, Jesus placed the stake into Satan's heart. The liberation had begun.

> He [Jesus] went to Nazareth, where he had been brought up, and on the Sabbath day he went into the synagogue, as was his custom. And he stood up to read. The scroll of the prophet Isaiah was handed to him. Unrolling it, he found the place where it is written:
>
> "The Spirit of the Lord is on me,
>   because he has anointed me
>   to preach good news to the poor.

He has sent me to proclaim freedom for the prisoners
and recovery of sight for the blind,
to release the oppressed,
to proclaim the year of the Lord's favor."

Then he rolled up the scroll, gave it back to the attendant and sat down. The eyes of everyone in the synagogue were fastened on him, and he began by saying to them, "Today this scripture is fulfilled in your hearing."

—LUKE 4:16–21

And off the kingdom went. When there is a reigning kingdom that enslaves, there is no peace without war. "'Do not suppose that I have come to bring peace to the earth. I did not come to bring peace, but a sword'" (Matt. 10:34). Jesus waged war successfully by going after the very heart of the dark kingdom, Satan himself.

He sent out seventy-two to spread the news about his own kingdom. The first thing they said when they returned was, "Lord, even the demons submit to us in your name" (Luke 10:17). To which Jesus replied, "I saw Satan fall like lightning from heaven."

Notice how he frames his ministry in terms of this confrontation.

Then they brought him a demon-possessed man who was blind and mute, and Jesus healed him, so that he could both talk and see. All the people were astonished and said, "Could this be the Son of David?"

But when the Pharisees heard this, they said, "It is only by Beelzebub, the prince of demons, that this fellow drives out demons."

Jesus knew their thoughts and said to them, "Every kingdom divided against itself will be ruined, and every city or household divided against itself will not stand. If Satan drives out Satan, he is divided against himself. How then can his kingdom stand? And if I drive out demons by Beelzebub, by whom do your people drive them out? So then, they will be your judges. But if I drive out demons by the Spirit of God, then the kingdom of God has come upon you."

—MATT. 12:22–28

The battle lines are becoming clear. If you are not joining in the battle, if you sit idly by, you have aligned with the enemy. The problem is that *everyone* seemed to be aligning with the enemy. The Pharisees had the highest profile in this group, but even the disciples themselves were ambivalent. Contrary to the true ethos of the kingdom, they were anticipating actual physical thrones and jostled for the highest position (Matt. 20:20–28). Peter tried to dissuade Jesus from his mission, thus falling in line with the Satan-inspired tempters and hindrances (Matt. 16:23). Before the crucifixion they scattered (Mark 14).

The kingdom is coming with power, there is no doubt, but it is an odd kingdom that includes, at most, a few women and a person or two who had been healed. Such a kingdom is not very glorious. It also doesn't seem to fit the promises that the kingdom would overflow the boundaries of Israel and bless the entire world. So a wise student of Scripture looks for more.

All those promises meet at the cross. All the kingdom proclamations and acts converged at this liberating event. Yes, there would be peace, but it would be hard-won.

> He was pierced for our transgressions,
>   he was crushed for our iniquities;
> the punishment that brought us peace was upon him,
>   and by his wounds we are healed.
>
> —ISA. 53:5

Things were not exactly as they seemed. What looked like defeat was actually the place where righteousness and peace kissed (Ps. 85:10).

But now in Christ Jesus you who once were far away have been brought near through the blood of Christ. For he himself is our peace, who has made the two one and has destroyed the barrier, the dividing wall of hostility, by abolishing in his flesh the law with its commandments and regulations. His purpose was to create in himself one new man out of the two, thus making peace, and in this one body to reconcile both of them to God through the cross, by which he put to death their hostility. He came and preached peace to you who were far away and peace to those who were near. For through him we both have access to the Father by one Spirit.

—EPH. 2:13–18

To ensure that his people would not live in fear and go back to their idols as a result, this liberating event was accompanied by the giving of the Spirit. Unlike most coronations where the new king is given tribute, Jesus *gave* gifts to commemorate his ascension to the throne. The Spirit guaranteed that the King's new promises would be fulfilled.

Prominent among these promises was the forgiveness of sins. This is the first of the many other blessings we have in Christ. Without forgiveness of sins, there can be no peace in our relationship with God, and when there is no peace with God, we will have no peace. If you are finding peace elusive, either you still don't believe you are forgiven or you don't really care that you are. If you know that sin is your most profound problem, more critical than anything else that worries you, you will know a resolute peace.

Sin and guilt are where we are most susceptible to Satan's accusations. Without Christ, we have no defense against his accusations that we are guilty. But at the cross the Accuser stands accused. Part of the Spirit's mission is to assure us that Satan's condemnation is sure (John 16:11).

Can you see the possibilities for peace? No more imprisonment, no more guilt, and a God-given power to make peace in the name of Jesus.

A PERSONAL RESPONSE

Peace is possible. Even more, it is promised. I just have to keep remembering that peace can't be found in the world around me. Jesus himself is our peace (Eph. 2:14).

Do you sense yourself yearning to be an activist? I do. With the battle clearly portrayed, I am drawn away from my worries by a grand purpose. I want to be an activist who participates in the reign of the Prince of Peace.

CHAPTER TWENTY-SEVEN

PEACE FOR PEACEMAKERS

GOD'S PEACE IS on the move. All the cherished passages of Scripture have found their fulfillment in Jesus. He proclaimed "freedom for the prisoners and recovery of sight for the blind, to release the oppressed, to proclaim the year of the Lord's favor" (Luke 4:18–19). The peace is fundamentally found in our relationship with God, but peace with God affects everything. It is the harbinger of peace even within creation itself.

A shoot will come up from the stump of Jesse . . . .
He will not judge by what he sees with his eyes,
    or decide by what he hears with his ears;
but with righteousness he will judge the needy,
    with justice he will give decisions for the poor of the earth.
He will strike the earth with the rod of his mouth;
    with the breath of his lips he will slay the wicked. . . .
The wolf will live with the lamb,
    the leopard will lie down with the goat,

the calf and the lion and the yearling together;
  and a little child will lead them.
The cow will feed with the bear,
  their young will lie down together,
  and the lion will eat straw like the ox.
The infant will play near the hole of the cobra,
  and the young child put his hand into the viper's nest.
They will neither harm nor destroy
  on all my holy mountain,
for the earth will be full of the knowledge of the Lord
  as the waters cover the sea.

—Isa. 11:1, 3-4, 6-9

Lions and lambs—the era has already begun. This metaphoric language finds its fulfillment in the strong caring for the weak rather than oppressing them. Leaders have been wolves throughout history, and the predominant crime of humanity has been its oppression of weak and helpless lambs. The kingdom of heaven will bring an end to such oppression. It will come gradually, but it will certainly come.

The cross ushered in a new era of peace. This peace doesn't come all at once. God's strategy is to allow his people to participate with him in his reign. While he certainly could have concluded history with his death and resurrection, he does something even better by allowing us to contribute to his unfolding plan for peace.

PEACEMAKERS KNOW PEACE

For worriers and fearful people, the message is this: If you want peace, you must pursue peace. As you start to understand how the kingdom works, the connection makes sense. For example, the Sermon on the Mount, the most concise sermon for kingdom living, includes this hard saying: "For if you forgive men when they sin against you, your heavenly Father will also forgive you. But if you do not forgive men their sins, your Father will not forgive your sins" (Matt. 6:14–15).

We know that our forgiveness is fully dependent on God's mercy, but once we have tasted forgiveness we too will forgive. If we are reluctant forgivers, we simply do not know God's forgiveness. In a similar way, if we have known peace, we will be peacemakers. But there is more. There is a feedback loop in the kingdom. When we respond to God's grace by making peace with others, he gives us more peace. Do you want to know forgiveness more deeply? Study the character of God *and* practice forgiving others. Do you want to know peace? Study the Peace-giver *and* make peace. Then he will give you even more.

Let's say you are not reconciled with someone. If it is someone close to you—a neighbor, family member, person from church—you will have daily reminders of the fractured relationship and you will not have peace. Even if the unsettled relationship is with someone you haven't seen for years, you can see how that would disrupt peace. You would live with the sense that something isn't right. Maybe you wouldn't locate the problem in the broken relationship but you would still notice that there was a breach in shalom. There is a direct connection between broken relationships and a general uneasiness in life.

JESUS THE PEACEMAKER

King Jesus inaugurated the reign of peace. By his own self-sacrifice he conquered the powers that held us in bondage and fear. Jesus is the only reason we can talk about eroding fear and worry in our lives. The cross was where Jesus bore the penalty for sin, which included a violent breach in his unity with the Father, so we would no longer have to experience that separation and its attending anxieties.

There are some ways in which we cannot imitate Jesus Christ. Specifically, we are not righteous and are not called to bear the sin of others. Such a sacrifice would be unacceptable before God. But the disciples had a very clear understanding that there are many ways we can and must imitate Jesus. This is what disciples did with teachers, children did with fathers (Matt. 5:45), and, in the case of Jesus, kingdom citizens did with the King. We are called to follow the One who made us alive and liberated us from darkness. One of the most obvious ways we follow him is by seeking peace and unity, as much as we are able, in all our relationships.

Jesus has determined that the kingdom would advance in a revolutionary manner. We would turn the other cheek, go the extra mile, love enemies, love brothers and sisters deeply from the heart, and do the impossible—"being like-minded, having the same love, being one in spirit and purpose" (Phil. 2:2). This unity is so essential to the kingdom that Jesus prays for it with the knowledge that unity will be the living proof that he is the Messiah sent from God. He prayed, "May they be brought to complete unity to let the world know that you sent me and have loved them even as you have loved me" (John 17:23).

FOLLOW THE PEACEMAKER

So scan your relational terrain. Where is there disruption of peace? Remember, only peacemakers know peace.

Peace with those you have wronged. Start by considering people you have wronged and with whom you have never really reconciled. Whom do you avoid because you have damaged the relationship? Who might have something against you?

> Therefore, if you are offering your gift at the altar and there remember that your brother has something against you, leave your gift there in front of the altar. First go and be reconciled to your brother; then come and offer your gift.
>
> —Matt 5:23–24

It isn't easy sorting out the details of reconciliation. You will probably need the wisdom of others. If the list is long, you will need this wisdom all the more. Note, however, the urgency in Jesus' teaching. Reconciliation is a high priority in the kingdom. It announces that we have been reconciled to Christ, and it announces the reign of Jesus Christ while it invites people to live under that reign.

How many times in your life have people come to you and asked forgiveness? The number is probably zero. If someone has asked, no doubt you remember the occasion. It gave you an inkling of glory. You saw how life in the kingdom is the result of Jesus' covenant of peace with us (Ezek. 34:25). This is the opportunity you now have with others.

Peace with those who have wronged you. We have all wronged others, and we have all been wronged *by* others. After you have seen your own relational sins in high definition, you are authorized to consider those who have wronged you (Matt. 7:3–5). Once again, seek wise counsel on this: There might be some people you confront in love while you cover in love the sins of others. As a general rule, the closer the relationship, the more you lean toward speaking to the person.

Peace by pursuing unity in the church. With personal relationships made right, we turn our eyes to the church. We take peace out of the personal and psychological realm and into the ecclesiastical. Typically we think of peace as something within us more than around us, but Scripture makes both equally important. If we want to be peacemakers, we will go public. Unity is our goal.

Negatively, we shun factions, a party spirit (1 Cor. 3:4) and pride that ignores the poor (1 Cor. 11:20–21). We don't allow our freedom to become a stumbling block to others (1 Cor. 8:9–11). Positively, we value the gifts of others (Eph. 4:11–13). We pursue peace and unity on a small scale within our homes (Eph. 5:21–6:3), on a larger scale within the church (Eph. 2:19–22), and on an even larger scale in the world around us (Eph. 6:5–9).

His purpose was to create in himself one new man out of the two, thus making peace, and in this one body to reconcile both of them to God through the cross, by which he put to death their hostility.

—EPH. 2:15–16

Are we avoiding gossip and slander? What opportunities do we have to enhance unity in the church? Are we praying for peace and unity? Are we encouraging reconciliation when we see fractures?

This is the prominent way we do battle in the kingdom. Satan is the true anti-Christ, so it isn't surprising that he targets Christian unity (Eph. 4:26–27). Conversely, we put the kingdom of God on display in the simple act of living in harmony with those who aren't replicas of ourselves. In the New Testament church, the two groups on display were the Jews and Gentiles. If the gospel of peace brings unity to them, it can certainly bring unity to our own church—and everyone is watching.

His intent was that now, through the church, the manifold wisdom of God should be made known to the rulers and authorities in the heavenly realms, according to his eternal purpose which he accomplished in Christ Jesus our Lord.

—EPH. 3:10–11

Peace by doing peace and justice. There is one more place to consider. As we make personal relationships right and seek unity in the church, we also turn our eyes to the world. All people, after all, are created in the image of God, and God shows his grace to believer and unbeliever. Injustice is our target.

Justice and peace are intimate companions. The one implies the other. If there is justice, you will find people at peace. If there is peace, you will find people who act justly. Both are included in shalom.

In the Old Testament, especially in the book of Isaiah, the people were under the judgment of God because they had violated his peace through their many injustices. "Take your evil deeds out of my sight!" said the Lord. "Stop doing wrong, learn to do right! Seek justice, encourage the oppressed. Defend the cause of the fatherless, plead the case of the widow" (Isa. 1:16–17). The people, however, were concerned about their own kingdoms more than God's. The result: "'There is no peace,' says the LORD, 'for the wicked'" (Isa. 48:22).

Where are the weak being neglected in your church, community, or nation? Where are the strong using their power for their own advantage? Where is corruption keeping funds away from those who need them?

Fearful people don't tend to be activists. They would prefer not to stand out or come under the scrutiny of others. But life in the kingdom changes our natural bents. One woman took her young son into a drugstore to get a prescription filled. On their way to the counter, they had to pass a magazine rack stuffed with soft porn and barely covered hard porn. The next day, with someone else watching her children, the woman went back to the store, letter in hand, and graciously presented her concerns to the manager. The manager spoke that day with the store supervisor and had the material taken from the shelves.

Some people give money to rescue missions and pregnancy services. Some keep their eyes open for any group pursuing racial reconciliation. Others simply ask for prayer and advice from others on how to think wisely about justice.

> He has showed you, O man, what is good.
> And what does the LORD require of you?
> To act justly and to love mercy
> and to walk humbly with your God.
> —MICAH 6:8

A PERSONAL RESPONSE

"Great peace have they who love your law, and nothing can make them stumble" (Ps. 119:165). The goal is not the alleviation of anxiety so much as it is the pursuit of God's purposes. If God's ways mean an increase in fear and anxiety, so be it, but, of course, the opposite is true. As we apply the gospel of peace, we will know peace.

CHAPTER TWENTY-EIGHT

YESTERDAY AND TODAY

YOU SEE THE mountain you committed yourself to climb and it seems utterly impossible. You can't imagine how you will get to the top. But when you get to the base, you keep your eyes on the trail. When you are thinking about your next step, the trip isn't as hard as you thought.

That's what we are aiming for. Like a horse with blinders, we are seeing as far as the next step. Like a person with a lamp in the night, we are looking at the light on the next step rather than the darkness around us.

We honor God when we believe what he says. He says that *he* will worry about tomorrow—he cares for us—so we can focus on the work of the kingdom now. Manna will be there when we need it. Right now there is work to be done.

THE BURDEN OF YESTERDAY

But what if you already tried to climb the mountain and failed? Even worse, what if that mountain was the one where your climbing companion slipped and fell to his death?

What if you had a painful encounter with a dentist? If you had a number of good visits prior to your painful one, you might get a little nervous the next time but you would hardly even notice. However, if you had no prior acquaintance with dentists and your maiden voyage was painful, then "every" visit to the dentist has been bad. You will only go back again kicking and screaming, inebriated, or anesthetized.

A young girl is attacked by a dog. If she is able to fend off the dog herself, she probably won't avoid all dogs in the future. But if the dog is pulled off her, she is more likely to have longer-term fears. And what if the fears spread to the point where she is afraid of *any* animal, or any open space where something unpredictable could happen to her?

Women are more prone to panic attacks than men, and those who can stay in their house for work are more prone to them than those who leave the house every day.[1] Why women? No one really knows, but women certainly are more vulnerable than men to being overpowered, controlled, and oppressed. Why those who don't have to leave the house? Fears tend to lose their grip when people face them. As Emmi Bonhoeffer states, "From the very moment one feels called to act is born the strength to bear whatever horror one will feel or see. In some inexplicable way, terror loses its overwhelming power when it becomes a task that must be faced."[2] Conversely, when we experience past difficulties as uncontrollable and unpredictable, we are more likely to carry and accumulate fears and worries.

Small steps. If we knew the details about our pasts and were creative in making links between the past and the present, we could probably find *some* inciting event for our present state of high alert. When we find one, at least we realize that there is a logic to our fears. But making a connection, accurate or not, doesn't eliminate the fear. Only faith can loosen our fears and worries—faith in the One who is in control and will give us grace when we need it.

What does this have to do with the girl who is afraid of dogs and is rapidly becoming agoraphobic?

- The wisdom of other dog handlers can teach her how to avoid dangerous dogs and what to do if one is loose.
- Those strategies in themselves, however, will not guarantee safety. Fear relates to God and our relationship with him. This is the young girl's opportunity to learn that we live by trusting God. Her struggle will be that God doesn't promise to spare us the hardships of life. However, he does promise to be with us and give us the courage to go through difficult times.
- The process of change—also called sanctification—is gradual and progressive. Therefore, the goal is not to arrange an immediate encounter with the local German shepherd. Instead, parents can arrange much less intense encounters and gradually build up to the more fearful ones. *desensitization*
- The young girl's calling from God today can outweigh the fears of yesterday.

WHAT IS YOUR CALLING?

No matter where we start, we always get to today.

Steve would certainly fit the description of someone with obsessive-compulsive disorder. He could get stuck on anything. Should he date someone? Which church should he attend while he was at college? What major? He was plagued with questions about his salvation. There were no obvious connections to specific incidents in his past; from birth he just seemed to be a scrupulous, rule-oriented person. Like any natural tendency, there was something good about this, but Steve also trusted rules to ensure stability in his world.

His family and friends offered him wonderful counsel that consistently led him back to the grace of God in the gospel. Steve himself was the one who suggested that he was trusting in rules rather than in God. This, no doubt, was the foundation for his growth. But if you asked him what had been the most helpful tool, he would say, "What does God call me to right now?"

In other words, instead of living in the future, paralyzed with indecision, Steve started to open his eyes to the things that were right in front of him. Typically, that meant homework, doing his wash, listening to his roommate, or taking a break and playing basketball with some friends.

His motto? God will take care of the future; what is my calling now?

Why did he talk about calling? Because anything short of that was not enough to rouse him from his obsessive groove.

When you hear someone talk about calling in church circles, that person is usually a candidate for professional ministry. He was called to be a pastor. He has a clear sense that this is God's word to him, and to do anything else would be to disobey God. When used in this sense, *calling* fits the life of *every* Christian. It reminds us that everything we do as servants of Christ is because God calls us to it.

Steve is in good company. For years Elisabeth Elliot has exhorted us to "Trust God and do the next thing" when we are feeling overwhelmed and paralyzed. "Do the next thing" for Mrs. Elliot usually refers to ordinary steps of obedience regarding the tasks that are right in front of us. George MacDonald agrees.

"Your next duty is to determine what your next duty is. Is there nothing you neglect? Is there nothing you know you ought not to do? You would know your duty if you were earnest about it, and were not ambitious of great things."

"Ah, then" responded she, "I suppose it is something very commonplace, which will make life more dreary than ever. That cannot help me."

"It will be if it be as dreary as reading the newspapers to an old deaf aunt. It will soon lead you to something more. Your duty will begin to comfort you at once, but will at length open the unknown fountain of life in your heart." [3]

When Jesus walked the earth, his presence made it clear that nothing done in obedience to the Father is mundane or ordinary. Certainly there is no kingdom activity that is ordinary. So think of the endless possibilities. They will come into view when you think of ordinary tasks rather than dramatic ones. They will come into view when you pray and ask the King, "Now what?" You will find that the answer usually has something to do with loving and serving another person.

Fear of flying. Sometimes it can seem complicated. Bob is a business-man who refused to fly. He had his reasons: While in the military he wit-nessed plane and helicopter crashes. He was actually on a plane that had to make an emergency landing, when some men were injured.

Does God call him to fly? Not necessarily. It is not a clear command in Scripture. Yet his calling is, in part, to care about others. If his unwill-ingness to travel becomes a hardship on others, he should probably leave his job or, by faith, begin going on planes. As it happens, however, other people are willing to take the trips that otherwise would be assigned to him.

Is that the end of the story? Bob is scared of flying, God doesn't neces-sarily call him to fly, and his colleagues are willing to make adjustments. It could be the end of the story, but all roads point to Christ, and this one hasn't gotten there quite yet. Has Bob ever brought his fears to the One who said, "Do not be afraid"? Whether he ever flies or not, now is the time for Bob to honor Christ by taking his fears out of the closet and letting Jesus be Lord in that previously hidden area of his life.

Fears of death? Undoubtedly, Bob has them. What a perfect time to mine more of the riches of Christ. And since fears travel in packs, he will probably find others. What a pleasure for him to see the kingdom of Christ come into new places!

Should his goal be to get on a plane again? Perhaps. If so, he will want to think in terms of small steps. If and when he eventually takes his flight, it will be time for prayer and celebration. But his real goal is something much grander.

No fear with cancer. A good friend of mine was diagnosed with cancer. Since he had younger children, many people said it wasn't fair. My response was just to worry. Would the treatments work? Would they make him sick? What about his job? Should he take a leave of absence? Pursue disability? My mind reeled with worry-induced questions, some of them fueled by my fear of losing him.

His response? "Nothing has changed." His God was still both good and in complete control. Certainly, there were decisions he had to make and there were physicians to help him and his wife through them. But mostly he just did the next thing. He did what he believed God called him to do: read Scripture daily, pray with his children, be faithful at his job, and love those he had opportunity to love. His example in this was a witness to the grace of God. He is the man to whom I dedicated this book.

We are not our own, we are bought with a price (1 Cor. 6:19–20). Therefore, we don't have to aspire to great projects. We can just open our eyes and ask God what he wants us to do now, like an eager child who wants to help his mother. We ask for a task and when we do it, we come back with a smile on our face and ask, "Now what?"

TOO MANY CHOICES?

When you are earnest about pursuing your calling, your problem will no longer be that you don't know what to do in the present. The problem will be that there are too many things to do, and the cycle of worry can begin again.

Ugh. Now what? Granted, there are complexities to modern life. There are difficult decisions. Many tasks vie for our attention, and each wants to be done before all the others. When you get to that place of paralysis, ask for help. What do others see as "the next thing" in your life? How would they prioritize the tasks in front of you?

Next, you could receive wisdom from books on decision making. This is similar to asking a friend for wisdom, but a book is usually written by someone you don't know. Jim Petty is a long-time friend who has written *Step By Step: Divine Guidance for Ordinary Christians*, an aptly titled book on decision making that I would recommend.

The pitfall, as George MacDonald points out, is that we might be looking for God's direction on some great project. The ordinary is not good enough for us; our hubris wants something grandiose. But the ordinary done in obedience to Christ is beautiful, inspired, and oftentimes heroic.

A PERSONAL RESPONSE

Now I am thinking about how to help others. How can I help the man who fears flying? The girl afraid of dogs? Now that I know some things about fear, I could be dangerous! Give me an opportunity and hear me preach. The application of Scripture, however, is not something I should offer quickly and casually. My goal is to partner with people as they seek Christ for wisdom.

I need my own set of the blinders horses wear so that all I will see is the next step in front of me.

CHAPTER TWENTY-NINE

TOMORROW

Have you noticed one can't feel afraid, even if one wants to?
–LUCY TO EDMUND IN THE LAST BATTLE

WITH ALL THIS talk about today and living in the present, you might think that tomorrow is completely off limits, surrounded by police barricades breached only by God himself. Well, in the same way that there are wise ways to go into the past, there are wise ways to travel to the future. One way is to plan for the future with the recognition that "If it is the Lord's will, we will live and do this or that" (James 4:15). The other is to learn God's view of the future, which promises that there is something beautiful just ahead. You can *almost* see it.

Fear, anxiety, worry, and pessimism—they are all part of the same conglomerate. Fear and worry, of course, only envision the worst. When you know that the story will end well, it is almost impossible to be afraid.

WITNESSES TO TOMORROW

One of God's remarkable words to us has been that faith is *not* a leap into the unknown. Maybe some people can leap based merely on one person's word, but not anyone with a smidgeon of fear or anxiety. Faith, instead, is a shift of confidence and trust to One who has always proven faithful.

The evidence against *us* is that we have trusted in other gods, and they have proved unable to sustain us. We can more easily grab the morning mist than find peace when our gods are the people or things of this world. In contrast, the true God is faithful and he is willing to prove it in the courtroom.

Do you remember the heroes of the faith—the "cloud of witnesses"—mentioned by the writer of Hebrews in chapter 11? They are witnesses in the technical sense of the word. They were recipients of God's testimony about future realities, and they have been summoned for the defense. "Every matter may be established by the testimony of two or three witnesses" (Matt. 18:16). In this case, the writer of Hebrews recruits more than a dozen witnesses to make their testimony on God's behalf incontrovertible, and he has a numberless throng ready to be called if needed. Interestingly, the immediate context for the letter to the Hebrews is the yearning of some people for the old ways. When times were difficult they yearned for the familiarity of Old Testament religion. Such reverting to old routines is typical of fearful people who want security in what has been comfortable in the past. To counter this, the writer says that all those people from the past were looking *forward* to Jesus Christ and his kingdom.

"Faith is the substance of things hoped for, the evidence of things not seen" (Heb. 11:1, KJV). It can sound like blind confidence in our own wishful thinking, but this hope only comes when our eyes are wide open. Pay attention to the argument that God has been building over the centuries. He is the sovereign Lord who has been steering history to its wonderful climax. Come into the courtroom and see the evidence on display.

Noah is called forward. "By faith Noah, when warned about things not yet seen, in holy fear built an ark to save his family" (Heb. 11:7). Noah understood future events because God revealed them. He responded by building the ark. He believed God's word: There would be judgment for those who ignored God's warning but salvation for those who trusted God's foretelling of events.

Noah tells us two things. First, he says, God's revelation of the future is true. You can trust him. Second, he is a forerunner of Jesus, who believed, acted, and delivered a family much larger than Noah's.

Next, Abraham is brought forward.

> By faith Abraham, when called to go to a place he would later receive as his inheritance, obeyed and went, even though he did not know where he was going. By faith he made his home in the promised land like a stranger in a foreign country; he lived in tents, as did Isaac and Jacob, who were heirs with him of the same promise. For he was looking forward to the city with foundations, whose architect and builder is God.
>
> —HEB. 11:8–10

Abraham was a pilgrim, a vagabond with a purpose. God deliberately withheld full ownership of the Promised Land as a way to perfect Abraham's vision of the future. If he had received it immediately, Abraham was liable to look for nothing better. Instead, his wandering gave him opportunity to know God and trust him, and he became certain that an earthly dwelling was a mere signpost to an eternal dwelling with God.

He tells us that God is true to his word. Future promises are certain. His son Isaac was a kind of down payment on those promises.

What better witness could there be? Abraham was even willing to sacrifice his own son in obedience to God. He was certain that if God chose to take Isaac, he would surely raise him from the dead. The future was just barely out of plain view, but for Abraham, the promises of God filled in the details he couldn't see. And when you know the end of the story, there is nothing to fear.

We have heard this before. "'For I know the plans I have for you,' declares the LORD, 'plans to prosper you and not to harm you, plans to give you hope and a future'" (Jer. 29:11). Now the witnesses are lining up to persuade us.

The final witness is Jesus himself, "who for the joy set before him endured the cross, scorning its shame, and sat down at the right hand of the throne of God" (Heb. 12:2). Jesus himself testifies to things in the future. He endured the cross because he knew that the Father—and joy, as a result—were right on the other side of death. With these testimonies clearly in mind, we can enter into fearful places confident that nothing can nullify the promises of prosperity.

It is enough to make you wonder how people who know Jesus could ever worry, and how people who don't know Jesus could do anything *but* worry.

Do you notice that your body is wasting away? As we age, we lose more and more teeth, mobility, strength, and even organs. If life were just a downhill slide to physical disability and death, suicide at age thirty would be a reasonable option. But most people don't take their lives at the first hint of physical decline. Some hope that there is something better; we *know* that there is something better.

DO HOPE

All right, the witnesses have appeared. They have said what we have heard before, but the relentlessness of their testimony is compelling. Now we must do something. "Okay, you're right" is not enough. We must stand in protest against the kingdom of earth, which says that there is nothing more than today, so it's best to eat, drink, and be merry. We must *do* hope.

To begin, we confess that our fears and worries reveal us. We have bought the lie that tragedy is the last word. Though that might seem like a simple misunderstanding to be treated with a slight cognitive correction, the reality is that such a belief is highly personal. It says that God is neither good nor in control. We are essentially saying that God's promises aren't true; that he is a liar.

Can you see how repentance is usually the beginning of change? The reason why simple information doesn't dislodge fear is that our problem is rarely lack of knowledge. It is usually misplaced allegiances. You can be sure that misplaced allegiances are behind our indifference to God's wooing of his worried people. So, when in doubt, begin by your confessing sin against God, and you will immediately know the sweetness of forgiveness.

Next, believe what God says. Say it aloud. Confess your belief to others. It is the most reasonable and sane thing we can do. We have been given the evidence, and we know the alternative to trust. How could we do anything else but rest in him and his word?

Finally, do hope. In the same way that the witnesses in Hebrews acted on their hope, act on yours.

Abel offered God a better sacrifice than Cain did.

Enoch walked in hope his entire life.

Noah built an ark.

Abraham left his home and went to a foreign country.

Joseph spoke about the exodus of the Israelites from Egypt long before it happened, and gave instructions for his burial in that new land.

Moses refused to be known as the son of Pharaoh's daughter.

Rahab welcomed the spies and was not killed with her unbelieving countrymen.

"These were all commended for their faith, yet none of them received what had been promised. God had planned something better for us so that only together with us would they be made perfect" (Heb. 11:39–40).

A PERSONAL RESPONSE

How will I practice hope? I plan to take a sabbatical from worry and pursue an obstinate optimism. I anticipate falling on my face, but much less often than before.

- I have some reasons to worry in the near future. I plan to go completely against type and speak with hope to my wife when the threat comes closer.
- I know I have to practice, so I am going to meditate on passages like Psalm 27 and Psalm 46.
- I will speak about hope to my friend who has cancer.
- I will pray that I have the power to turn quickly to Christ when I am afraid.
- I will listen to worry and go after it at its roots.

How will you protest? How will you do hope?

CHAPTER THIRTY

LAST WORDS

TRACK YOUR FEARS with the light of Scripture and you are directed to God. Your fears are more about God than you realize. Along the way that light also helps you see yourself more clearly. What you see is that the world is organized into two kingdoms, and the boundary between those two kingdoms, as Alexander Solzhenitsyn observed, cuts right through each of our hearts. Our preference is to straddle that line, but our patient God keeps persuading us to be wholeheartedly devoted to his kingdom. There is no other way to distance ourselves from fear and anxiety.

So you turn. You turn and face God. You seek his kingdom. You seek it imperfectly but with perseverance. You listen, meditate, and act on what God says. No doubt your response will include some confession of sin and repentance. While you are engaged with God and the truth of his kingdom, you will notice that the scenery is changing. You are headed home—the place where his kingdom has come and God is with you in the fullest sense.

I remember being at work one Wednesday when weather reports forecasted a heavy snowstorm. Sure enough, it was heavy, my car got stuck, and I had to walk home in a blizzard. The snow itself didn't really bother me. What distressed me was the thought that my children had to drive home from school that day. How would they make it? They weren't skilled at driving in those conditions and I was disturbed—all right, I was worried to death—that they were in an accident or stuck somewhere.

As I trudged up to the house, I noticed the car they had driven to school. My heart leaped. It was as if I had been covered with a warm blanket. When I walked in the door, I saw that they were safe at home. "The chicks are all in the roost," my wife said. For the rest of the afternoon we sat in the living room watching a driving snowstorm, drinking hot chocolate, thankful that we had food and shelter, and enjoying each other's company. It was a glimpse of home, a glimpse of eternity. It was one of the best days of my life.

The kingdom has come and it gives us glimpses of home. When you are home, you have peace. It is no longer just a rumor. Peace is available. It is one of those features of the kingdom that God is pleased to give us. The apostle Paul knew it even when things were tough.

May the God of hope fill you with all joy and peace as you trust in him, so that you may overflow with hope by the power of the Holy Spirit.

—ROM. 15:13

The God of peace be with you all.

—ROM. 15:33

Grace and peace to you from God our Father and the Lord Jesus Christ.

—1 COR. 1:3

Now let Jesus have the last word.

While they were still talking about this, Jesus himself stood among them and said to them, "Peace be with you."

—LUKE 24:36

"Peace I leave with you; my peace I give you. I do not give to you as the world gives. Do not let your hearts be troubled and do not be afraid."

—JOHN 14:27

"I have told you these things, so that in me you may have peace. In this world you will have trouble. But take heart! I have overcome the world."

—JOHN 16:33

On the evening of that first day of the week, when the disciples were together, with the doors locked for fear of the Jews, Jesus came and stood among them and said, *"Peace be with you!"* After he said this, he showed them his hands and side. The disciples were overjoyed when they saw the Lord.

Again Jesus said, "Peace be with you! As the Father has sent me, I am sending you." And with that he breathed on them and said, "Receive the Holy Spirit. If you forgive anyone his sins, they are for-given; if you do not forgive them, they are not forgiven."

Now Thomas (called Didymus), one of the Twelve, was not with the disciples when Jesus came. So the other disciples told him, "We have seen the Lord!"

But he said to them, "Unless I see the nail marks in his hands and put my finger where the nails were, and put my hand into his side, I will not believe it."

A week later his disciples were in the house again, and Thomas was with them. Though the doors were locked, Jesus came and stood among them and said, *"Peace be with you!"*

—JOHN 20:19–26, *author's emphasis*

"The Lord bless you and keep you;
the Lord make his face shine upon you and be gracious to you;
the Lord turn his face toward you and give you shalom."

—Num. 6:24–26

NOTES

Chapter 1: A World of Fear

1. "The Bridal Gown" in *Ask the Bones,* Arielle North Olson and Howard Schwartz (New York: Viking, 1999), 125.
2. "The Handkerchief" in *Ask the Bones,* 73.
3. "Jack Frost, a Russian Folk Tale," in *Short and Shivery: Thirty Chilling Tales* Retold by Robert D. San Souci (New York: Doubleday, 1987), 9.
4. "The Ghost's Cap," in *Short and Shivery,* 22.
5. Of course, one purpose of scary stories is to get kids to be good. As every dictator knows, fear is a powerful way to control others. [See Marc Siegel's *False Alarm: The Truth about the Epidemic of Fear* (New York: Wiley, 2005).] But that does not explain why children seem attracted to the stories.
6. *The Philadelphia Inquirer,* "There's nothing funny about fear of clowns," Alex Waterfield, January 15, 2006.

Chapter 2: *Your* Fear

1. L. Wagner-Martin, *Sylvia Plath: A Biography* (New York: Simon and Schuster, 1987), 89.

Chapter 3: Fear Speaks

1. Mitch Albom, *Tuesdays with Morrie* (New York: Bantam, Double-day, Dell, 1997).

Chapter 4: Anxiety and Worry Chime In

1. Sigmund Freud, *Introductory Lectures on Psychoanalysis,* translated by James Strachey (New York: Worton, 1966), 393.

Chapter 5: Do Not Be Afraid

1. "Of seditions and troubles," (1625), from *The London Series of English Classics,* J. W. Hales and C. S. Jerram, Eds., *Bacon's Essays, Vol. II, 5ᵗʰ Ed.* (London: Spottiswoode, 1882), Internet book digitized by Google.
2. Essays, 1625, "Of seditions and troubles."

Chapter 7: The God of Suspense

1. N. T. Wright, *Following Jesus: Biblical Reflections on Discipleship* (Grand Rapids: Eerdmans, 1994), 68.

Chapter 12: Grace for Tomorrow

1. I am indebted to John Piper's book *Future Grace* for highlighting this basic idea.

Chapter 18: Fear of Death

1. The poem, "Death."
2. "A serious consideration of death can, strange as it may seem, be a source of joy and hope." John Garvey, *Death and the Rest of Life* (Grand Rapids: Eerdmans, 2005), 6.
3. Ernest Becker, *The Denial of Death* (New York: Simon & Schuster, 1973).
4. A. Norenzayan and I. G. Hansen, "Belief in supernatural agents in the face of death," *Personality and Social Psychology Bulletin*, Vol. 32, No. 2 (2006), 174–187.

Chapter 19: Fear of Judgment

1. http://www.carm.org/creeds/heidelberg.htm.

Chapter 21: Already Dead

1. "The Weight of Glory," in *A Weight of Glory and Other Addresses,* edited by Walter Hooper, rev. ed. (New York: Macmillan Publishing, 1980).

Chapter 28: Yesterday and Today

1. See Susan Mineka and Richard Zinbarg, "A contemporary learning theory perspective on the etiology of anxiety disorders," *American Psychologist,* 61, January 2006, 10–26.
2. Emmi Bonhoeffer, *The Auschwitz Trials,* quoted in *The Elisabeth Elliot Newsletter,* November–December 2001.
3. Cited in Elisabeth Elliot, *Secure in the Everlasting Arms* (Ann Arbor: Servant Publications, 2002), 71.

EDWARD T. WELCH is the author of such best-selling titles as: *Depression: A Stubborn Darkness, Addictions: A Banquet in the Grave, Blame It on the Brain,* and *When People Are Big and God Is Small.* He received a PhD in Counseling Psychology (Neuropsychology) from the University of Utah, and an MDiv from the Biblical Theological Seminary in Hatfield, PA. Welch is a licensed psychologist and works as a counselor, faculty member, and director of the School of Biblical Counseling at the Christian Counseling & Educational Foundation in Glenside, PA. His written work and speaking ministry, which are characterized by sound biblical exposition and paired with dynamic practical application, are in great demand by today's modern church. Ed is married to Sheri and has two amazing daughters. He is also the glad owner of a growing guitar collection and competes in the Master's swim event where he happily placed fourth in the country.